Environmental Degradation and Protection

Volume II

Environmental Degradation and Protection

Volume II

Editors :

K.K. SINGH
A.K. SINGH
ALKA TOMAR
VINOD SINGH

MD Publications Pvt Ltd
New Delhi

Published by
MD Publications Pvt Ltd
"MD House"
11, Darya Ganj
New Delhi-110002
Tel. : +91-11-41562846, 41563325
Fax : +91-11-29235450
E-mail : contact@mdppl.com
Website : www.mdppl.com

ISBN : 978-81-904551-5-2 (Volume 2)
978-81-904551-3-8 (Set of 2 Volumes)

Printed and Published by **MD Publications Pvt Ltd** at Times Press, New Delhi

CONTENTS

FOREWORD

Preservation and protection of the environment is not an option any more, it is the only way out. Our existence is at stake. It is we who stand to disappear, and not the biosphere. Nature is too powerful to let us misbehave for long, Like any good mother, she knows when to threaten and when to punish.

Providing sufficient food, shelter and clean environment to the people is becoming exceedingly difficult as the earth's natural endowments are progressively degraded and depleted due to our excess usage of resources. Depletion of natural resources is a fact of life, but it is its current rate that is alarming. A rate that is directly reflective of rapid population growth, increasing urbanization and indiscriminate industrial development.

Natural calamities such as floods, droughts, tsunamis, earthquakes and volcanic eruptions, seem to be recurring more frequently these days. This is a indicator that all is not well with our only home - the earth. What we are witnessing today are changes that could seriously threaten our collective future.

Every year over 1.5 million hectares of forest disappears. About 12000 million tonnes of fertile soil is washed away. More than 1000 species of animals and 2500 species of plants face extinction. Thousands of human beings are displaced into homelessness by natural and man-made disasters while the several others are not even that fortunate to survive. Millions are affected by the unscientific and indiscriminate use of insecticides and pesticides and are dying of diseases spawned from the abuse of nature.

Our current scenario hence warrants serious alarm and more urgently - action. This book entitled **'Environmental Degradation and Protection'** helps us to do that.

It not only highlights major environmental degradation issues, but also suggests strategies, technologies and techniques for protection, conservation and judicious utilization of natural resources as well as sustainable development. It no doubt is a pertinent addition in the existing literature on Environmental Science.

This reference book covers wide range of topics like the depletion of natural resources, acid rains and its harmful effects, degraded ecosystems, watershed for land and water management, disaster management, indoor pollution, land degradation, nanotechnology, macrophyte decomposition and water quality, ozone layer depletion, equipments and techniques to assess and monitor pollution, landfill leachates, xenophobic exposure in organisms and women & environment.

The compilation is, undoubtedly significant. It presents highly complex fields like Agriculture, Environmental Engineering, Ecology, Biotechnology, Hydrology and Social Sciences in an understandable, reader friendly manner. The technical information contained herein is useful in understanding the science behind degradation of natural resources. The book is sure to help both scientists and environmental activists in working towards assessing degradation of natural resources and monitoring pollution problems and more specifically environment protection. It gives the required lesson that the fundamental principle in developing a rational approach in environmental degradation that management is the principle of relating environmental quality standards to the demands of legitimate beneficial use of the natural resources.

The efforts made by Dr. K.K. Singh, Dr. A.K. Singh, Mrs. Alka Tomar and Dr. Vinod Singh, in the compilation and meticulous editing of the book are commendable.

Dr. (Mrs.) Iqbal Malik
Founder and Director
Vatavaran, New Delhi

PREFACE

Environment is under constant threat from mans' own activities. Population explosion, rapid industrialization, unplanned urbanization and intensive agriculture have caused tremendous damage to our environment. Ignorance towards laws of nature and over-exploitation of natural resources has further aggravated the problem. Development oriented exploitation of non-renewable (coal, ores, petroleum etc.) and renewable (air, water, plants and animals life etc.) natural resources have lead to discharges of waste products, which polluted air, water and land. Sometimes wastes are discharged at a rate beyond the carrying capacity of the environment ultimately degrading the quality of the environment. The degradation has not only led to short-term health and social impacts but also to long-term deterioration of the natural resource base. Faced with such imminent threat, there is a growing realization that rational utilization of environmental endowments of life support system like water, air and soil is a must for sustainable development.

Environmental protection, proper waste utilization and the conservation of natural resources emerged as key of national priorities. However, one must recognize that the situation has not reached the point of no return and by resorting to appropriate environmental management, by integrating the inseparable economic and environmental systems and by creating awareness among the people we can choose ecologically compatible paths of development. The solution for the environmental problems lie in the participation of scholars and practitioners from various disciplines such as biologists, physical scientists, earth scientists and social scientists for requisite and much needed implementation of available technologies in the various streams of environment.

An attempt, therefore, has been made through this book to provide a gist of available waste utilization and environment conservation technologies and tools for improving the quality of life of the people in general and proper strategic environmental protection and management in particular. The contents of the book provide up-to-date, comprehensive and integrated knowledge of ecosystem and the factors concerned with the deterioration of the environment with a view to manage the development programmes in such a way that environmental degradation may not upset the balance of nature. Each chapter of the book is well written by the leading experts and scholars having long standing experience in their respective fields. The treatment of all the topics is in a cogent, lucid style aimed at enabling the reader to grasp the information quickly and easily.

The book is divided into two sections. The first section embodies various fundamental aspects of environmental degradation and depletion of natural resources. The second section deals with various equipments and tools required for assessing and monitoring environmental problems. It is hoped that this comprehensive publication in two volumes would be a reference document to serve the needs of environmentalists, entrepreneurs, researchers, students, consultants and decision makers, as it deals with a wide array of environmental issues and themes.

The editors express their deep sense of appreciation to all the authors for their valuable contribution in the form of chapters. We are also thankful to all the fellow friends whose tireless efforts facilitated us to bring out this publication in time. All the other individuals and organizations who directly or indirectly contributed to this book deserve overwhelming appreciation. We are also thankful to Shri V.K. Gupta, Publisher, M.D. Publications Pvt. Ltd., New Delhi for excellent production of the book.

Editors

LIST OF CONTRIBUTORS

A.K.Singh, Asst. Professor, Department of Physics, Dronacharya College of Engineering, Farrukhnagar, Khetanwas, Gurgaon, Haryana.

Ajay Kumar Naithani, Department of Geology, Garhwal University, Srinagar Garhwal-246174, Uttaranchal.

ALEYA Lotfi, Laboratoire de Biologie Environnementale, Universite de Franche-Comte, 1 Place Leclere, 25030 Besancon Cedex France.

Alka Tomar, Dy.Director & Head, Centre for Media Studies (Research House), Community Centre, Saket, New Delhi-110017.

Amit Krishna De, Executive Secretary, The Indian Science Congress Association, 14, Dr. Biresh Guha Street, Kolkata-700017, West Bengal.

B.A.K. Prusty, Environmental Impact Assessment Division, Salim Ali Centre for Ornithology and Natural History, Anaikatty (PO), Coimbattore-64108, Tamil Nadu.

Basudeo Prasad, Scientist & Head, Environmental Monitoring Instruments Division, C.S.I.O., Chandigarh-160030.

Eline Meulenberg, ELTI Support VOF Drieskensacker 12-10 6546 M H. Nijmegen, Thc Nothorlands.

F.A.Lone, Division of Environmental Sciences, S.K. University of Agricultural Sciences and Technology, Shalimar Campus-191121, Jammu Kashmir.

G.S. Kanade, Scientist, National Environmental Engineering Research Institute (NEERI), Nehru Marg, Nagpur-440020, India.

Girish H.Pandya, Dy. Director, National Environmental Engineering Research Institute (NEERI), Nehru Marg, Nagpur-440020, India.

Inderpal Rai, Assoc. Professor, Department of Home Science, JNV University, Jodhpur, Rajasthan.

J.C.Sharma, Department of Soil Science and Water Management, Dr. Y.S.Parmar University of Horticulture and Forestry, Nauni-Solan-173230, Himachal Pradesh.

Jean-Louis Morel, Laboratoire Sols et Environment, 2 Avenue Foret de Haye 54505 Vandoeuvre, France.

Joseph Toscano, Manager (Quality Control), Bharat Petroleum, Mumbai, Maharashtra.

K.K.Singh, Project Directorate (Res.), Agriculture and Soil Survey, Krishi Bhawan, Bikaner, Rajasthan.

KHATTABI Hicham, Laboratoire de Biologie Environmentale, universite de Franche-Comte, 1, Place Leclerc, 25030 Besancon Cedex, France.

M.A.Khan, Division of Environmental Sciences, S.K. University of Agricultural Sciences and Technology, Shalimar Campus-191121, Jammu & Kashmir.

Mahadevi Singh, Teacher, Sophia Sr. Secondary School, Bikaner-334002, Rajasthan.

N.R. Nadarajan, Environmental Impact Assessment Division, Salim Ali Centre for Ornithology and Natural History, Anaikatty (PO), Coimbatore-64108, Tamil Nadu.

P.A.Azeez, Principal Scientist, Environmental Impact Assessment Division, Salim Ali Centre for Ornithology and Natural History, Anaikatty (PO), Coimbatore-64108, Tamil Nadu.

Paromita Ghosh, Scientist B., G.B.Pant Institute of Himalayan Environmental and Development, Garhwal Unit, Srinagar Garhwal-246174 (Uttaranchal).

R.P.Bajpai, Director, Central Scientific Instruments Organization, Chandigarh-160030.

Sanjeev K. Chaudhary, Department of Soil Science and Water Management, Dr. Y.S.Parmar University of Horticulture and Forestry, Nauni-Solan (HP)-173230, Himaçhal Pradesh.

Subodh Kumar Maiti, Asst. Professor, Centre of Mining Environment, Indian School of Mines, Dhanbad-826004, Jharkhand.

V.Gayathri, EIA Division, Salim Ali Centre for Ornithology and Natural History, Anaikatty, Coimbatore-641108, Tamil Nadu.

V.K. Kandawar, Scientist Environmental Engineering Research Institute (NEERI), Nehru Marg, Nagpur-440020, India.

V.M. Shinde, Scientist, National Environmental Engineering Research Institute (NEERI), Nehru Marg, Nagpur-440020, India.

Vinod Singh, Lecturer, Department of Geography, Govt. Dungar College, Bikaner-334001.

Y.P.Sundriyal, Department of Geology, Garhwal University, Srinagar, Garhwal-246174, Uttaranchal.

CHAPTER 1

ECOLOGICAL IMPACT ASSESSMENT OF SURFACE MINING PROJECT

Subodh Kumar Maiti
Centre of Mining Environment
Indian School of Mines, Dhanbad-826 004.

ABSTRACT

Two Ecological Impact Assessment (EcoIA) procedures are discussed. One is Species level approach (SLA) that is commonly being used for most of the EcoIA. Other approach is Habitat evaluation system (HES) that has been developed by US Army crop engineers. In second approach, rather than considering species alone, it considers the habitat as a whole. Both the processes have 6-step procedures, but approaches are different. In HES to reduce subjectivity, value functions curves are used for each important ecological attribute. In both the processes, a systemic baseline quantitative evaluation of ecological status is crucial. The depth baseline studies depend on requirements of project. Three stages of baseline data generation have been discussed.

A case study by using species level approach has been discussed. Advantages and disadvantages of HES approach were also discussed. Relevant portion of The Forest (conservation) Rules, 1981 which required for EcoIA also discussed. Mitigation measures for ecological impacts for mining project also given.

Key Words: Ecological impact assessment, species level approach, habitat evaluation system, monitoring, mitigation.

Introduction

Ecological Impact Assessment (Eco IA), an important component of any EIA, is often carried out mechanically. Mining industry is only an intermediate user of land, but land degradation caused by it is so devastating that an altogether new ecosystem is developed in the derelict site. The main thrust should be on habitat quality assessment and how it will help to ecosystem regeneration.

This paper stresses the need to carry out focused Eco IA. This is of paramount importance in mining, particularly surface mining, which invariably inflicts significant damages on the receiving ecosystem. This article, apart from highlighting the principal ecological impacts caused by surface mining, attempts to chalk out the steps that would, in the author's opinion, overcome the shortcomings of existing processes and practices. Highlighting cases from Indian Coal sector the author encapsulates a holistic view of the problems and proposes pragmatic solution.

It has been stressed that in order to make Eco IA effective, an appropriate procedure needs to be adopted. While, fulfillment of legislative requirement cannot be overlooked, ensuring data adequacy within the allocated finance poses a major challenge.

The author stresses that unless a freehand is given to the assessor in planning and executing impact assessment studies, there is little chance of improvement in the Eco IA study effectiveness. Only with effective coordination with appropriate feed-forward and feed-back mechanisms can an EOIA be turned into an effective tool for ensuring environmental sustainability.

Ecological Impact Assessment (Eco IA) "*is a formal process of defining, quantifying and evaluating the potential impacts of defined actions on ecosystem (Canter, 1996). The basic components of an EcoIA are baseline studies, impact assessment, impact prediction and evaluation, and mitigation measures.* Some researchers incorporated the monitoring component also (after suggested mitigation measures) as feed-back to the EIA process.

Significant irreversible ecological damage is often associated with surface mining. A part and parcel of surface mining activities is stripping of overburden. Such activities lead to near-total destruction of ecological habitat forcing total destruction of two of the most basic ecosystem components viz., plants and decomposers. At times even some consumers are badly affected. This calls for development of a new land-habitat for development of a fresh ecosystem, which, for habitat quality variation, can sustain an ecosystem that is at significant variance with the premining ecosystem.

A unique feature of Eco IA of mining projects is that such assessment lays stress not only on identifying the key parameters of ecosystem regeneration but also assessing the impacts on these parameters.

Ecological impact assessment - Some case examples

Under the EIA notification 1994, Ecological components include only floral and faunal aspects and that too a project specific extent. While conducting an Eco IA, floral and faunal components are studied in both the core and buffer zones. The study is usually conducted by taking representative samples from the core zone (within the project area) where detailed quantitative data are collected. Similar studies are also conducted for buffer zone. Following steps are followed in the field:

(*a*) The project-influence-zone is classified according to the premining land uses (e.g. forest land, agriculture land, pastureland, barren area etc.). If need arises certain sub-classification is also resorted to. For example a forest area may be sub-categorized on the basis of the age of plantation, whether natural forest or an afforested area, dominance (mono or multiculture) etc. A real life example of ecological status (baseline) assessment is presented in Table 1. In bigger projects involving larger area a little more extensive study may be expected and detailed quantitative ecological parameters which are studied in the field are given in Table 2.

Table 1 : What do we actually measure in the field?

Location	Name of species	Relative dominance	Girth (cm)	Height (m)
Old teak plantation area	*Tectona grandis*	69 %	7.10	7-8
	Diospyros montana	2.75 %	20.32	10-12
	Phyllanthus officinalis	6.9%	2.54	5-6
	Wrightia tinctoria	1.2%	1.80	3-3.5

Trees less than 2m height: *Diospyros, Termelia, Zizyphus, Ixora.*

Table 2 : Structural parameters in 5 forests in Singrauli region

Forest type	% of Shorea	Cover	Canopy height (m)	Density (trees/ha)		Basal area (m^2/ha)	No of species, 0.1ha	Shannon Wiener's index
				G≥ 10cm	G≥ 30cm			
Open mixed forest	0	0.57	24	410	230	25.9	12	2.62
Open mixed forest	7.5	0.67	25-27	400	350	24.2	14	3.29
Sal forest	73.7	0.64	23-25	990	590	30.5	5	1.13
Acacia-hardwickia forest	3.1	0.53	10	1300	460	14.8	12	2.92
Mixed forest with Sal	17.5	0.66	16-18	1140	530	20	18	3.45

(*b*) If diversion of forestland is involved, legislative requirements for ecological status assessment of the area as per the provision of Forest (Conservation) Rules 1981 (Rule 4) is provided in Table 3.

Table 3 : Details of forest land involved

Requirements	What do we supply?	Utility in EIA in India?
(*a*) Legal status of the forest (namely reserve, protected/ unclassed etc.)	Certificate from Revenue officer/ DFO	Minimal
(*b*) Details of flora and fauna existing in the area	List is usually appended as Annexure to EMP report	During selection of plant species for restoration of the area; idea of natural seed banks.
(*c*) Density of vegetation	Density in terms of plants/ha or as crown density (CC).	Base line data bank; goal to achieve by reclamation;
(*d*) Species-wise and diameter-wise abstract of trees	Supplied in tabular form	Vale of plantation stock;
(*e*) Vulnerability of the forest area to erosion, whether it forms a part of a seriously eroded area or not.	More of subjective assessment	Helpful for assessment of water quality; should be considered in EIA, but not actually considered.
(*f*) Whether it forms a part of National Park, wildlife sanctuary, nature reserve, biosphere reserve etc, if so, details of the area involved.	Certificate from DFO	Poorly assessed in EIA; the information is seldom incorporated in mitigation planning.
(*g*) Itemwise break-up of the forestland required for the project/ scheme for different purposes.	Supplied by the Project proponents	Aid to reclamation planning
(*h*) Rare/ endangered species of flora and fauna found in the area.	?	?
(*i*) Whether it is a habitat for migrating fauna or forms a breeding ground for them.	?	?
(*j*) Any other significance of the area relevant to the proposal.	?	?

(c) The impact assessment is carried out in simplistic terms that how much trees were felled/ destroyed by comparing tree density in the project site and buffer zone (forest area far off from project site). A case example is presented below for the assessment of ecological impacts in WCL area conducted by Ramprasad *et al.*, TFRI, Jabalpur.

Case Study: Quantification of impacts of a Mining project on tree density

The purpose of this study was to get the clearance of the project from MOEF. The ecological impact was assessed as per the guidelines given in Forest (Conservation) Rules 1981 (Rule 4) for diversion of forestland for non-forestry purpose. The total vegetation was divided into two categories Teak (*Techtona grandis*) and non-teak species and tree sizes were classified on the basis of diameter at breast height (DBH). The leasehold size (read as project area) was less, hence total number of trees were estimated by counting, where as for baseline quadrate method was used for estimation of tree density and size classifications. Table 4 shows the tree density and size in leased out areas and Table 5 shows the tree density and size distribution in a control site, which was selected 5-6 km away from the leased out areas.

Table 4 : Standing trees (Leased out area)- Project site (215.77ha). Methods: Total count

Tree size (DBH)	Teak (*T. grandis*)	Non-Teak species	Total
Less than 20 cm	12,830 (59)*	61,772 (286)	74,602 (345)
21cm - 30 cm	15,374 (72)	52,788 (244)	68,162 (316)
> 31 cm	3,063 (14)	9,220 (43)	12,283 (57)
Total	**31,267 (145)**	**1,23,780 (573)**	**1,55,047 (718)**

Table 5 : Standing trees (5-6 km away from project site) - baseline or control site

Tree size (DBH)	No of Teak/ha	No of Non Teak /ha	Total (plants/ha)
< 20 cm	876	1155	2031
21-30 cm	93	372	405
> 30 cm	85	121	206
Total	**1054**	**1640**	**2702**

Figure in parenthesis shows no. of trees/ha. [Method: 20 quadrate each of 100 m x 100m size].

Table 6 : Quantification of loss. area damaged due to project 215.77ha

Density of species (trees/ha)- Control area	Total no of tree species would have been present, without project (A)	Existing number of plant in project site (B)
Teak 1054	Teak - 1054 x 215.7 = 2,27,421	
No-teak 1640	Non-teak: 1640 × 215.77 = 3,53, 862	
Total	**5,81,283**	**1,55,236**

Number of trees lost due to direct/ indirect activity of the project is (A-B)

= 5,81,283 -1,55,047 = **4,26,236** Nos.

Table 6 reveals the following important conclusion and likely del impacts of the proposed project :

(*i*) At the control site located about 5-6 km distance from the project site, tree density is about 4 times (2702 trees/ha) more than that of the project site (718 trees/ha).

(*ii*) This is predominantly teak area, therefore teak poles and trees are 9-10 times more in control site than project site.

(*iii*) Even in respect of non-teak species, it is about 3 times more in control site than project site.

(*d*) After impact assessment and prediction is over, an assumption is made that by following the mitigation measures suggested in EMP, the ecosystem will be restored. But the ground reality of ecosystem restoration in overburden dumps and species composition may be understood from the case example presented in Table 7.

Table 7 : Comparison of tree composition (dominance %) between mining sites and a nearby natural forest (ECL area)

Plant species	Mining site	Natural forest
Acacia auriculiformis	58%	-
Eucalyptus	24%	-
Alstonia scholaris	12%	-
Azadirachta indica	6%	-
Bassia latifolia	-	56%
Anacardium occidentalis	-	19%
Shorea robusta	-	12.5%
Terminelia arjuna	-	6.25
Albizzia lebbek	-	6.25%

Suggested Measures for Improving Eco IA

The ecological impact assessment for a mining project could systematically carried out by six-step or six-activity model is suggested by Canter (1996) for planning and conducting ecological assessment studies which is presented in Table 8. These 6-steps are discussed as :

Table 8 : Conceptual approach for study of ecological impacts of mining projects

Step	Methodology
1. Identification of biological impacts of the proposed project	Interaction matrix, Simple and descriptive checklist, Network etc
2. Description of existing biological condition (*Baseline studies*)	Field survey
3. Procurement of relevant laws, regulations, guidelines etc.	-
4. Impact prediction	Land use or habitat change
5. Assessment of predicted significant impacts	Magnitude and sensitivity/ or value of ecological system
6. Mitigation measures	Reclamation/ restoration

Step-1 : Identification of biological impacts of the proposed project

The first step is to quantitatively identify the potential impacts of the proposed project (or activity) on biological resources, including habitat and species. Table 9 exemplifies the impacts of mining on biological resources. Each of the activities has a negative direct or indirect effect on the flora and fauna.

Diverse sources of useful information are available. How a particular activity is going to affect biological resources may be identified by the conventional impact identification methods such as: *Interaction matrix, Simple and descriptive checklist, Network etc.* Table 10 delineates probable ecological impacts that could be assessed with lesser degree of subjectivity.

Table 9 : Impacts of Mining on Ecosystem (Flora and fauna)

Pre-production (development phase) - short duration • Impact on vegetation • Removal of vegetation, topsoil and subsoil	• Loss of terrestrial habitat • Loss of standing crop, aesthetics and ameliorative properties of ecosystem. • Total loss of decomposers components including nutrients pool • Fragmentation of ecosystem. • Invasion of weeds
Production phase	• Deposition of settable dust and retardation of growth • Rapid invasion of unwanted weeds (*Lantana, Eupatorium* etc) due to modification of habitat (rocky) • Scarcity of moisture limits normal succession process; • Alteration of landform and creation of rock habitat encourages vigorous growth of weeds that permanently occupies the site and never allows other late successional species to establish. • Increase in anthropogenic disturbance to the surrounding ecosystem components; • Increase in run-off and loss of fine textured soil forming materials. • Habitat transformed into stony surface, higher compaction, either very high or very low infiltration, increase in temperature and encouragement of shallow rooted plants. • Lowering of water table;

Contd.

Post production (Reclamation)	• Changes in landform and topography; (natural angle of repose in external dumps around 34-36°); • Reduction of local species and diversity in species, implying increased dissimilarity of ecosystem (reduced ecosystem stability) • Slow recovery of decomposer cycles; • Development of impoverished habitat; • Enhanced recycling of heavy metals in ecosystem; • Slow regeneration of water table;
Impacts on wildlife	• Direct → Destruction of animal habitat. • Indirect→Interference with → Breeding, Feeding, Migration etc.

Table 10 : How far is it practically possible to conduct EcoIA of an opencast mining project?

1. Quantification of biological impacts	• Year-wise habitat degradation (excavation, dumping and ancillary development). • Loss of trees (timber) • Reduction in diversity of fauna (including avifauna- quantitative); • Invasion of unwanted weeds/ shrubs (area wise, density); • Reduction in crop yield/ productivity (effect of production); • Overall loss of habitat due to indirect activities.
2. Description of ecological environment setting	• Yes, all in quantitative terms (density, diversity, frequency, timber value, sensitive species, red data-book category species, key stone species etc).

Contd.

3. Procurement of laws and guidelines	• Yes
4. Impact prediction	• Macroscale - loss of habitat/ chance in habitat; • Reduction in habitat quality and suitability for vegetation growth; • Area invaded by weeds/ loss of habitat other than direct mining activities;
5. Assessment of predicted significant impacts	• Fragmentation of ecosystem (macro-scale); • Micro-scale- quantification of species lost.
6. Mitigation measures (most valuable) - repair the damage by reclaiming the area; assertion the recovery by the continuos monitoring.	• Successful recovery of ecosystem depends on:- surround seed banks; dumps morphology; nature of spoil materials; planting practices; amendments uses; after-care of reclaimed sites.

Step-2 : Description of existing biological condition (Baseline studies)

The description of the environmental setting (also referred to as "baseline", "existing", "background" or "affected environment") is an integral part of an environmental impact study. This involves three phases of study in terms of intensity of study.

- Phase -I: Habitat survey.
- Phase -II: Species composition.
- Phase -III: Quantitative informations.

Phase-I: Habitat survey

It includes a general description of habitat or vegetation type within a study area and an attempt to fit these informations to a standard classification so that they can be easily understood and compared. The classification may be - woodland (or forest), shrubs-land, Grassland or pastureland etc. The Phase-I survey, better to call as reconnaissance survey is done easily with the help of topo-sheet or landuse map of the area. The types of vegetative cover can be marked directly in the topo-sheet. Or *sometimes type of the forest - tropical throne forest (6A), C1, C2, DS1, DS2 or, dry tropical forest (5A), C1 (1a, 1b), C2, C3 etc. (The Forest type of India, 1968).*

Phase-II: Plant and animal community composition-species list

Floral components

The list of plants should have local names (in vernacular or English), botanical names and family. Such components may include:

Floral components	*Faunal components*
• Tree species	• Amphibians,
• Shrubs	• Reptiles
• Herbs (Leguminous herbs).	• Fishes
• Grasses, Climbers	• Birds
• Succulents (Cactus),	• Mammals.
• Others: Moss, Ferns etc.	

The list should be supplemented with qualitative description such as :

Degree of occurrence (C,O, R). or by + notations:

- C = common, occurring in many localities in large number; (+++)
- O = Occasional, occurs in several localities in small number. (++).
- R = rare, highly localized, restricted by scarcity of habitat or low number (+).

Habitat: Openland, forest area, roadside, aquatic, wetland etc.

Red-data book species list: Threatened, Endangered or critically endangered species, if any.

Phase-III: Community attributes

It involves more intensive sampling to provide details quantitative information on species and/or community attributes.

- Vegetation structure in terms of Phenology and phenograms, Abundance, life-form (growth form-Phaenrophyte, Chaemephyte, Hemicryptophyte, Cryptophyte, Geophye and Therophyte), verticle structure (stratification), Vitality, Disseminule type, and age structure.
- Individual tree: Aerial height, DBH, CC etc.
- Biomass and net primary productivity
- Quantitative character - Density, Dominance (crown cover and basal cover), Frequency, Importance value and Species diversity.

The study of community structure can be useful in woodland survey, but is less commonly applied to other communities.

Diversity and similarity

Shannon-Index or Shannon- Weaver index

Any ecosystem comprises of a long number of plant and animal species that forms diversity. Diversity is measure by Shannon - Weaver index (H) .

$$H = -\sum \frac{ni}{N} \ln \frac{ni}{N}$$

Where: H is species diversity, ni = proportion of individual species and

N = total number of individuals of all species.

Simpson index of diversity (D)

The Simpson's index measures the probability that two specimen picked at random in a community belong to different species.

$$D = 1 - \sum_{i=1}^{n} (P_i)^2$$

Where Pi = ni/N.The Simpson index ranges between a value of 0 (low diversity) and a maximum of 1-1/S.

Similarity index

Similarity index is used to compare two ecosystems. It is also useful for comparison of species diversity of an polluted site and unpolluted sites. The expression of similarity index is

$$S = \frac{2C}{A + B} \times 100$$

Where S = percentage similarity; A = no. of species in mining site, B = no. of species in non-mining sites C = no. of species common to both sites. Table 4 shows that practically there is no similarity of vegetation composition between a nearby natural forest and reclaimed mining area.

Faunal survey

In general, animals are more difficult to sample than plants. Most of the studies contain only a faunal list. It can be argued that the ecological value of a site can be determined largely from a vegetation study, because most resident animals depend on plants for food and shelter. **Census survey** method is common in the study of birds and animals.

Valued Ecosystem components (VECs) and key biological process

"Key species" should be selected on the basis of their economic importance, protected status, rarity, sensitivity to specific impacts or on their representativeness of other species which use a common environmental resource (Guilds).

Step-3 : Procurement of relevant laws, regulations, guidelines etc.

Although, the Forest (Conservation) Act, 1980 and the Wildlife (Protection) Act, 1972 are the principal laws on biodiversity maintenance, a host of other laws regulating diverse activities ranging from land acquisition to mine closure may influence the course of actions and decisions taken for ecological management of mining projects. It is important to procure the relevant regulations and make a synthesis of them to ensure that legislative compliance is essential while practicing ecological management.

Step-4: Impact prediction

The most technically demanding step in addressing the biological environment is the prediction of the impacts of the project-activity. Impact prediction for the biological environment is generally focused on **land-use or habitat changes.** Some important changes that affects faunal population are:

- Loss of habitat
- Habitat fragmentation and isolation
- Reduction of habitat quality and suitability
- Pollution
- Disturbance.

Some additional issues that need to be addressed at this stage include:

- Likelihood of impact- in a relative scale: high, medium or low;
- Duration of Impact: Short-term or Long-term; (anticipated duration).
- Reversibility of the impacts;
- Relative resiliency of individual plants or animals within the study area;
- Potential mitigation measure for a given project type;

The list of potential effects on the biological system could be used as an information source.

Step-5: Assessment of predicted significant impacts

Predicted impacts should usually be considered a function of magnitude and sensitivity or value of the ecological system affected. Interpretation of the anticipated impacts of a proposed project (or activity) should be considered in terms of the following:

Individual plant species	• Role of the individual species food-web relationship. • Resiliency of the plant.
Effects on general characteristics of the affected habitat	• Resiliency of the habitat. • Reduction in species diversity. • Economic importance.
Effects on overall ecosystem.	• Fragility of the environmental setting. • Interruption in natural succession process.

Identification of suitable Indicator species is an important aspect.

- Functional aspects: Change in biomass, productivity etc.
- Traditional approach: Just to quantify impacts (may be in terms of reduction in density of plants species, for example) before (baseline or control area) and after impacts occurs (project site or impact zone) due to activity/ or proposed action.

Drawbacks:

- Lack of replication.
- Identification of suitable site (baseline or control site).

GIS based techniques: Overlays the maps of before and after projects. It also help to identify any fragmentation of habitat.

Drawback: Identification of suitable control sites.

Step-6 Mitigation measures

Mitigation measures for biological impacts can include:

- Avoidance of Impacts
- Minimize the impacts
- Ameliorate the impacts and
- Habitat replacement/ restoration.

A summary of some mitigation measures, which relate to biological system or biological impacts, is presented in Table 11.

Table 11 : Summary of Biological mitigation measures

Ecological impacts	Possible mitigation measures
Erosion and sedimentation	• Surface runoff must be collected in sediment pond; construction of garland drains; • Disturbed surface must be revegetated.
Destruction of vegetation	• Affected land must be restored to at least to pre-mining capacity or better. • Where possible, topsoil must be removed, segregated, stored, and re-disturbed within a minimum time. • Topsoil and subsoil may be removed separately and replace in sequence. • Native vegetation or appropriate substitutes after mining must be established.
Disturbance of aquatic organisms and aquatic habitats	• A regulatory programme designed for restoration, protection, enhancement, and maintenance of aquatic life must be implemented. • Surface and underground mine opening must be cased and sealed to prevent escape of acid and toxic discharge. • Buffer strips must be left between mining operations and waterways.

Contd.

Loss of wildlife and wildlife habitat	• A wildlife protection plan is required as part of any mining permits application. • Wildlife agencies must be consulted. • Timing, shaping, and sizing operations must be conducted to avoid breeding or nesting season and trees, protecting key food, cover, and water resources.
	• Fencing will keep large mammals from direct contact with toxic chemicals in sedimentation ponds and from roadways to reduce the number of road-kills. • Revegetation must use species with high nutritional or cover value. • Topsoil handling and replacement prior to revegetation must be conducive to wildlife. • Topsoil storage must be covered with vegetation, thus providing cover for wildlife. • A 30-m buffer zone on each side of streams must be undisturbed.

Limits of acceptable changes (LACs)

In some biological impact assessment, LACs have been defined for specific environmental components, with agreement on subsequent mitigation measures. For example, LACs were defined for

- Percentage vegetation cover,
- The average size of bare patches,
- Width of footpath; Corridors etc.

Others

- Creation of buffer zones around the project.
- Transplanting of habitat, seeds, ecological value of added trees.

Step-7: Monitoring

Some basic questions to be asked before any monitoring programme.

Who will monitor?

What parameters to be monitored?

Methods of monitoring.

When to monitor?

Duration of monitoring.

How this monitored data will be used? Who will use?

- Monitoring should be done by implementing authority or project authority.
- Monitoring activities should reveal the degree of effectiveness of mitigation measures.
- The monitoring database may be useful for future EIA studies.

Methods: Methods similar to those used for baseline studies.

- Photographs and permanent quadrate sites can be useful to record changes.

- Comparison should be made between the monitoring data and data obtained from control/ reference sites

Drawbacks of existing ecological impact assessment methods

Although, there is no dearth of theoretically appealing Eco IA methods in available EIA literature, application of such methods in Indian mining projects lead to few successes. Such limitations owe their origin to the fact that ecosystem degradation due to mining activities are caused by large scale land degradation causing loss of habitat. Thus, when the project activities cease on a land area the reclamatory task focuses on generation of a new habitat, which, because of moisture, nutrient and other ecological stresses, are bound to be different from the pre-mining habitat. Conventional methods of Eco IA fail to address this unique feature of mining activities and are, therefore, of little practical relevance. The focus of Eco IA under such situations must be on avoidance and minimization of impacts. That is, the Eco IA for mining projects must accept the hard reality of habitat loss being inseparably connected with mining activities, especially the surface mining activities. Once this reality is understood and accepted the Eco IA logically focus on creation of new habitat with the objective of accelerating the process of establishing a self-sustaining ecosystem in the regenerated habitat. In other words, the effectiveness of the new habitat in developing a productive ecosystem should be the central theme of Eco IA for surface mining projects. In order to be effective for changed paradigm of Eco IA as proposed above, the habitat based method of ecological impact assessment, as suggested by many EIA scholars including Canter (1996) is more applicable than the conventional methods.

HABITAT-BASED METHOD FOR ECOLOGICAL IMPACT PREDICTION (CANTER, 1996)

Habitat Evaluation System (HES)

The HES method was developed in 1976 by US Army Corps Engineers (USA). The fundamental assumption-underlying HES is that the presence or absence, abundance, and diversity of plant population in a habitat or community are determined by basic biotic and abiotic factors that can be readily quantified. HES does not treat individual species, although techniques can be modified to evaluate habitats for specific species.

The HES procedure involves six-steps for evaluating impacts of a development project. These steps are presented in Table 12.

Table 12 : Steps involved in evaluating ecological impacts of surface mining projects

Steps of HES	Methodology
1. Obtaining habitat type or land-use (area in ha)	Land use for both project area (core zone) and buffer zone is obtained from land use map. Subsequent changes during the project (involvement of forest land, area of compensatory afforestation, external dumping area, internal dumping area) after project could be accurately predicted.
2. Deriving habitat quality index (HQI) scores	Crucial step for the successfulness of HES. Determination of key variables that effect ecosystem health and functioning are important which may be of project specific, location specific or both. Some of the **HQ indicators** for coalmine overburden dumps that

Contd.

	influence ecosystem development are listed below: • Dump heights and slope • Source of natural seed banks • Matching landscape • Stone content in the rooting depth (up to 100 cm) • Bulk density (g/cc) • Field moisture content (%) • Infiltration rate (cm/hr) • pH • Organic carbon content (%) • Available N & P • CEC • Microbial activity • Density of VAM spores • Types of amendments envisaged • Problems of toxic metals
3. Deriving habitat unit values (HUVs)	HUV = HQI x habitat size
4. Anticipated HUVs during the project and without project	Changes in land use during project life, 5-years reclamation plan preparation
5. Using HUVs to assess impacts of project alternatives (even in terms of reclamation alternatives)	Estimate impacts in terms of change in habitat value (HV)
6. Determining mitigation requirements.	Reclamation/ restoration practices

Step-1: Obtaining habitat type or land-use (area in ha)

The study area needs to be delineated in terms of habitat type. The land -use habitat pattern may be presented for the existing condition, and project for future with project and without project.

- Defining the study area
- Delineating cover type
- Selecting evaluation species. - Sensitive species, key species, species with high public interest, economic values, or both; ecological interest (food-web). A typical HES study will incorporate 4 to 6 species.

Terrestrial - Natural Forest, plantation area (afforested area), grassland (grazzing land), shrub land (bushes); Aquatic - Stream, lakes, wetland (marshy land) etc.

Step-2: Deriving habitat quality index (HQI) scores

Derive the HQI scores for each land-use category or habitat type. Data are obtained on several key viable for each habitat type from field measurement, literature, and historical information. Assign weightage for key variable.

Important stages:

- Identification of key ecological attributes for particular habitat.
- Assignment of relative weights to each variable. Table 13 explains the variable and their relative weights for a forest ecosystem. In other types of ecosystem like grassland, productivity may be important variable. The assignment of relative weight will be site specific.

Table 13 : Landuse type (Forest land]

Key variable	**Relative weights**
Tree Species association .	20
Fruit trees (Fauna attracting)	20
Canopy cover	30
Large tree (ex. > 30cm DBH)	30
Percentage ground cover	10
Total	100

In the next step, value function curve is developed for each key variable for the said **habitat.** Thus in an area, if there are other kinds of habitats like plantation area, wetlands etc, then the key variables are to be identified and value function for each variable should be developed for the particular habitat. The values may be convert into HQI score.

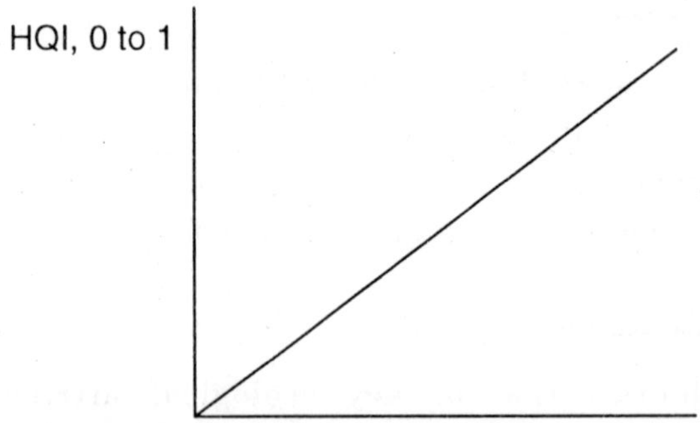

Number of Species association and types

HQI score based on scale 0 to 1 (maximum value, or height rating). HQI scores for a given habitat is assigned a weight between 0 and 100. Conversion of HQI score is given in Table 14.

Table 14 : Landuse type: Forest land (Sampling plot 100m × 100 m; 20 plots)

Key variable	Field data	HQI score (value function curve)	Weights	Wt. HQI score
Species association	*Teak-Sal-Mohua*	0.80	20	16.0
Fruit trees (Fauna attracting)	6 (2 good, 2 moderate, 2 not so important)	0.60	20	12.0
Canopy cover	80% (Good is >60%)	1.00	30	30.0
Large tree (ex. > 30cm DBH)	10 trees (5 is over 45 cm)	1.00	30	30.0
Percentage ground cover	60% (palatable, and 3 species rich)	0.80	10	08.0
Total HQI score				96.0

Aggregate HQI= 0.76 (Before project) and 96.0

Step-3: Deriving habitat unit values (HUVs)

The size of the given habitat is multiplied by aggregated HQI score to produce a Habitat Unit value (HUVs) for the habitat.

Thus HUV = Habitat Quality Index (HQI) x habitat size (acre or ha).

Step-4: Projecting HUVs for with project and without project

Project the habitat Unit Value (HUV) over the project life and for various alternatives (reclamation/ restoration scenario). HUV must be derived for each time increment, usually 10-yr interval, over the project life against without project and each alternative plan (ex. even for alternative reclamation plan).

Step-5: Using HUVs to assess impacts of project alternatives

Impact = With-project HUV- Without Project HUV.

Step-6: Determining mitigation requirements.

Envisage mitigation plan. Mitigation may be defined as "any measure taken to return the 'with project' environmental quality of the area to the same level as the 'without project' condition" (Canter, 1996).

Advantages and Disadvantages of HES over conventional EIA

Advantages

(*i*) Highly dissimilar environmental characteristics are quantifiable in standardized terms (Habitat Quality Index). Adverse and beneficial effects are clearly identified in comparable terms.

(*ii*) The system provides an objective method for comparing environmental effects of project alternatives (better to use reclamation alternatives) and various mitigation measures.

(*iii*) HES results are reproducible. Functional curves are based on quantitative measurements of key variables, which are converted to an HQI score. Thus, once key variable are identified, the HQI is fixed.

(*iv*) Use of the HES is rapid and efficient and requires a minimum of field and laboratory data on terrestrial habitat. Data for most aquatic functional curves can be obtained from historical data sources.

(*v*) HES is a flexible method. If Ecologists in a specific geographical area feel that the functional curves do not correctly represent conditions of that area, curves can be altered and reweighted.

Disadvantage

(*i*) The curves and weights assigned to each variable are subjective to some extent. The subjectivity needs to be dealt with caution in order to avoid bias.

Conclusions

(*i*) More than three decades of global experience with EIA has amply demonstrated the multiple weaknesses of conventional EIA methods in assessing ecological impacts. Such weaknesses are more conspicuous in surface mining projects where *habitat destruction is inevitable, however a new habitat which heterogeneous substratum is given back to the Nature.*

(*ii*) Over the years a general contentious has emerged about the structure and sequence of EIA process (Sinha 2001). However, in India only the baseline studies are conducted in a comprehensive manner. *Other sequential steps, particularly the prediction and evaluation of impacts, are poorly understood and hence, are presented vaguely.*

(*iii*) Vast improvement in mitigation planning may be achieved by restoring to quantitative techniques where due care should be taken to allow for *risks and uncertainties like accumulation and transfer of toxic metals to the ecological food chain, invasion of unwanted weeds (pathaneium), withering of tree species etc.*

(*iv*) While habitat based system of ecological impact assessment seems to be a promising technique for overcoming the limitations of the conventional techniques, care should be taken to document the thought process that goes into quantifying the ecological impacts. Otherwise, the inherent subjectiveness of the habitat evaluation system may be buried under the spurious objectiveness.

(*v*) A disquieting feature of the Indian EIA/EMP reports is that the reclamation plans developed for mining projects are seldom based on the prediction and evaluation of ecological impacts. The reclamation plans so developed are thus poor in both form and content. Adopting an appropriate Eco IA method may go a long way in improving the reclamation plan towards regenerating both flora and fauna to match with the local ecological setting.

References

Canter Larry, W. (1996) *Environmental Impact Assessment* (2nd ed), McGraw Hill Inc. Singapore.

Environmental Assessment Source Book (vol.1,2,3) Published by The World Bank, Washington, D.C., 1991.

Gilpin, Alan (1994). *Environmental Impact Assessment-Cutting edge for the twenty first century.* CUP, London.

Glasson J., Riki Therivel and Andrew, Chadwick (1998) *Introduction to Environmental Impact Assessment,* Research Press, England, 1998.

Jain, R.K., Urbane, L.V., Stacey, G.S. and Balbach, H.E. (1993) *Environmental Impact Assessment.* McGraw Hill Inc. New York.

Maiti, S.K. and Sinha, I.N (2004) Ecological Impact assessment of Mining project: A pragmatic approach: Conference on " *Technology & management of sustainable exploitation of minerals and natural resources* (TAMSEM 2004), Dept of Mining Engg, IIT Kharagpur, Feb 5-7, 2004.

Morris, P. and Therivel, Riki (1995) *Methods of Environmental Impact Assessment,* UCL press, London.

Paul, A. Erickson *(1994). A Practical Guide to Environmental Impact Assessment,* Academic Press.

Sinha, Indra N. (2001) A framework of EIA for Environmental Sustainability. ENVIS monograph No. 8, Pub by ENVIS Centre of Mining Environment, CME, ISM, Dhanbad.

Therirvel, Riki Wilson, E., Thompson, S., Heaney, D. and Pritchard, D. *(1992). Strategic Environmental Assessment.* Earthscan, London.

Westman, Walter E. (1995) *Ecology, Impact Assessment & Environmental planning.* John Wiley and Sons, USA.

CHAPTER 2

ROLE OF EARTH SCIENCE IN DISASTER MANAGEMENT

Ajay Kumar Naithani and Y.P. Sundriyal

Department of Geology, P.B. No. 86, H.N.B. Garhwal University, Srinagar (Garhwal), Uttaranchal-246 174.

ABSTRACT

Natural disasters can be broadly classified into the domains of "geological" "climatic" and "marine" disasters. While avalanche / landslide; earthquakes and volcanic eruptions are included under geological disasters; blizzards, flood, drought, hurricane / tornadoes / cyclones and El Nino / La Nino, that are purely "climatic (atmospheric) disasters". Tidal waves, coastal erosion and tsunami can be termed broadly as marine phenomena with geological inputs. Extra-terrestrial impacts can be clubbed with the atmospheric (climatic) disasters as they can be monitored using satellites. This broad classification must ensure their grouping for monitoring and tackling by appropriate component professional agencies, unlike the present set up. Earth science related knowledge and R & D are pre-requisite to the understanding of natural hazards – their genesis, occurrence, mitigation and efficient management are based on this knowledge. Hazards never come without a brief or a protracted warning. Wasting that reaction period is at the root of our failure. This reaction time must be catalogued and valued. As a Chinese proverb puts it "Disasters offer new opportunities also". It is time for us to think a bit more scientifically and systematically to put in place a system of monitoring the nature in order to understand its dynamics with the object of forewarning major calamities that may befall us.

Key Words : Disasters, earth science

Introduction

Disaster is commonly used to denote any odd event, either natural or man-made, which plays havoc with the lives of the people. There is hardly any part of the globe whether in Asia, Africa, and Oceania or elsewhere, which is really free from natural disasters of one kind or the other. Human vulnerability to disasters especially natural disasters is an old-age phenomenon. A disaster results in disruption of normal pattern of life, which is usually grave, quite and sudden. It disrupts the socio-economic structure, health and communication systems, and also the essential services of the affected area. In practical terms, a disaster needs as accurate and precise focus with the regards to the requirements of the situation, because when it strikes, it not only leaves a devastating impact on human psyche but also creates panic among the people and the government. Disasters continue to strike into increased economic impact and their effects have continued to inflict unacceptable pressure on a world population which is already finding it difficult to make ends meet. The biggest sufferers are the least developed nations and specially economically weaker sections of the society.

The world's worst disasters occur between the tropic of Cancer and the tropic of Capricorn and this is the area, which contains the poorer countries of the world. Some of these countries remain in the category of developing nations primarily because of the severity and magnitude of the disasters, and we must say that disasters are a strong aggravating factor in the differences between wealthy nations and poor nations. The south Asia tops the list of fatalities due to natural disasters and, in fact world's some of the worst natural disasters have occurred in this part. If the menace of natural disasters could be contained, the course on the economies of many of the Asian countries would be overcome. A qualitative (subjective) assessment of the relative intensity of natural disasters faced by some of the most affected countries of Asia is given in Table 1. It is important to understand why the natural disasters seem to strike the Asian region, more than they strike other part of the world? Phenomenal increase in the population of Asia has driven people to the places where no one ever lived. Populated areas, especially those already vulnerable and under pressure of population are gradually turning hostile, thanks to intense human interference. The other reason is the deforestation, unplanned growth and proliferation of non-engineered constructions, which make disaster prone areas more vulnerable.

Types of Disasters

Disaster can be classified as (*a*) high probability, high risk natural events disaster like sea water rise, (*b*) high probability, more frequent, but less catastrophic events like earthquake, cyclone, landslide, tsunami, volcano and avalanches and (*c*) low probability, high risk events like impact of comets on earth.

Sea Water Rise

Sea water rise has the potential of drowning small island states. Since, one third of human population lives within 60 km of world's coastline, sea level rise may threaten the lands and lives of about one billion or a quarter of the world population. Sea water rise is known to take place firstly by the thermal expansion of the seawater and secondly because of the melting of ice from the high altitudes due to global warming (Bhadur and Naithani, 1999). It has been estimated

Table 1 : Qualitative assessment of intensity of natural hazard faced by some countries of Asia

Country	Earthquake	Floods	Landslides	Cyclones	Volcanoes	Drought	Tsunamis
Bangladesh	L	S	L	S	-	S	L
Bhutan	M	L	M	-	-	-	-
India	M	S	M	M	-	S	-
Indonesia	S	M	L	L	M	M	L
Malaysia	-	M	L	-	-	-	-
Myanmar	S	M	-	M	-	M	-
Nepal	M	M	M	-	-	M	-
Sri Lanka	-	M	S	M	-	M	-
S –Severe; M – Moderate; L- Low							

Source : Bhandari, 1999

that during the last century, the global sea water level rose by 10 to 25 cm. Of this, about 5 cm could perhaps be attributed to the thermal expansion and remaining 5 to 10 cm to deglaciation. It is therefore, important to pursue which suggest that by the year 2050, the sea level rise may vary between 23.8 cm and 116.7 cm and may vary from 56.2 cm to 345.9 cm in the year 2100 (Singh, 1996).

Earthquakes

Earthquakes are considered to be one of the most disastrous phenomenon and is usually sudden, with little or no warning. Earthquakes may be defined as the motion of the earth, usually resulting from the sudden release of stress. Well known on the basis of geological features and past occurrence of earthquake. If the quake is of sufficient magnitude it causes collapse of building and possible destruction of life and property. The severity of an earthquake depends on the amount of energy released, and is expressed in term of amplitude of the largest wave recorded on the seismograph, denoted by magnitude M. The severity of an earthquake is also indicated in terms of observed impacts on the environment, extent of damage caused to various structures, and human perception (Srivastava, 2004). This is the Modified Mercalli (MM) Scale. It is not yet possible to predict the magnitude, time and place of occurrence of earthquakes but earthquake prone areas are generally well defined.

The occurrence of earthquakes can be explained by the theory of plate tectonics. Plate tectonic theory is based on an earth model characterized by a small number of lithospheric plates (there are 7 major plates and many smaller ones) 70 to 250 km thick that float on a viscous under-layer called the asthenosphere. These plates, which cover the entire surface of the earth and contain both the continents and seafloor, move relative to each other at rates of upto ten cm/year. The region where two plates come in contact is called a plate boundary, and the way in which one plate moves relative to another determines the type of boundary: spreading, where the two plates move away from each other; subduction, where the two plates move toward each other and one slides beneath the other; and transform, where the two plates slide horizontally past each other. Deep oceanic trenches characterize subduction zones. Most of the volcanic islands or volcanic mountain chains are generally associated with the many subduction zones in the world oceans. Although, an earthquake can be caused by volcanic activity, movement along the fault zones associated with the plate boundaries generates most of the earthquakes. Most strong earthquakes, representing 80% of the total energy released World wide by earthquakes, occur in subduction zones where an oceanic plate slides under a continental plate or another younger oceanic plate (Gzovsky, 1962; Udias, 2000).

Almost, 75% of earthquake energy is released around Circum-Pacific belt, 20% in the Alpine – Himalayan belt and remaining 5% through the mid-oceanic ridges and other stable continental regions. The world's largest recorded earthquakes have all been megathrust events occurring where one tectonic plates subducts beneath another. These include : 1952 Kamchatka earthquake of magnitude 9.0; the 1957 Andrean Islands of Alaska earthquake of magnitude 9.1; 1960 Chile earthquake of magnitude 9.5; 1964 Prince William Sound, Alaska earthquake of magnitude 9.2 and 2004 Sumatra earthquake of magnitude 9.3. (Radhakrishna, 2005). Sumatra earthquake has broken a sector of the plate boundary extending some 1000 km, with vertical displacement of up to 20 m. It may also be noted that never before an earthquake of this size occurred in this part of the world.

Earthquake can be devastating to people as individuals, to families, to the social fabric at every level and to the economic life of the community. About 75% of all fatalities have been attributed to collapse of buildings. An earthquake disaster may also destroy or damage certain critical infrastructure i.e. lifeline, disrupting communication and supplies, water and gas lines, hospitals and fire station, etc. Earthquakes damage machinery, structures and industrial processing plants. One of the most severe follow-on disasters triggered by earthquakes is fire. Densely packed modern urban districts at one extreme and "shanty town" settlements of the poorer sections of urban sprawl at the other, both may well provide the potential for a conflagration following an earthquake. About 200 large magnitude earthquakes (M>6.0) occur in a decade and on an average about 18000 people die each year due to this disaster throughout the world. In the Indian Subcontinent, more than 60,000 people were killed since the beginning of recorded history. Around 56% of India total area is susceptible to seismic disturbances (Naithani, 2000). Himalayan region is very sensitive from earthquake point of view. The past recorded major earthquakes from the Indian Himalayan region is given in Table 2.

Despite much scientific and human endeavor, prediction and prevention of earthquake has proved to be a distant dream. Increasing frequency of tremors reminds us to find alternative approaches to strengthen our buildings' capabilities, which can increase capacities of our settlements at large to resist and face such tectonic waves of motions. One of the important aspects of the occurrence of earthquakes and damage due to them is that they teach us certain important lessons. If we take care of the various lessons taught by the past earthquakes, we can minimize considerably the damage resulting from earthquakes.

Table 2 : Main devastating earthquakes in the India Himalayan Region

S.No.	Year	Place	Intensity	Magnitude	Death
1.	1803	Garhwal	IX	8	200
2.	1826	Kashmir	X	8	1000
3.	1833	Nepal-Bihar	X	8	-
4.	1885	Kashmir	IX	8	3000
5.	1897	Shilong	IX	8.7	1600
6.	1905	Kangra	XII	8.6	19,000
7.	1906	Kangra	VIII	6.3	9
8.	1918	Istrimangal (Assam)	IX	7.6	-
9.	1934	Bihar-Nepal	X	8.4	11,000
10.	1947	Assam	X	7.9	-
11.	1950	Assam	XII	8.7	1526

Contd.

Table 2 Contd...

12.	1963	Badgaam	VII	5.1	79
13.	1967	Anantnag	VII	5.6	1
14.	1975	Kinnor	VIII	6.8	48
15.	1986	Dharmasala	VII	5.7	2
16.	1988	Bihar-Nepal	VIII	6.6	1004
17.	1991	Uttarkashi	VIII	6.6	712
18.	1999	Chamoli	VIII	6.8	104

Source : Seeber and Armbruster, 1981; Khattri and Tyagi, 1983; Ni and Barazangi, 1984; Khattri, 1987; Gupta, 1992; Narula *et.al.* 1995; Naithani, *et.al.* 2004.

Tsunami

Tsunami is a name of Japanese origin given to waves caused as a result of earthquakes beneath the sea bottom. Tsunamis or tidal waves are the seismic sea waves of long period, produced by a submarine earthquake, underwater volcanic explosion, or massive gravity slide of seabed sediments. However, earthquakes are responsible for almost 85 to 90% of the major tsunamis generated. For an earthquake to create a tsunami, it is important that the earthquake fault disrupts the ocean bottom. This would normally happen due to normal faulting or thrust faulting. In the open ocean such waves are barely noticeable even through they may be traveling at 700 – 900 km h^{-1}. On reaching shallow waters along the coastline, the energy of deep-sea waves gets transformed into very forceful tidal waves of great height (upto 30 m) and cause severe damage in coastal areas. There are frequent occurrences in certain locations bordering the Pacific Ocean, especially Japan. Table 3 gives a list of large tsunamis in the past.

Tsunamis in the Indian Ocean are however rare. The mid-oceanic ridges do not generate large enough earthquakes to create tsunamis. The 26th December 2004 Sumatra earthquake (M~9.3) (Raval, 2005) is now recognized to be the second largest earthquake to have been ever recorded, and the Andaman earthquakes of magnitude 7.3 soon after the Sumatra earthquake was an aftershock of the Sumatra earthquake, created tsunami waves which are estimated to have killed more than 2,30,000 people in Indonesia, Sri Lanka, India, Thailand and many other regional countries. In India, Nagapattinum, along the eastern coastline of India suffered the greatest damage and has reported the maximum number of dead. Tsunamis are not so uncommon in India as we are made to believe. Dr. Mihir Guha, formerly of the

Table 3 : List of large tsunamis in the historical past

Date of Events	**Damages Observed**
November 1, 1775	The great Lisbon earthquake generates a wave up to 20-feet high that strike coastal Portugal, Spain, and Morocco.
August 27, 1883	The eruption of the volcano Krakatau generates a massive wave that sweeps over the shores of nearby Java and Sumatra, killing 36,000 people.
June 15, 1896	The Sanriku tsunami strike Japan without warning. A wave estimated at more than 70 feet high hits a crowd gathered to celebrate a religious festival, killing more than 26,000 people.
December 17, 1896	Tsunami washes away part of the embankment and main boulevard of Santa Barbara, California.
January 31, 1906	A devastating offshore quake submerges part of Tumaco, Colombia and washes away every house on the coast between Rioverde, Ecuador and Micay, Colombia. Death toll estimated at 500 to 1,500.
April 1, 1946	Alaskan earthquake generates a tsunami that destroys North Cape Lighthouse, killing five. Hours later, the wave arrives at Hilo, Hawaii, killing 159 people and causing millions of dollars damage.

Contd.

Table 3 Contd...

May 22, 1960	A wave reported as up to 36-feet high kills 1,000 in Chile and causes damage in Hawaii, where 61 die and in the Philippines, Okinawa and Japan as it sweeps across the Pacific.
March 28, 1964	Good Friday earthquake in Alaska sends out a wave swamping much of the Alaskan coast and destroying three villages. The wave kills 107 people in Alaska, four in Oregon and 11 in California as it sweeps down in West Coast.
August 16, 1976	Tsunami kills more than 5,000 people in the Moro Gulf region of the Philippines
July 17, 1998	An offshore quake triggers a wave that strikes the north coast of Papua-New Guinea, killing some 2,000 people and leaving thousands more homeless.

Source : **Gupta, 2005**

Indian Meteorological Department has reported (The Hindu, 26.12.2004) that a tsunami struck Bengal (Present day Bhola district in Bangladesh), killed several lakhs of people. Tsunamis affecting the Indian / South Asian Coastal region in the past are: 1524, Near Dabhol, Maharashtra; 2 April 1762, Arakan Coast, Mayanmar; 16 June 1819, Rann of Kachchh, Gujarat; 31 October 1847, Great Nicobar Island; 31 December 1881, Car Nicobar Island; 26 August 1883, Krakatoa (Indonesia) volcanic eruption; 28 November 1945, Mekran Coast (Arabian Sea), Baluchistan. For a tsunami to hit Indian coast, it is necessary that a tsunamigenic earthquake occurs and its magnitude should be larger than 7, in an area from where tsunamis could propagate to the Indian coast. With experience and available data, two regions in the Indian Ocean capable of generating tsunamis are identified. One is Java-Sumatra seismic belt extending to Andaman and Nicobar and further north and other is the Makran coast and extension of 1819 and 2001 Kachchh and Bhuj earthquake faults respectively into Arabian Sea. These are also the tsunamigenic areas which could generate tsunamis for the rest of the Indian Ocean rim countries.

Volcanic eruption

Volcanic eruption is a naturally occurring phenomena at the earth's surface through which, solid and gaseous materials erupt. Approximately, 600 volcanoes are active or have erupted out of which about 50 volcanoes erupt every year. At present, about 10% of the world's populations lives on the area near potentially dangerous volcanoes. Short-term forecasts, within hours or months may be made through volcano monitoring techniques, including seismic ground deformation studies and observation and recording of geo-electric and geo-chemical changes.

Landslide

The landslide is among the serious and frequent disasters occurring in mountainous regions of the world. According to the Working Party on the World Landslide Inventory (1990), a landslide is "the movement of a mass of rock, earth or debris down a slope". This is the informal definition adopted by the Working Group and suggested for use in the International Decade for Natural Disaster Reduction (1990-1999). Landslides are a major problem in mountainous regions of India such as the Himalayas, Nilgiri Hills, Western Ghats, Northern region and Vindhyanchal, disrupting communication routes, increasing the sediment load on rivers and resulting in additional expenditure for the state exchequer on landslide control. The incidence of landslides in Himalaya is high to very high; in Northeastern Hills is high; in Western Ghats & the Nilgiris is moderate to high and in Eastern Ghats & Vidhyachals is low. Landslides take place most frequently during the monsoon rains, as water is an important catalyst for initiating landslides. In the Himalaya, the winter rains and at high elevations, frosts action and snow also contribute to landslides. Inherent geological characteristics of the strata and geometry of slope control the stability of the slope and in turn landslides. Active tectonic movements, such as the movement across faults and uplift of topography, occurring at a rate of 20 mm to 50 mm per year in the Himalaya, result in weaknesses across certain tectonic zones that are prone to extensive landslides and other types of mass movement. Deforestation, as a result of the falling trees for timber and removal of vegetation cover for development activities such as building roads, dams and settlements are also responsible for the increased rate of soil erosion and destabilization of slopes prone to landslides. On an average the damage caused by landslides in the Himalayan range is estimated to cost more than one billion US$ besides causing more than 200 deaths every year. This is considered as 30% of such types of losses occurring world-wide. In India alone, the cost of restoration works and associated economic losses due to landslides have been estimated conservatively to Rs 200 crores per annum (Naithani, 1999).

Snow avalanches

Snow avalanche is a natural disaster of snow bound mountains caused by structural failure of snow cover resting on steep slope. Snow avalanches are common in the Himalaya, especially the Western parts of Himalaya, i.e., snowy regions of Jammu and Kashmir, Himanchal Pradesh, Uttaranchal and also in some part of Sikkim and Arunanchal Pradesh. Topographic or terrain features and meteorological factors contribute to avalanche formation. Snow avalanches are of four types: dry snow directed action types, dry snow delayed action type, wet snow direct type and wet snow delayed type. Wet snow avalanches are more dangerous than dry snow avalanches (Upadhyay, 1995). Failure may occur as a consequence of: extreme stresses caused by intense snowfall, movement of human beings, animal or vehicles and by sound waves; metamorphic activities forming a weaker layer, which can fracture due to the load of snow above; excessive melting of upper layer when melt-water percolates underneath and lubricates snow or soil surface to trigger off slab avalanche.

Fractured snow pack runs down the slope, usually on specified path. Boulders, stones, loose soil, trees etc. also roll down with flowing snow gathering huge momentum and causing loss of life, destruction and damage of structure and disruption of communications or power supply system. Sometimes, if the avalanche falls in a lake or reservoir it blocks a river or stream, it can result in a flash flood. The Western Himalayas have many avalanche prone sites where hundreds of lives are lost and essential services disrupted every year.

Tackling of landslides and snow avalanches can be done through: preparation of hazard zonation maps; research and development work in control measures; instrumentation and modeling for risk assessment; training programmes on capacity building for landslides and avalanches studies and transfer of knowledge to user agencies. Stringent rules and strict enforcement are required to stop indiscriminate quarrying, mining, blasting and to prevent deforestation in vulnerable areas.

Retreat of glaciers

Glaciers have retreated over the past century in the mountainous regions of the globe, and in some cases glaciers retreated over several kilometers. Himalayan glaciers composed of the great part of the cryosphere in the low-mid latitude and high elevation besides the Antarctica and north-polar region. Presently, there are more than 5218 glaciers occupying an area of 38221 km^2, which is 9.04% of the total area of the Himalaya (Ravishankar and Srivastava, 1999). The field evidence gathered to date for the western Himalayan indicates a lack of synchronicity in the commencement of the recession from the little Ice Age maximum (Table 4). Large size terminal moraine indicates that the glacier occupied this part for a long time. If there is no break in the continuity between the oldest and the youngest terminal moraines, indicates that the retreat has been gradual. The presence of lateral moraine at lower altitudes, about 1,800 m is a proof of the existence of Pleistocene glacier upto that level (Table 5).

The glaciers by and large, are witnessing recession due to global warming (Prasad and Naithani, 2001). Over the past

Tabel 4 : Records of retreat of some Indian Himalayan Glaciers

Glaciers	Period	Years	Retreat of Snout (in Mts.)	Average (m/yr.)
Triloknath (H.P.)	1969 –1995	27	400	14.81
Pindari (Uttaranchal)	1845–1966	122	2840	23.27
Milam (Uttaranchal)	1849–1997	149	2472	16.59
Ponting (Uttaranchal)	1906–1957	52	262	5.04
Glacier No.3, Arwa Valley (Uttaranchal)	1932–1956	25	198	7.92
Shankalpa (Uttaranchal U.A.)	1881–1957	77	518	6.73
Chota Shigri (H.P.)	1962–1995	34	225	6.62
Bara Shigri (H.P.)	1906–1956	51	1750	34.31
	1957–1977	21	250	11.90
	1978–1995	18	650	36.11

Contd.

Zemu (Sikkim)	1909–1965	57	56	0.98
	1966–1975	10	320	32.00
	1977–1984	8	193.9	24.24
Gangotri (Uttaranchal)	1966–1971	6	138.85	23.14
	1972–1977	6	7.0	1.16
	1978–1989	12	364	30.33
	1990–1999	10	190	19.00

Source : Vohra, 1981, Ravishankar and Srivastava, 1999 and Naithani *et al.,* 2001

Table 5 : The presence of Terminal moraines at lower elevation is a proof of the existence of Pleistocene glacier upto that level (Data from Garhwal Himalaya)

Name of Glacier	Pleistocene Terminal moraines	Altitude (m)	Source of River	Present snout	Altitude (m)
Gangotri	Sukhi below Jhala	3061	Bhagirathi	Gaumukh	4120
Chorabari	Mundkata Ganesh	1800	Mandakini	Near Chorabari Tal	3840
Satopanth	Hanuman Chatti	2600	Alaknanda	Above Vasudhara fall	3800
Rishi Ganga	Upto Tapoban	2000	Rishiganag	Snout of South Rishi Bamak	4600
Sili Samudra	Upto Sutol	2200	Nandakini	Snout of Sili Samudra Bamak	3800

Source: Kushik (1972)

hundred years the global mean temperature has increased by about 0.5^{0}C. This is due to emission of green house gasses and mainly due to the rise in CO_2 concentration (Plass, 1962). Scientists from all over the world agree that global warming is still continuing and the volume of snow and ice is decreasing. The discharge from the snowfields and glaciers is also decreasing as a result of which many countries are going to face a deficiency of water particularly during dry season and our country is no exception in this regard. There is a growing need for glacier information in the context of climate change, and water resource needs and management. The role of snow has a far-reaching significance in the impact of avalanches on civil construction, protection of villages in the higher reaches, safety of roads as well as railways construction and defense installations in strategic areas.

Cyclone

Cyclone (depression or hurricane) is defined as an enclosed area of low pressure revealed by the pattern of pressure distribution, and has a characteristic pattern of wind circulation (anticlockwise around low pressure areas in the northern hemisphere). Hurricances are the intense tropical cyclones of Caribbean region and on the northeastern coast of Australia (Queensland). Similar types of storm in other parts of the world are known as 'typhoon' (western Pacific) and 'Cyclone' (Bay of Bengal). Every year these sudden, unpredictable, violent storms with winds bring widespread devastation to coastlines and islands lying in their erratic paths. Bay of Bengal and Arabian Sea are such important regions in the world where severe tropical cyclones usually originate in the months of May, November and December. While Bay of Bengal and Arabian Sea amount to only 3% of global ocean waters they account for about 13% of world cyclones. As a matter of fact, Indian coastline is affected by cyclones and related storm surges several times every year (Pisharoty, 1993). They are well known for their extreme destructive potential and impact on human activities. Associated with the severe cyclones are strong winds, storm winds, storm surges along the coast and there is heavy rainfall, which result in destruction to life and property. Proper prediction of this natural disaster requires understanding of its genesis, movement and landfall. Floods generated by cyclone rainfall are more destructive than winds. Most casualties are caused by coastal inundation by storm tides. The collapse of buildings, falling trees, flying debris, electrocution, aircraft accidents and disease from contaminated food and water in the post-cyclone period also contribute to loss of life and destruction of property. The damage survey due to major cyclone in India is presented in Table 6.

As prevention of formation of tropical cyclone is not in the realm of possibility. However, the loss of human lives and destruction of properties can be minimized by adopting prescribed shot viz. cyclone warning system and long term measures for risk reduction. Some structural i.e. construction of cyclone shelters, embankments, dykes, reservoirs, and coastal afforestation and non-structural, i.e., creation of proper awareness, training and education of people and introduction of insurance are the preventive measures that can be undertaken to mitigate the suffering of cyclone affected people. Strike implementation of the Coastal Regulation Zone (CRZ) norms is one of the remedies for future disasters. The CRZ notification (dated 19.2.1991 and subsequent amendments) was issued by the Ministry of Environment and Forests (Department of Environment, Forests and Wildlife), Government of India. Developmental activities in coastal region have adhered to the norms laid out in the CRZ notification which has four categories namely CRZ I, CRZ II,

Table 6 : Major Cyclones recorded in India.

Year of occurrence	Location of land fall	Damage Observed
1977	Machilipatnam, AP	Lifeline, Residential Buildings, Industrial Structures, etc.
1977	Nagapatnam, TN	Lifeline, Residential Buildings, Industrial Structures, etc.
1984	Sriharikota, AP	Roofing, Elevated Water Tanks, Communication Towers, Industrial Structures, 606 people loss their life, etc.
1989	Kavali, AP	Microwave Tower, Large Industrial Structures, Dwellings.
1990	Guntur, AP	Lifeline, Residential Buildings.
1993	Karaikal, TN	Residential Buildings, Industrial Structures.
1994	Madras, TN	Lamp masts, Hoarding, Dish Antennae.
1996	Kakinada, AP	Residential Buildings, Industrial Structures, Lamp Masts, Transmission and Communication Towers.
1998	Porbandar, Gujarat	Residential Buildings, Industrial Structures, Lamp Masts, Communication Towers, Port and Marine Structure.
1999	Orissa	Residential Buildings, Industrial Structures, Transmission and Communication Towers. Port and Marine Structure.

Source : Lakshmanan, 1998

CRZ III and CRZ IV. The notification imposes restrictions on certain activities in the coastal regions lying between High Tide Line (HTL) and Low Tide Line (LTL) and between HTL and 500 m landward of HTL and the CRZ I encompasses areas, which are ecologically sensitive and the contiguous area between HTL and LTL. No new construction is permitted within 500 m of the HTL. The CRZ II includes areas, which are already developed close to the shoreline, as in the case with coastal cities and towns. In this zone, construction of buildings can be taken up only on the landward side of the existing road. The areas covered under CRZ III include stretches that are relatively undisturbed (urban areas which are not substantially built up and rural areas). The land here upto 200m from the HTL is to be declared as "No Development Zone". Designated authorities can permit construction of hotels, beach resorts, dwelling units in the area lying between 200m and 500m (from the HTL). Andaman, Nicobar, Lakshadweep archipelago and other offshore islands come under the CRZ IV. The restriction on developmental activities is similar to that the CRZ III. In the case of developed (cities and towns) areas, for which there is practically no set back line (CRZ II), it is imperative to have other protective measures like preserving the existing mangroves and sand duns, planting casuarinas trees etc. Emplacement of hard structures like sea walls can be the last option, that too in places where it is absolutely necessary to save some important structures, at any cost. This may be even at the cost of loosing the adjacent beaches / structures.

Flood

Whenever, the magnitude of flow of water exceeds the carrying capacity of the channel within its banks, the excess water overflows on the flood plains and causes floods. There can be several causes of excess flow – heavy rainfall and cloudburst, the melting of snows on a large scale with attendant bursting of dams built of ice blocks, sudden and excess release of impounded water behind dams and bursting of man-made or landslide-built dams. The main types of flood are (a) Flash floods, (b) River floods and (c) Coastal floods. Floods, results of natural and physical phenomena, very much depend upon the pattern of rainfall, the topography of the land and the river channel configuration. The human intervention through unplanned and improper activities in the flood plains further aggravates the problem of flood. It should therefore, be understood that there can really be no such thing as an "absolute control" or "full proof protection" for all magnitude of floods for all times to come. So long the mankind is not in a position to modify the rainfall pattern or its distributions; floods are bound to occur. Major floods may result in physical damage, deaths and injuries, problems in drinking water supply and food shortages. In Himalayan region, flash floods is the significant disaster occurring in the river valleys. On an average, at least one event is reported every year from some part of the Himalaya (Naithani, 2003). Although, these phenomena are well known to the local people, they are sudden and unpredictable and may cause loss of life and property. In August 2004, a lake (Parechu) was formed in the Tibetan region, which might outburst and create serious problems in the downstream of Himachal Pradesh. This lake outburst/ landslide dam will result downstream flooding as a result of dam failure. The stability of this lake will depend on a number of factors such as the volume, texture, sorting of the dam materials, capacity of storage, nature of seepage water, rate of sedimentation and amount of water flow into lake. Depending on such conditions, the lake will be breached from within a few days to a few years. Through, controlled blasting we can save the life and property of the people downstream from this lake. The events

Table 7 : A List of cloudburst and flash floods caused by landslide and debris flow dam failures in the Western Indian Himalaya.

Name of Events	Year	Dammed River	Location	Losses
Gohna	26.08.1895	Birehi	Chamoli (U.A.)	Due to early warning not a single life was lost, despite the height of the floodwater in the Alaknada rose by 20 metres at Chamoli and very much more in the Ganga at Hardware.
Pehalgam	1963	Lidar River	68 km from Srinagar (J&K)	Uprooted a hotel and some large trees, killing several people.
Belakuchi	20.07.1970	Alaknanda	Chamoli (U.A.)	Belakuchi village wiped out, also washed away a 7 km stretch of road and 15 vehicles and killed about 100 people. The upper Ganga canal downstream from Hardwar was closed for 75 days.
Kandoliya stream	10.08.1978	Bhagirathi	Uttarkashi (U.A.)	The motorable road between Bhatwari and Tehri was breached in several places. Damage was caused to Maneri Bhali hydroelectric project, part of Uttarkashi town and Bhatwari village.

Contd.

Table 7 Contd...

Karmi	23.07.1983	Karmi stream	Almora (U.A.)	Landslide and debris flood killed 25 persons, 6 houses washed away, heavy loss of agricultural fields.
Soldam stream	29.09.1988	Sutlej	H.P.	The cloudburst washed away 15 houses and an apple orchard, 32 people were killed. The flash flood downstream washed away a 2 km stretch of road and a bridge over the national highways.
Maling stream	31.07.1991	Spiti	H.P.	It was a glacial lake outburst flash flood event. The failure of the temporary dam responsible for damage to a road section, a bridge and farm land downstream.
Jhakri	24.02.1993	Sutlej	H.P.	The blockade created a lake about 12 km long and 15 to 20 km wide. However, timely action, which consisted of cutting a channel through the dam drained the stored flow out and thus averted a flash flood downstream.

Contd.

Table 7 Contd...

Naptha	08.07.1993	Sutlej	Bhabanagar (H.P.)	A temporary natural dam was created with the formation of a 6 km long lake. The raised water level entered in some hydroelectric power installations, which remained inoperative for three months.
Rohtang	September 1995	Bias	North of Manali	The brusting of the dam generated a flash flood, causing a sudden increase in runoff that swelled into the dry paleochannel of the Bias river. This swept away several establishments, including a hotel, tourist resort and government installations that were located on the old paleochannel of the river. At the same time, downstream near Kulu, a landslide on the road cutting near the river killed 60 people.
Bangut	11.08.1997	Satluj	Kinnaur-Shimla	Damming of river Satluj and consequent flash flood in the downstream causes 140 lives loss, apart from this huge loss of the property and agricultural land.

Contd.

Table 7 Contd...

Chirgoan	11.08.1997	Andhra-Neogli-Khad stream	Shimla	In 10 minutes of massive flash flood swept away civil and government buildings, including a 15 MW power house, taking over 200 human lives.
Budakedar	11.08.1997	Balganag-Dharmganga	Tehri (U.A.)	The flash flood washed away 80 grain grinder, 6 bridges, electric line, transformer, irrigated agricultural fields and 400 mts stretch of road.
Sutlej flash flood	30.07.2000	Sutlej	H.P.	This flood washed away many bridges and a national highway in several places and killed about 200 people.

Source : Bhandari and Gupta, 1985; Nand and Prasad, 1972; Chansarkar, 1975; Krisnashawamy, 1980; Anbalagan, 1990; Naithani, 2003.

of flash flood from the Western Indian Himalaya are presented in Table 7.

It is, however, well recognized that flood management namely living with flood situation, but with maximum mitigation of its adverse effects on mankind, can be achieved (Lal, 1999). The concept of flood management aims for such planned measures which ensure profitable and economic utilization of the flood plains and water resources for the benefit of mankind. Since, the start of the National Flood Management on a planned basis in 1954, the main thrust of flood management efforts has been on structural measures to modify the floods and flood protection works. The disaster due to flood and erosion can be grouped into two parts namely structural and non-structural measures. Structural measures include: construction of embankments, raised platforms for affected villages, bank protection measures, channel improvements, town/ village protection works, ring bounds, diversion works, storage reservoir and detention basin. In view of cost effectiveness of non-structural measures and speedier implementation, the main thrust is expected to be now on the non-structural flood management measures. The non-structural measures include: watershed management, modifying the susceptibility to flood damage through flood plain zoning, regulation land use in different flood zones, broad methodology of flood plain zoning. In view of the ever-increasing flood damage reported by States, it is necessary to overcome the resistance to flood plain zoning measures and appreciate the advantages of planned activities in flood plains. The State Governments should identify the flood plains immediately, get the flood risk maps prepared and demarcate in the field and publicise this widely for information of all concerned, including the inhabitants in the flood plains.

Drought

A drought can be defined as a lack or shortage of water in a region for an unusually long period. Drought is relative term denoting a period during which rainfall is either totally absent or substantially lower than usual for the area in question, so that there is a resulting shortage of water for human use, agricultural, or natural vegetation and fauna. There are three types of droughts namely, meteorological caused by reduction in rainfall, hydrological caused by reduction in water resources and agricultural caused by loss of crop yields. Two thirds of India come under arid and semi arid regions and dry sub-humid conditions (Singh, 1995). All these areas are prone to droughts.

The severity of drought largely depends on the degree of moisture deficiency; rainfall and duration of dry spells; extent of irrigation facilities and size of the affected area. Drought devastates crops and brings hard time; leads to famines, economic destabilization, forced migration, malnutrition/ epidemics and loss of lives. These causes are interacting with each other and exacerbate drought conditions. Approximately, 50 million people in India are affected by drought every year, yet its disastrous consequences do not seem to have been adequately recognized (Dhameja, 2000). The ever-worsening drought scenario in the states of Gujrat, Rajasthan, Andra Pradesh and Orissa is indicative of the fact that drought management in the country is just a reactive exercise where relief and recovery schemes are implemented merely to meet the short-term requirements of the disaster. Socio-economic system plays a very vital role in the relief and rehabilitation measures during famines but drought mitigation largely depends upon the government policy and their proper implementation. In case of meteorological drought, Section 18 of national water Policy (GOI, 1987) dealing with drought management. Under this policy drought prone areas should be made less vulnerable to drought associated problems through soil moisture conservation measures, water harvesting of the ground water potential and the transfer of surface water from surplus area, where feasible and appropriate.

Drought is more of a man-made disaster resulting from a total mismanagement of our water resources. The big dams and irrigation projects can solve this problem and our traditional rainwater harvesting techniques are needed for domestic and agricultural purposes. Modern day science and technology should be made use of to look for alternative means of water conservation. Eighty per cent of the agriculture in the country is still dependent on ground water resources. Hydro-geomorphological maps can be prepared which will give an idea of the potential zones where water resources could be available. For this type of work, remote sensing data, geographical information system network and resource mapping have been found very useful. Scientific methods can certainly improve the traditional systems by identifying locations and means for water harvesting and developing land use patterns.

Desertification

The spread of desert-like conditions, particularly in arid or semi-arid areas, due to the influence of human activity and climatic changes is known as desertification. Deserts may be thought of in terms of biomes in which evaporation exceeds the average precipitation. The desert conditions are likely to develop wherever precipitation is less than 250 mm/yr. Desertification worsens the condition of poor, brings malnutrition and disease, and destabilizes the socio-economic bases of a country.

El Nino and La Nina (Double Trouble Twins)

El Nino and La Nino are known to influence weather across the globe. Since, about half of La Nina in the recent decade has followed El Nino as their shadows, they have come to be known as the mirror image of El Nino. El Nino occurs when a large mass of water in equatorial pacific region gets heated, the hot water then migrates eastward towards the west coast of South America, in the absence of usual easterly trade winds. The warm water layer which could be as much as one hundred metre thick covers the cold water along the coast line, thereby destroying the food chain and killing fishes, sea birds etc. Moisture rich warm air current produces devastating storms causing submergence of large tracts of coastal areas, drawing all that comes on its way. Impact of climatic hazards such as El-Nino are not factored into the Indian projections of drought or flood by our Meteorological Department, although the pioneer who conducted the initial research on El Nino was a Britisher, assigned with the Indian Meterological Department for the purpose in the beginning of last century. So far as India's agricultural remains a gamble with the monsoon, global phenomenon like El Nino cannot be ignored.

La Nina is characterized by unusually cool water temperature in the same area of tropical equatorial pacific that was warm during El Nino. An upsurge of water from the lower depth, which is even cooler because of the strong easterly trade winds, pushes warmer surface water westward towards Asia.

Impact of comets

Global catastrophes due to impact of comets has the potential for killing more than a quarter of the world population, and the probability of that happening (low) multiplied by the extremely high mortality, yields an average fatality rate that probably exceeds that of the other natural disasters of any scale (Morrsion *et al.* 1994). Arther C. Clark has recently predicted that in the year 2019, a major meteor impact will occur on the North Polar Ice Cap. There will be no loss of human life due to direct hit, but the resulting tsunamis will cause considerable damage along the coasts of Green Land and Canada.

Damages due to Natural Disasters

Major disasters, be it natural or man made, inflict huge damages to life and property. The average estimated cost of damage from natural disasters is million of dollars every year, which are off-course the statistics of immediate losses. No attempt has been made to calculate the long-term costs and there are also some cases for which it would be perhaps impossible to do so. Take for instance, the great Okhimath and Malpa tragedy of August 1998 in Uttaranchal. The villages of Bhenti and Kothi located on the left bank of river Madhyamaheshwar and Malpa, located on the right bank of river Kali got obliterated from the map of India by a natural disaster. During the International Decade for Natural Disaster Reduction (IDNDR, 1990-1999), the combined cost of disasters worldwide was estimated at US$ 741 billion by the Centre for Epideminology of Disaster in Belgium. The Indian Ocean tsunami has been called one of the world's worst natural disaster, which killed 2,30,000 peoples. 6,00,000 or more killed in Tasgshan in 1976 China earthquake and 2,00,000 or so on two occasions in the 1920s. Iran lost an estimated 50,000 people to a quake in 1990 and further 26,000 in December 26th 2003 earthquake. It is not even that Indian Ocean's deadliest disaster, for cyclones have often brought worse, most notoriously in 1970 when Bangladesh lost about 5,00,000 people (The Economist, 1 January, 2005, pp. 9). In the global context, the flood is the major disaster, accounting for nearly 30% of all deaths, damage and affected population. Drought accounts for around 20% of all the disaster damages, but does not result in too many deaths. Most of the natural disaster individual events in the world have killed only a small fraction of world's population: earthquake (2 million), cyclone (300,000), landslide (100,000), tsunami (100,000), volcano (30,000 immediate deaths, 92000 immediate plus secondary deaths), avalanche (20,000) (Cornell, 1982 Encyclopedia Britannica, 15th ed.). Be that so, it remains a fact that more attention is needed to counter numerous smaller events which are catastrophic for individual victims and which collectively mean a big drag on natural economies. So to reduce the impact of disaster, there is a necessity for coordinated international action in order to strengthen all aspect of disaster management, wherever this is possible.

Role of Earth Science in Disaster Mitigation

There are number of questions related to natural disaster which only earth scientist can answer for satisfactory engineering and technology interventions to develop. For instance, how the forces acting within the crust of the mother earth and the movement of the planets around it, combine to create earthquakes? Why the earthquake belts and the belts of volcanoes coincide, as they seem to do? Why the extinct volcanoes are slowly but surely becoming active? How an earthquake triggers a landslide or a tsunami? How does a volcano induce a tsunami? Why the track of a cyclone plays dice with planet earth? Which areas are landslide and avalanche prone?

Natural occurrences such as floods, earthquakes, cyclone, landsides, avalanches etc. simply cannot be stopped. What can be done, however, is to take preventive measures at various levels of society in order to make the impact of such natural hazards as harmless as possible for people and peoples' properties. At present more attention is needed to counter numerous smaller events such as earthquake, landslide, snow avalanche, flood, volcano, drought and tsunamis, which are catastrophic for individual victims.

Disaster mitigation is a major component of disaster management plan. In simple words, mitigation entails measures that could reduce the severity of the impact of a disaster on an area of populace. Structural mitigation strategies encompass land use control, construction of model disaster resistant houses, reduction in maritime activities, suitable building codes and architectural design of buildings and construction of rock fall barriers. Watershed management, channel improvement, alternative cropping pattern, livestock management and soil conservation techniques are also important components of disaster mitigation.

Good management of natural hazards makes economic sense. People must be educated and involved in this management with maturity and sensitivity. There is a necessity to set up Rural Science Centres to educate the masses in their regional languages to face such hazards. Training programmes should be organized on disaster management including sociological / psychological implications, security aspects and hierarchy of action-plan in case of a disaster and concurrently, strengthen and sensitise the administrative machinery to cope with such crisis situations. Introducing relevant concepts and imparting basic information at the school level is also extremely important in this context.

Earth scientist can do microzonation of the vulnerable areas. In this vulnerable building stock are identified in each microzone for suitable remedial steps. The site-specific data obtained by microzonation studies are used for landuse planning and town planning as well as earthquake resistant design of building for the benefit of common people. Earth scientist can publish leaflets, brochures, manuals about hazard resistant construction and general disaster problem including planning and preparedness in different regional languages and which can be distributed to general public in disaster prone areas.

Conclusions

The future scenario of natural disasters is likely to be too much worse if one were to go by the past history and the present trend of degradation. Despite the frightening picture, there is, however, a ray of hope which comes from the mind boggling advances in science and technology which seem to have the potential to reverse the decline, ushering a safer and more prosperous world habitat. Research in the field of modern services and technology and utility of the innovative and empirical methods to combat disasters can shape the disaster management strategies anew. Several new developments in this area could be cited. Thus, tsunami is predicted, earthquakes are properly monitored and calibrated for their magnitude, geographic location and focal mechanism and warning on cyclones, blizzards, tsunami etc. is given in sufficient advance. Need based reorganization of our scientific establishments and responsibility assignment are the need of the hour, if we have to safeguard our populations living in the hinterland as well as along the coastal tracts of India. There must be a clear-cut distinction of geological hazards on one side and atmospheric-marine disaster on the other, with provision for accurate data generation and timely data sharing. A confluence of modern technology and traditional wisdom can be attempted. The traditional practices to combat disasters are cost effective, environment friendly, sustainable, quite scientific and participatory. Their revival could prove to be a boon for disaster management activities. Natural hazards will continue to occur despite all the modernity and millions of dollars spent on their prediction. What is more important is to take steps to mitigate the severity of such disasters through social planning and preparedness, through proper and adequate emergency response exercises. A geologist, with his better knowledge of ground conditions, is in a better position to be of assistance to the community.

References

Anbalagan, R. (1990): Hazards of Erosion and sedimentation due to cloud burst in small catchment- A case study from Kumaun Himalaya, India. *In: Ecohydrology of High Mountain Areas* (Ed. S.R. Chalise) ICIMOD, Nepal, pp., 433-438.

Bhadur, J. and Naithani, A.K. (1999) Glaciers beating retreat. Down to Earth, New Delhi, April 30, 1999, pp., 27-34.

Bhandari, R.K. (1999) Natural disasters in Asia and the IDNDR stimulus. Proc. of the 11th Asian Regional Conference, Seoul, Korea, 16-20 August, 1999.

Bhandari, R.K. and Gupta, C. (1985) Problems of landslides in Himalaya and future directions. *In : Environmental Regeneration in Himalaya*. (Ed. J.S. Singh) Gyanodaya Prakashan, Nainital, pp., 39-57.

Chansarkar, R.A. (1975) Geological and geomorphologic factors in landslides investigations. In: Proc. Seminar on landslides and toe erosion problems with special reference to Himalayan region, Gangtok, pp., 54-66.

Dhameja, A. (2000) Coping with drought. Employment News, 10-16 June 2000 pp., 1 & 3.

Gupta, G.D. (ed.) (1992) *Himalayan seismicity* Geological Society of India, Bangalore.

Gupta, H.K. (2005) A Note on the 26 December 2004 tsunami in the Indian Ocean. Geological Society of India, Vol. 65, pp., 247-248.

Gzovsky, M.V. (1962) Tectonophysics and earthquake forecasting. Bull. Sci.Soc.Amm., 152: 485-86.

Kaushik, S.D. (1972) A glaciological study of the Garhwal Himalaya. Geol. Surv. Ind. Misc. Publ. No. 15, pp., 73-76.

Khattri, K.N. (1987) Great earthquakes, seismicity gaps and potential for earthquake disaster along the Himalayan plate boundary. Tectonophysics, 138: 79-92.

Khattri, K.N. and Tyagi, A.K. (1983) Seismicity patterns in the Himalayan plate boundary and identification of the areas of high seismic potential. Tectonophysics, 96: 281-297.

Krishnaswamy, V.S. (1980) Geological aspects of landslides with particular reference to Himalayan region. In State-of-the-art report. Proc. Intl. Symp. on landslides, Vol.2, New Delhi.

Lakshmanan, N. (1998) R & D towards cyclone disaster mitigation to buildings and structures – past, present and the future. *In : Natural Disaster Management and Mitigation*, (Eds. N. Mehrotra and B.G. Panicker), Manipal Institute of Technology, Karnataka, pp., 3-7.

Lal, R. (1999) Integrated watershed management in the global ecosystem. Springer Publ., Germany.

Morrison, D., Clark, R. Chapman and Paul Slovic (1994) Impact hazard in hazards due to comets and asteroids (Ed. Tom Gehrels). The University of Arizona Press, Tucson.

Naithani, A.K. (1999) The Himalayan landslides. Employment News, New Delhi, 20-26 February, 1999, pp., 1-2.

Naithani, A.K. (2000) Himalayan seismicity. Employment News, New Delhi, 28 October – 3 November 2000, pp., 1-2.

Naithani, A.K. (2003) Flash floods in the Himalaya. Employment News, New Delhi, 3-9 May 2003, pp., 1-2.

Naithani, A.K., Joshi, V., Kimothi, M.M. and Garg, J.K. (2004) Chamoli earthquake of 29th March 1999 Garhwal Himalaya, India: An observation. J. Science and Culture, 70(1-2) : 21-31.

Naithani, A.K., Nainwal, H.C., Sati, K.K. and Prasad C., (2001) Geomorphological evidences of retreat of Gangotri glacier and its characteristics. Current Science, 80(1) : 87-94.

Nand, N. and Prasad, C. (1972) Alaknanda Tragedy, A geomorphological appraisal. J. Nat. Geog., 18 (3) : 205-212.

Narula, P.L., Shome, S.K., Kumar, S. and Pande, P. (1995) Damage patterns and delineation of isoseismals of Uttarkashi Earthquake of 20th October, 1991. Memoir Geol. Soc. Ind., 30: 1-17.

Ni, J. and Barazangi, M. (1984) Seismotectonic of the Himalayan collision zone: geometry of the underthrusting Indian plate beneath the Himalaya. J. Geophysics Res., 89: 1147-1163.

Pisharoty, P.R. (1993) *Tropical Cyclone*. Bharatiya Vidya Bhawan, Mumbai.

Plass, N., 1962: Carbon dioxide and the climate. *In : Study of Earth* (Ed. J.F. White). Prentice-Hall Inc., N.J., 224-238.

Prasad, C. and Naithani, A.K. (2001) Global warming and the Himalayan environment. (in Hindi). J. Vigyan Garima "Shindu", New Delhi, 36 : 58-61.

Radhakrishna, B.P. (2005) O, horrible! Most horrible! Devastating Tsunami Strikes Coastline of India on 26th December 2004. Geological Society of India, 65 : 129-134.

Raval, U. (2005) Some factors responsible for the devastation in Nagapattinam region due to Tsunami of 26th December 2004. Geological Society of India, 65 : 647-649.

Ravishankar and Srivastava, D. (1999) Glaciated regime, environmental interaction and Himalayan ecosystem. Invited paper, Symp. Snow, ice and glaciers: A Himalayan Perspective, GSI, Lucknow, 9-11 March 1999, pp., 1-7.

Seeber, L. and Armbruster, J.G. (1981) Great detachment earthquakes along the Himalayan arc and international review. Am. Geophysical Union, Morris Ewing Series, 4 : 259-277.

Singh, T. (1995) *Drought Disaster and Agricultural Development in India*. People's Publishing House, New Delhi.

Singh, V.P., (1996) *Hydrology of Disasters*. Kluwer Academic Publishers, Netherlands.

Soman, K. (2005) Disaster management effects – some thoughts on where to begin. Geol. Soc. Ind., 65 : 770-772.

Srivastava, H.N. (2004) *Earthquakes: Forecasting and Mitigation.* National Book Trust, New Delhi.

Udias, Agustin, (2000) *Principles of Seismology.* Cambridge University Press, pp., 1-475.

Upadhyay, D.S. (1995) *Cold Climate Hydrometeorology*. New Age International Publishers, New Delhi, pp., 1-345.

Vohra, C.P. (1981) Himalayan glaciers. *In : The Himalaya Aspect of Change*, (Eds. J.S. Lal and A.D. Moddie) Oxford University Press, Delhi, pp., 138-151.

CHAPTER 3

ENVIRONMENTAL CRISIS IN RELATION TO INDOOR POLLUTION

Amit Krishna De

The Indian Science Congress Association,
14, Dr Biresh Guha Street, Kolkata-700 017.

ABSTRACT

Indoor air pollution contributes to lung disease, including respiratory tract infections, asthma, lung cancer, hypersensitivity and pneumonitis. In addition, it can cause headaches, dry eyes, nasal congestion, nausea and fatigue.

Biological pollutants, including molds, bacteria, viruses, pollen, dust mites, and animal dander promote poor indoor air quality and may be a major cause of days lost from work and school. In office buildings, heating, cooling, and ventilation systems are frequent sources of biological substances that are inhaled, leading to breathing problems.

Radon, a naturally occurring gas, can enter the home through cracks in the foundation floor and walls, drains, and other openings. A recent report estimates that radon is responsible for a large number of lung cancer deaths each year in the United States.

Environmental tobacco smoke (ETS) also called "secondhand smoke," a major indoor air pollutant, containing about 4,000 chemicals that cause lung cancer and heart disease deaths.

Formaldehyde found primarily in adhesive or bonding agents, may cause health problems, such as coughing, eye, nose, and throat irritation, skin rashes, headaches, and dizziness.

Asbestos fibers found in the home, including roofing and flooring materials can be inhaled into the lungs and can cause asbestosis (scarring of the lung tissue), lung cancer and mesothelioma, a relatively uncommon cancer of the lining of the lung or abdominal cavity.

Heating systems and other home appliances using gas, fuel, or wood, can produce several combustion products, of which the most dangerous are carbon monoxide and nitrogen dioxide. Carbon monoxide can impede coordination, worsen cardiovascular conditions, and produce fatigue, headache, confusion, nausea, and dizziness. Nitrogen dioxide irritates the mucous membranes in the eye, nose and throat and causes shortness of breath after exposure to high concentrations. Prolonged exposure to high levels of this gas can damage respiratory tissue and may lead to chronic bronchitis.

This article discusses in brief the adverse health effects of major indoor pollutants and suggests some ways of controlling them.

Key words: Indoor pollution, Biological pollutants, radon, Environmental tobacco smoke, Formaldehyde, carbon monoxide, asbestos, lead, health effects.

Introduction

Pollution may be a problem in the place we expect to be safest from harm — our homes. Indeed, many of the regulated outdoor pollutants are commonly found at higher levels indoors. Since, we spend 90% of our time indoors, and most of that at home, the quality of our residential environment is a serious health concern. Indoor pollution problems can cut across housing type, age, cost, location and condition. A brand-new house can make its occupants sick. So, can an energy-efficient, 15-year old tract house and so can a restored century house, a well-maintained, 70-year old, suburban double, and a dilapidated, inner-city row house. However, low-income, deteriorated housing poses the greatest risks. In Japan the adverse health effects caused by indoor air pollution are termed "sick building syndrome" (Nakazawa *et al.*, 2005).

On an average, we spend more than 90% of our time indoors and 65% of that time at home. That means daily exposure to levels of indoor air pollution that can be two to five and sometimes more than 100 times higher than outdoor levels. Young children, the elderly, and people with chronic health problems may be especially susceptible to the effects of indoor pollutants and they are also the people who spend the most time in the house. Asthma, for example can be aggravated by exposure to allergens and irritants in the home environment.

Unfortunately, it's often difficult to detect exposure to indoor air pollution because many of the contaminating substances give no warning and produce vague or sometimes similar symptoms that are difficult to pinpoint to a specific cause. Or, they produce symptoms years later when it's even more difficult to identify the source. The main sources of indoor pollution is given in Table 1 (De, 2000a).

Table 1 : Main Sources of Indoor Pollution.

Sources	% Contribution to Indoor Pollution
Ventilation	55
Building Materials	5
Biological	5
Outdoor Pollutants	10
Indoor Pollutants	15
Miscellaneous	10

According to a report from the US Government Accounting Office, an estimated 20% of all schools in the

United States have indoor air problems and 25% have unsatisfactory ventilation. Recent research has shown that indoor pollutants such as dust mites, molds, mildew, animal dander, insect waste and body parts (especially from cockroaches), and tobacco smoke have been strongly associated with increased respiratory problems for people with asthma, as well as people with allergies. This is especially alarming in light of the fact that asthma is on the rise, affecting an estimated 14.6 million people - 4.8 million of whom are under the age of 18. Today, asthma is the sixth-ranking chronic condition in the country and the leading serious chronic illness of children in the world.

Those with asthma, allergies and other forms of lung disease are not the only ones affected by poor air quality. Many more may be at risk for health problems related to indoor air pollution. Some of the most prevalent and harmful pollutants present in a typical house include those like :

1. Asbestos
2. Biological Pollutants
3. Carbon Monoxide
4. Formaldehyde/Pressed Wood Products
5. Household Cleaning and Maintenance, Personal Care, or Hobbies
6. Lead
7. Nitrogen Dioxide
8. Radon
9. Pesticides
10. Respirable Particles
11. Secondhand Smoke/Environmental Tobacco Smoke
12. Stoves, Heaters, Fireplaces and Chimneys

A details account is now given on some of the major indoor pollutants:

A. BIOLOGICAL POLLUTANTS

Biological pollutants, such as molds, mildew, bacteria, pollen, dust mites, and animal dander (tiny scales from hair, feathers, or skin), which promote poor indoor air quality and may be a major cause of days lost from work and school. Pollens originate from plants; viruses are transmitted by people and animals; bacteria are carried by people, animals, and soil and plant debris; and household pets are sources of saliva and animal dander. The protein in urine from rats and mice is a potent allergen. When it dries, it can become airborne. Mold, mildew, and fungi can be introduced into the home by either natural ventilation or through the air intake of a ventilation system (De 2000a).

Two conditions are essential to support biological growth (*i*) Nutrients and (*ii*) Moisture. Bacteria, fungi and molds find nourishment and can flourish in improperly maintained air ducts, air conditioners, humidifiers, dehumidifiers, air-cleaning filters, carpets and in improperly ventilated places where moisture is likely to collect, such as bathrooms, kitchens, laundry rooms and basements. In office buildings, heating, cooling and ventilating systems are frequent sources of biological substances which, when inhaled, lead to breathing problems. They can travel through the air and are often invisible. They enter the respiratory system either alone or by attaching themselves to particles of dust.

Health Effects

When biological agents are allowed to flourish in poorly maintained ventilation systems, severe health problems can result that can be experienced throughout an entire building. Infectious and noninfectious diseases can be caused by the various biological agents. Some biological contaminants trigger allergic reactions, including hypersensitivity, pneumonitis, allergic rhinitis, and some types of asthma. Infectious illnesses, such as influenza, measles, and chicken pox are transmitted through the air. Molds and mildews release disease-causing toxins. Symptoms of health problems caused by biological pollutants include sneezing, watery eyes, coughing, shortness of breath, dizziness, lethargy, fever, and digestive problems.

Allergic reactions occur only after repeated exposure to a specific biological allergen. However, that reaction may occur immediately upon re-exposure or after multiple exposures over time. As a result, people who have noticed only mild allergic reactions, or no reactions at all, may suddenly find themselves very sensitive to particular allergens.

Some diseases, like humidifier fever, are associated with exposure to toxins from micro-organisms that can grow in large building ventilation systems. However, these diseases can also be traced to micro-organisms that grow in home heating and cooling systems and humidifiers. Children, elderly people, and people with breathing problems, allergies, and lung diseases are particularly susceptible to disease-causing biological agents in the indoor air.

There is convincing epidemiological evidence that 'dampness' in buildings is associated with respiratory effects. In order to identify health-relevant exposures in buildings with 'dampness', a study 'Dampness in Buildings and Health' (DBH) was conducted among 10,851 children (1-6 years) in Sweden (Bornehag *et al.*, 2005). The prevalence of wheezing during the last 12 months of the children was found to be 18.9% and doctor-diagnosed asthma 5.4%. Rhinitis during the last 12 months was reported for 11.1% of the children and eczema during the last 12 months 18.7%. Water leakage was reported in 17.8% of the buildings, condensation on windows in 14.3%, and detached flooring materials in 8.3%.

Furthermore, it was found that the combination of water leakage in the home and PVC as flooring material in the child's or parent's bedroom was associated to higher prevalence of symptoms among children. The study showed that moisture-related problems in buildings are a risk factor for asthma and allergic symptoms among preschool children.

Some suggestions - Control of moisture levels in the home is key to controlling many biological pollutants (Nero, 1988). Moisture can invade the home through many sources, including leaks and seepage and even through some appliances. Standing water, water-damaged materials, or wet surfaces serve as breeding grounds for molds, mildews, bacteria, and insects. Additionally, house dust mites and cockroaches thrive in damp, warm environments. Humidity levels can be reduced by installing and using exhaust fans in the kitchen and bathroom, venting clothes dryers outdoors, ventilating attics and crawl spaces, cleaning humidifiers on a regular basis, and cleaning and drying (or replacing) water-damaged carpets and building materials as soon as possible after the damage occurs. Keeping a house clean in general reduces the amount of pollens, animal dander, cockroach dust and dust mites present.

Poorly maintained ventilation systems cultivate the population of biological agents. Good ventilation is important in preventing the build-up of biological particles. Controlling dust is very important for people who are allergic to animal dander and mites. These actions can eliminate much of the moisture that builds up from everyday activities. Another benefit of using kitchen and bathroom exhaust fans is that they can reduce levels of organic pollutants that vaporize from hot water used in showers and dishwashers. At the office, maintenance of the ventilation system should be undertaken regularly and the filters should be kept clean while in operation, so that there is an adequate regular exchange of air throughout the building.

House dust mites, pollens, animal dander, and other allergy-causing agents can be reduced, although not eliminated, through regular cleaning (Nero, 1988). People who are allergic to these pollutants should use allergen-proof mattress encasements, and avoid room furnishings that accumulate dust, especially if they cannot be washed in hot water. Bedding should be washed in hot water (at least 130 degrees F) at least every 7 to 10 days to kill dust mites. Synthetic bedding can be used instead of wool blankets or feather-stuffed pillows and comforters, which do not stand up to washing. Allergic individuals should also leave the house while it is being vacuumed because vacuuming can actually increase airborne levels of mite allergens and other biological contaminants. Using central vacuum systems that are vented to the outdoors or vacuums with high efficiency filters may also be of help.

B. RADON

Radon is a radioactive gas that is found in the earth's rock and soil. It is formed by the natural breakdown of radium, which is itself a decay product of uranium. Radon arises from uranium, which is present in small amounts in the soil and rock throughout the earth's crust, but particularly in volcanic rocks such as granite and in dark shales such as those underlying west-central Ohio. As uranium undergoes natural radioactive decay, it gives off radiation and transforms into a series of elements, which include radon. Radon enters the home through cracks in the foundation, floor drains, sump pumps, and other openings. As radon decays, it forms radioactive by-products called either "progeny," "decay products" or "daughters" which, if inhaled, can damage lung tissue and cause lung cancer (Pawel and Puskin, 2004).

Radon radiation is measured in Pico curies (trillionths of a curie) per liter of air (pCi/L). The average outdoor radon level is about 0.4 pCi/L; the average indoor level is about 1.3 pCi/L. Lifetime exposure to 4 pCi/L means a 50% added lifetime risk of lung cancer.

Homes with elevated levels of radon have been found in all countries, and therefore all homes should be tested for radon, regardless of their geographic location. Testing for radon is neither difficult nor costly. Most people can use low-cost, do-it-yourself kits. Nearly one out of every 15 homes in the United States has radon levels above 4pci/L. Indoor radon exposure is estimated to be the second-leading cause of lung cancer, responsible for thousands of deaths each year in the United States alone.

Water is another possible pathway for bringing radon into the home. Water, when in contact with rock containing uranium, absorbs the radon gas. The radon is then carried into the home and released into the air in household dishwashers, faucets, showers, or washing machines. Water-related radon problems usually involve deep private wells rather than community water supplies. In some unusual situations, radon may be released from home construction materials such as stone used to build fireplaces or solar heating storage systems (De, 2000a).

Health effects

Invisible and odorless, radon is a health hazard when it accumulates to high levels inside homes or other structures. When radon is inhaled, its radioactive breakdown products deliver a radioactive assault to the lungs, which increases the risk of lung cancer. Radon may be the leading cause of lung cancer among nonsmokers. But because smoking substantially increases the susceptibility to radon damage to the lungs, most lung cancer deaths due to radon are among smokers. Radon is estimated to be the second leading cause of lung cancer in the U.S. today, causing thousands of deaths each year. Cigarette smoking remains the primary cause.

Some suggestions: There are two basic strategies for reducing indoor radon: 1) To stop radon from getting in and 2) To remove it if it does get in (Nero, 1988). Radon entry can be stopped by sealing entry points. Radon levels can be lowered through a variety of repairs, from sealing cracks in floors and walls to change the flow of air into the building (e.g., covering sump pumps, sealing crawl space soil), using sub-slab ventilation to draw off radon before it enters, and reducing air pressure differences between the basement and surrounding soil which drives radon in. Removing radon involves increasing ventilation of the basement.

Today's technology can reduce indoor radon levels to below 4 pCi/L; in most cases, to 2pCi/L or less. A variety of methods are used to reduce indoor radon levels, from sealing cracks in floors and walls to changing the flow of air into the home. Simple systems, known as sub-slab depressurization, use pipes and fans to remove radon gas from beneath the concrete floor and foundation before it can enter the home. Radon is vented above the roof, where it safely disperses. Lowering high radon levels requires technical knowledge and special skills.

- Sub-slab depressurization uses pipes and fans to remove radon gas from beneath the concrete floor and foundation before it can enter the building. Radon is vented above the roof, where it safely disperses.
- Soil depressurization is used to ventilate the soil surrounding the home so that radon is drawn away before it can enter the structure.

C. COMBUSTION PRODUCTS

Combustion products — dangerous gases and particles — can be generated by household appliances, such as furnaces, water heaters, gas stoves, space heaters, and fire places (De, 2000a). If these appliances are not adjusted properly and/or they are not exhausted or vented adequately, they can release carbon monoxide, nitrogen dioxide, other gases, and small particles into the indoor air. Hydrocarbons and nicotine are mostly emitted from tobacco smoke. Smoke also comes from automobile exhaust, specially, if there is a garage inside the house.

(*i*) Carbon monoxide is a colorless, odorless gas formed due to incomplete burning of carbon. It is a product of motor vehicle exhaust, which contributes about 60% of all CO emissions nationwide. High concentrations of CO generally occur in areas with heavy traffic congestion. In cities, as much as 95% of all CO emissions may emanate from automobile exhaust. Nearly 300 people die every year from carbon monoxide exposure related to residential combustion appliances, and thousands of others become ill or seek medical attention.

Any fuel-burning appliance that is not adequately vented and maintained can be a potential source of CO, including:

- Gas appliances (furnaces, ranges, ovens, water heaters, clothes dryers, etc.)
- Fireplaces, wood and coal stoves, space heaters
- Charcoal grills, automobile exhaust fumes, camp stoves, gas-powered lawn mowers, and power tools

Health effects - Carbon monoxide enters the bloodstream through the lungs and reduces oxygen delivery to the body's organs and tissues. The health threat from CO is most serious for those who suffer from cardiovascular disease.

CO combines with the hemoglobin of the blood and interferes with its ability to deliver oxygen throughout the body. Lower concentrations can cause headaches, dizziness, nausea, confusion, fatigue, and chest pain, symptoms which are sometimes confused with the flu or food poisoning. At higher levels of exposure, healthy individuals are also affected. Visual impairment, reduced work capacity, reduced manual dexterity, poor learning ability, and difficulty in performing complex tasks are all associated with exposure to elevated CO levels.

(*ii*) Nitrogen dioxide is a colorless and odorless gas that can irritate the mucous membranes in the eyes, nose, and throat. High concentrations can cause shortness of breath and may also increase the risk of respiratory infection and emphysema. Particulate matter from incompletely burned fuels can lodge in the lungs and irritate or damage lung tissue.

Some Suggestions: Furnaces and chimneys should be professionally inspected annually. Carbon monoxide detectors should be installed, but not in lieu of an annual furnace inspection. Signs of incomplete combustion or poor venting of flue gases may be foul smells from the appliance or unusual condensation and black soot on walls and windows. Other steps to be taken to reduce exposure to combustion products in homes include: not using unvented space heaters, installing and using exhaust fans over gas stoves, making certain that the doors on wood stoves and fire places are tight-fitting and that the wood burned is properly dried and not painted or treated.

As the symptoms of carbon dioxide poisoning are similar to other illnesses, such as the flu. Low-level exposure to carbon monoxide over a long period of time can be just as harmful as high concentrations over a short period of time -

particularly to infants and children. The gas appliances should also be checked regularly.

(*iii*) Tobacco smoke: Tobacco smoke is one of the most common indoor air quality problems. It contains over 4,000 compounds, at least 40 of which are known human carcinogens. Exposure to environmental tobacco smoke is responsible for approximately 3,000 lung cancer deaths each year in nonsmoking adults and impairs the respiratory health of many more children. Infants and young children whose parents smoke in their presence are at increased risk of lower respiratory tract infections. Secondhand smoke - the smoke from someone else's cigarette, cigar or pipe - contains some 4,000 chemicals, including nicotine, formaldehyde, carbon monoxide, and other known cancer-causing agents. While smokers themselves face serious health risks from tobacco, it is now clear that even people who don't smoke may be threatened. Exposure to secondhand smoke may have certain harmful - possibly even fatal - health effects such as lung cancer and heart disease. Secondhand smoke, also known as environmental tobacco smoke, comes from two sources: mainstream and sidestream smoke. Mainstream smoke is what smokers pull through the mouthpiece when they inhale or puff. Nonsmokers are exposed to mainstream smoke when smokers exhale. Sidestream smoke goes directly into the air from the burning end of the cigarette. Sidestream smoke has large amounts of certain noxious compounds and continuously pollutes the air. Persons exposed to secondhand smoke at work are at increased risk for adverse health effects. Levels in restaurants and bars were found to be 2 to 5 times higher than in residences with smokers and 2 to 6 times higher than in office workplaces (Shopland, 2001).

Health effects

Secondhand smoke has been classified as a Group A

carcinogen, a rating used only for substances proven to cause cancer in humans places (De, 2000b). It is estimated to be responsible annually for approximately 3,000 lung cancer deaths, 35,000 - 62,000 cardiovascular disease deaths. Secondhand smoke is a direct health threat to people who already have heart and lung disease, and increases the risk of serious respiratory disease during the first two years of a child's life. Children exposed to secondhand smoke experience many severe health problems. In the first two years of life, babies of parents who smoke at home have a much higher rate of lung diseases such as bronchitis and pneumonia. Several studies have noted an aggravation of asthma in children of smoking parents. A very critical observation is that children of parents who smoke have a slower rate of growth in lung function as the lung matures. It has been suggested that this may lead to increased susceptibility to developing lung disease in adult life. A study found that nonsmokers exposed to environmental smoke were 25% more likely to have coronary heart diseases compared to nonsmokers not exposed to smoke (He *et al.,* 1999). Secondhand smoke exposure may cause buildup of fluid in the middle ear.

Some Suggestions: Smoking at home should be avoided. Smoking should not be allowed particularly if children are present, particularly infants and toddlers. Ask smokers to go outside while they smoke. If someone must smoke inside, limit them to rooms where windows can be opened or fans can be used to send the smoke outside. Help people who are trying to quit smoking places (De, 2000b).

D. PESTICIDES, BUILDING MATERIALS AND CONSUMER PRODUCTS

A wide variety of pesticides, building materials and consumer products used in and around the home contain toxic ingredients, which can contaminate the indoor environment. Although, indoor exposures are generally quite low, they are consistently higher than outdoor concentrations, and can be substantial following remodelling, pesticide application, or other product use. Toxic chemicals that can be emitted from numerous consumer products, building materials and pesticides are given below:

(a) Pesticides

Nearly, 80% of most people's exposure to pesticides occurs indoors. Measurable levels of up to a dozen pesticides have been found in the air inside homes. The amount of pesticides found in homes appears to be greater than can be explained by recent pesticide use in those households; other possible sources include contaminated soil or dust that floats or is tracked in from outside, stored pesticide containers, and household surfaces that collect and then release the pesticides. Pesticides used in and around the home include products to control insects (insecticides), termites (termiticides), rodents (rodenticides), fungi (fungicides), and microbes (disinfectants). They are sold as sprays, liquids, sticks, powders, crystals, balls, and foggers.

Health Effects

There are many types of pesticides, with active ingredients that work in different ways places (De, 2005). Potential health effects from exposure to pesticides include headache, respiratory and skin irritation, dizziness, muscular weakness and nausea. In addition to the active ingredient, pesticides are also made up of ingredients that are used to carry the active agent. These carrier agents are called "inerts" in pesticides because they are not toxic to the targeted pest; nevertheless, some inerts are capable of causing health problems. Some pesticide active ingredients and inert compounds are considered carcinogenic. The effect of

Chlorpyrifos and Pentachlorophenol residues, used as fungicide and herbicide, persist upto two weeks after application, exposing people to levels far above those recommended limits. Incidentally, Pentachlorophenol was used as a wood preservative until the 1970s. Of particular concern are exposure of pregnant women and their fetuses because little is known about the potential development hazards of such exposure (Berkowitz *et al.*, 2003). Assessment of airborne organophosphorus pesticides in houses of young children (1-6 years old) and childcare facilities was conducted following pesticide applications in an agricultural community in Japan. Estimated daily inhalation exposures were inversely correlated to the proximity of their activity location to the pesticide-applied farm (Kawahara *et al.*, 2005).

Suggestions

There is a clear need for more data on pesticide exposure among pregnant women because fetuses are known to be particularly vulnerable to environmental toxicants. Use of alternative methods, such as Integrated Pest Management, which uses less toxic substances, should be encouraged to reduce pesticide exposure. The following guidelines to be followed for reducing exposure to pesticide in the home :

- Use strictly according to manufacturer's directions.
- Mix or dilute outdoors.
- Apply only in recommended quantities.
- Increase ventilation when using indoors. Take plants or pets outdoors when applying pesticides/flea and tick treatments.
- Use nonchemical methods of pest control where possible.
- If you use a pest control company, select it carefully.

- Do not store unneeded pesticides inside home; dispose of unwanted containers safely.
- Store clothes with moth repellents in separately ventilated areas, if possible.
- Keep indoor spaces clean, dry, and well ventilated to avoid pest and odor problems.

(b) Formaldehyde

It is an important chemical used widely by industry to manufacture building materials and numerous household products. It is also a by-product of combustion and certain other natural processes. It is found in wood products (e.g., fiberboard, plywood and particle board), building materials, smoking, household products, fuel-burning appliances, like gas stoves or kerosene space heaters. Formaldehyde, by itself or in combination with other chemicals, serves a number of purposes in manufactured products. For example, it is used to add permanent-press qualities to clothing and draperies, as a component of glues and adhesives, and as a preservative in some paints and coating products.

In homes, the most significant sources of formaldehyde are likely to be pressed wood products made using adhesives that contain urea-formaldehyde (UF) resins. Pressed wood products made for indoor use include: particleboard (used as subflooring and shelving and in cabinetry and furniture); hardwood plywood paneling (used for decorative wall covering and used in cabinets and furniture); and medium density fiberboard (used for drawer fronts, cabinets, and furniture tops). Medium density fiberboard contains a higher resin-to-wood ratio than any other UF pressed wood product and is generally recognized as being the highest formaldehyde-emitting pressed wood product. Urea-formaldehyde foam insulation (UFFI) was generally not used after the 1980s because of problems with formaldehyde "off gassing" into the indoor air; now, years after installation, "UFFI homes" are generally not a problem.

The patterns of residential exposure and the health effects of the mix of exposures at residential levels are not well established, but some studies have found worrisome associations with serious illness, particularly in children. The chemicals typically measured in residential indoor air, depending on level and duration of exposure and the sensitivity of the exposed population, can have a range of short and long-term health effects, from eye irritation to neurotoxicity to cancer.

Health effects

Exposure to formaldehyde vapors can cause eye, nose and throat irritation; coughing; skin rashes; headaches; dizziness; nausea; vomiting and nosebleeds. Formaldehyde has also been shown to cause cancer in laboratory animals, and the U.S. Environmental Protection Agency (EPA) ranks formaldehyde as a probable human carcinogen. However, the most recent EPA estimate of the lifetime cancer risk associated with exposure to formaldehyde in homes is equal or less than 1 chance in a million of developing cancer.

Some Suggestions

When considering purchases, read ingredient lists and warnings. For example exterior-grade pressed wood products emit less formaldehyde and newer water-based finishes eliminate problems with solvents. Label warnings should be taken seriously. Painting / polishing furnitures should be done outdoors, if possible. The children, the elderly and people with chronic illnesses should be kept out of the work area. Protective gear should be worn. The closets and cupboards should be ventilated aggressively with fans, when finished. Hazardous products should not be used while pregnant, smoking, consuming alcohol, eating or wearing contact lenses (Nero, 1988).

Some studies suggest that coating pressed wood products with polyurethane may reduce formaldehyde emissions for some period of time. To be effective, any such coating must cover all surfaces and edges and remain intact. Increase the ventilation and carefully follow the manufacturer instructions while applying these coatings. Maintain moderate temperature and humidity levels and provide adequate ventilation. The rate at which formaldehyde is released is accelerated by heat and may also depend somewhat on the humidity level. Therefore, the use of dehumidifiers and air conditioning to control humidity and to maintain a moderate temperature can help reduce formaldehyde emissions. (Drain and clean dehumidifier collection trays frequently so that they do not become a breeding ground for micro-organisms.) Increasing the rate of ventilation in your home will also help in reducing formaldehyde levels.

(c) Asbestos

Asbestos — a family of naturally-occurring mineral fibers — was commonly used in boiler and furnace insulation, floor tiles, roofing, siding, and other materials in houses built before the 1950s, but was not entirely banned until the late 1970s. Although, there may be many sources of asbestos in houses, there is an exposure pathway only if the asbestos-containing material is disturbed and microscopic asbestos fibers are released into the air. If the asbestos is firmly embedded in the product, such as in vinyl-asbestos floor tile or asphalt-asbestos roofing material, or if the material is covered, such as intact boiler pipe insulation, there is likely minimal current exposure. However, dangerous amounts of asbestos fibers may be released if the material is demolished, sawed, drilled, or sanded.

The principal forms of asbestos include chrysotile, crocidolite, amosite, tremolite, actinolite, and anthophyllite.

All but chrysotile are classified as amphiboles, which tend to have a thin, needle-like appearance. Chrysotile breaks into curly fibers. There is evidence that amphibole asbestos fibers are more potent for causing mesothelioma than chrysotile fibers.Common products that might have contained asbestos in the past, and conditions which may release fibers, include:

- Steam pipes, boilers, and furnace ducts insulated with an asbestos *blanket* or asbestos paper tape. These materials may release asbestos fibers if damaged, repaired, or removed improperly.
- Resilient floor tiles (vinyl asbestos, asphalt, and rubber), the backing on Vinyl sheet flooring, and adhesives used for installing floor tile. Sanding tiles can release fibers. So may scraping or sanding the backing of sheet flooring during removal.
- Cement sheet, millboard, and paper used as insulation around furnaces and wood-burning stoves. Repairing or removing appliances may release asbestos fibers. So may cutting, tearing, sanding, drilling, or sawing insulation.
- Door gaskets in furnaces, wood stoves, and coal stoves. Worn seals can release asbestos fibers during use.
- Soundproofing or decorative material sprayed on walls and ceilings. Loose, crumbly, or water-damaged material may release fibers. So will sanding, drilling, or scraping the material.
- Patching and joint compounds for walls and ceilings, and textured paints. Sanding, scraping, or drilling these surfaces may release asbestos.
- Asbestos cement roofing, shingels, and siding. These products are not likely to release asbestos fibers unless sawed, drilled or cut.
- Artificial ashes and embers sold for use in gas-fired fireplaces. Also, other older household products such

as fireproof gloves, stove-top pads, ironing board covers, and certain hairdryers.

- Automobile brake pads and linings, clutch facings, and gaskets.

Asbestos may also occur naturally. Ultramafic or serpentine rock material often contains asbestos. This type of rock is found in many parts of California, and is especially abundant in the costal regions. Asbestos may be found in dust from unpaved roads or driveways surfaced with ultramafic or serpentine rock.

Health effects

From studies of people who were exposed to asbestos in mines, factories and shipyards, we know that breathing high levels of asbestos fibers can lead to an increased risk of:

- lung cancer;
- mesothelioma, a cancer of the lining of the chest and the abdominal cavity; and
- asbestosis, in which the lungs become scarred with fibrous tissue.

Over a period as long as 20 or 30 years, breathed-in asbestos fibers in the lungs can increase the risk of lung cancer and mesothelioma (cancer of the lining of the chest and abdominal cavity). Smoking dramatically increases the risk of lung cancer from asbestos exposure. Average indoor asbestos levels are extremely low and so the related health risk is assumed to be low from the mere presence of asbestos-containing material. However, exposure levels can increase if the material is disturbed (Gaensler, 1992).

Some Suggestions

Generally, it is best to just leave asbestos-containing material alone unless it must be disturbed for furnace replacement or for other repair or renovation. It may often be safer to cover the asbestos-containing material with an exposure barrier than to remove it. If removal or substantial covering is required, a licensed asbestos contractor should do the work.

(d) Lead

Leaded paint was used in most houses and apartments built prior to the 1950s and in some until 1978. Leaded paint is most likely to be found on siding, porches, windows, kitchen and bath walls, and trim. Deteriorated or improperly removed leaded paint can contaminate household dust and soil. In the past, automotive sources were the major contributor of lead emissions to the atmosphere. As a result of regulatory efforts to reduce the content of lead in gasoline, the contribution from the transportation sector has declined over the past decade. Today, metals processing is the major source of lead emissions to the atmosphere. The highest concentrations of lead are found in the vicinity of nonferrous and ferrous smelters, battery manufacturers, and other stationary sources of lead emissions.

Children are poisoned by exposure to lead in peeling paint, and in lead-contaminated dust and soil. Children swallow lead that gets on their hands, toys, and pacifiers. Most children are poisoned by normal hand-to-mouth contact with lead-contaminated dust and soil around the house; some children eat paint chips and dirt. Other lead hazards include lead dust brought home on work clothes and lead in hobby and craft materials. Although, drinking water is generally not a major source of lead poisoning, there are some public water systems, that have found elevated tap levels under worst-case testing. Corrosion control measures have been instituted to reduce the leaching of lead from the house plumbing system.

Health Effects

Exposure to lead occurs mainly through the inhalation of air and the ingestion of lead in food, water, soil, or dust. It accumulates in the blood, bones, and soft tissues. Because, it is not readily excreted, lead can also adversely affect the kidneys, liver, nervous system, and other organs. Excessive exposure to lead may cause neurological impairments such as seizures, mental retardation, and/or behavioral disorders. Recent studies also show that lead may be a factor in high blood pressure and subsequent heart disease.

Childhood lead poisoning has been declared by the U.S. Public Health Service to be "the most common and societally devastating environmental disease of young children." Elevated blood lead has been associated with developmental delays, deficits in intellectual performance and neurobehavioral functioning, decreased stature, and diminished hearing acuity. Even at low doses, lead exposure is associated with damage to the nervous systems of fetuses and young children, resulting in learning deficits and lowered IQ.

Children between the ages nine months and three years are at the greatest risk because they have a high degree of hand-to-mouth activity, they absorb ingested lead more efficiently, and because of the heightened vulnerability of their developing nervous system to lead toxicity. However, lead accumulated during childhood can remain stored in bone for many years and may be released from bone latter in life. This may happen during pregnancy and thus poison the fetus. There is also speculation that adult neurotoxic effects may occur when lead is released from the bone as part of the aging process.

Over the past 15 years there has been a dramatic 77% decline in children's average blood-lead levels, due primarily to the elimination of lead from gasoline. However, for poor and minority children living in deteriorated housing, the rates remain at epidemic levels. Even children in well-maintained housing can be put at risk by lead-contaminated soil and by lead dust generated during home repair, renovation, and remodeling.

Average adult blood lead levels are low and adult lead poisoning is overwhelmingly related to occupational exposure. However, adults can poison themselves (and their children) at home when engaged in renovation projects that involve torching, heat gunning or power sanding leaded paint.

Some Suggestions

The general lead hazard control strategy is to clean up immediate lead hazards and to prevent the creation of new lead hazards. In addition, good nutrition should be provided to reduce the child's absorption of ingested lead. Here are some lead hazard control tips:

- Improper removal of leaded paint can spread dangerous lead dust; do not dry scrape, sand, torch or heat gun leaded paint.
- Cover or block children's access to damaged leaded paint; clean-up paint chips immediately.
- Wash children's hands, toys, and pacifiers frequently; provide meals and snacks high in iron and calcium and low in fat.
- Wash floors, window sills and window wells frequently with automatic dishwasher or other high-phosphate or lead-specific detergent to clean lead dust
- Cover bare soil — plant grass or other plants or cover with wood chips, gravel, top soil, sand, bricks; use washable mats, leave shoes at door.

- Do not bring work shoes or work clothes that may have lead dust into the house.
- Use only cold tap water for consumption; run water before using.

In any event, the decline in average blood-lead level is not likely to continue at the same dramatic pace because the major control actions — elimination of lead from gasoline, paint, plumbing components, and food cans, and the more strict industrial release standards — have already had their effect.

References

Berkowitz, G.S., Obel, J., Deych, E., Lapinski R., Godbold, J., Zhisong, L., Landrigan, P. and Wolff, M.S., (2003) Exposure to Indoor Pesticides During Pregnancy in a Multiethnic Urban Court. Environmental Health Perspectives, 111(1): 79- 84.

Bornehag, C.G., Sundell, J,., Hagerhed-Engman, L., Sigsggard, T., Janson, S. and Aberg, N. (2005) 'Dampness' at home and its association with airway, nose, and skin symptoms among 10,851 preschool children in Sweden: a cross-sectional study. Indoor Air, 15 (suppl. 10) : 48-55.

De, A.K., Datta, N.C., Mitra, A., and Sinha, T.R.C., Ed., (1997) Sustainable Development & Environment Cosmo Publishing, Delhi, 1997.

De, A.K. (2000b) Tobacco & Smoking, Books For All, Delhi.

De, A.K. (2000a) *Environmental Pollution and Individual Man.* Mother Publishing, 34/2A Jhamapukur Lane, Kolkata.

De, A.K. (2005) *Emerging Pollutants : Impact on Agriculture, Health and Environment.* Allied Publishers , New Delhi (in press).

Gaensler E.A., (1992) Asbestos exposure in buildings. *Clin Chest Med.* 13(2): 231-42.

He, J., Vupputuri, S., Allen, K., *et al.* (1999) Passive Smoking and the Risk of Coronary Heart Disease-A Meta-Analysis of Epidemiologic Studies. New England Journal of Medicine, 340: 920-926.

Kawahara, J., Horiskoshi, R., Yamaguchi, T., Kumagai, K., Yanagisawa, Y. (2005) Air pollution and young children's inhalation exposure to organophosphorus pesticide in an agricultural community in Japan. Environ Int. June 23.

Krishna Murali, K.V.S.K., Air Pollution and Control, Published by Kausal & Co., Kakinada.

Nakazawa, H., Ikeda, H., Yamashita, T., Hara, I., Kumai, Y., Endo, G. and Endo, Y. (2005) A case of sick building syndrome in a Japanese office worker. Ind. Health. 43(2):341-345.

Nero, A.V., (1988) Controlling Indoor Air Pollution, Scientific American, 258(5): 42-48.

Pawel, D.J. and Puskin J.S. (2004). The U.S. Environmental Protection Agency's assessment of risks from indoor radon. *Health Phys*. 87(1): 68-74.

Shopland, D. (2001) Smoke-Free Workplace Coverage. *J. Occupational and Environmental Medicine,* 43(8): 680-686.

Spengler, J.D. and Sexton, K. (1983) Indoor Air Pollution : A Public Health Perspective. Science, 221 (4602), 9-17.

CHAPTER 4

ENVIRONMENTAL IMPACT OF NANOTECHNOLOGY

Inderpal Rai
Department of Home Science
JNV University, Jodhpur, Rajasthan.

ABSTRACT

In the two decades since the birth of the Nanotechnology revolution, it has been a strict case of small is beautiful. President Clinton, while launching the National Nanotechnology Initiative, now third in the research funding pecking order in the US behind the war on cancer and the Star Wars programme, gushed about the potential. Tiny sensors would, in the future speed through arteries detecting cancers at an early stage, exotic new lightweight materials would be 10 times the strength of steel. The whole world caught the Nanotech bug, quietly ignoring the early but serious question marks over safety. In May 2004, the European Commission put the industry's value today at Euro 2.5 billion worldwide. By 2011, it could hit the US$1 trillion mark.

A new report says the laws on safety and Nanotechnology are not up the job and must be reviewed. The 29 July 2004 report from the Royal Society and Royal Academy says there are uncertainties about the potential effects on human health and the environment of manufactured "Nanoparticles" and "nanotubes" – ultra small pieces of material – if they are released. The report recommends that the UK Government should fund a programme of research to understand the effects of such particles on humans and the environment.

The report says as a precautionary measure releases to the environment be minimized until the effects are better understood. The report recommends that the Health and Safety Executive should review existing regulations and consider setting lower exposure levels for manufactured Nanoparticles, in order to provide the proper protection for workers in, for example, university laboratories.

Key Words : Nanotechnology, impact on environment

Introduction

Nanotechnology -- or Nanotech, for short -- is a new approach to industrial production, based on the manipulation of things so small that they are invisible to the naked eye and even to most microscopes. Nanotech is named after the nanometer, a unit of measure, a billionth of a meter, one one-thousandth of a micrometer. The Oxford English Dictionary defines Nanotechnology as "the branch of technology that deals with dimensions and tolerances of less than 100 nanometers, especially the manipulation of individual atoms and molecules." Nanotech deals in the realm where a typical grain of sand is too huge (a million nanometers in diameter). A human hair is 200,000 nanometers thick. A red blood cell spans 10,000 nanometers. A virus measures 100 nanometers across, and the smallest atom (hydrogen) spans 0.1 nanometers.

Nanotechnologists foresee a second industrial revolution sweeping the world during our lifetimes as individual atoms are assembled together into thousands of useful new products. The pressure for rapid development of Nanotech is enormous. The surprising properties of materials at the nano scale have opened up a new universe of industrial applications and entrepreneurial dreams. Largely unnoticed, hundreds of products containing nano-sized particles have already reached the market-- metal surfaces and paints so slick they clean themselves when it rains; organic light-emitting diodes for computer screens, digital cameras and cell phones; sub-miniature data storage devices; speciality lubricants; long-mileage vehicle tyres; nano-reinforced plastics for stronger automobile fenders; light-weight military armor; anti-reflective and scratch-resistant sun glasses; super-slippery ski wax; powerful tennis rackets and long-lasting tennis balls; inkjet photographic paper intended to hold an image for 100 years; high-contrast MRI scanners for medical diagnosis; efficient drug and vaccine delivery systems; vitamins in a spray; invisible sunscreen ointments containing nano particles of titanium or zinc; anti-wrinkle cosmetic creams; and so on.(Peter Montague, RACHEL'S ENVIRONMENT & HEALTH NEWS, Environmental Research Foundation http://www.rachel.org April 28, 2005,Published May 5, 2005).

Benefits of Nanotechnology

Nanotechnology creates and uses new structures, devices and systems that have novel properties and functions because of their small size. In other words, it is technology that enables investigation and manipulation of materials and processes on a tiny scale that is much, much smaller than micro technology. Benefits are seen as smaller, faster, smarter, cheaper, safer, and cleaner products and processes.

Current Applications

Engineering and industry-

- Glass, Building materials
- Ceramics
- Eyeglasses

- Transformed titanium dioxide (TiO_2)
- Textiles
- Coatings
- Tennis rackets
- Car tyres

Cosmetics-

- Sunscreen
- Anti-ageing cosmetics
- Sprays

Food and Agriculture-

- Pesticides in nano-capsules for controlled release
- Smart fields and Smart herds (sensors for crops and livestock surveillance)
- Aquaculture (mass vaccination of trout)
- Aviculture (antibiotic delivery)
- Atomically modified rice.
- 'Consumer designed' food and beverages. Take-home beverages to be made using microwave oven with appropriate program. Similarly, variable texture of ice cream, to be made as soft as desired. Trials by Kraft, Unilever and Nestle.
- Packaging (plastic) that recognizes the condition of the food within.
- Nano barcodes (radio frequency) Quantum dot tags (cadmium selenide) for remote identification. Walmart and Tesco are working on this.

Nano pharmaceuticals-

- Drug delivery in nano-capsules- about 20% of pharmaceuticals so far

- Micro fluidics for testing and delivery
- Nano-constructed biocompatible tissues.
- Synthetic DNA

Military applications-

- Sensors for surveillance and control

(NANOTECHNOLOGY: The Fourth Technological Revolution? *By Vinod Moonesinghe,* Information Officer at EFL and editor of *Biosphere.)*

Some of the real Nanotech products that are already in the market:

- Sunscreen makers have found that nano-scale particles cover the skin more thoroughly and do not reflect light. So, Procter & Gamble is adding nano-size particles to its sunscreen lotions, with significantly better results.
- With a rubber core that uses tiny "nanoclay" particles to form an airtight seal, Wilson's tennis balls retain their air pressure twice as long as ordinary balls.
- Eddie Bauer, Lee Jeans and others are selling stain-free and wrinkle-resistant slacks developed by Nano-Tex. Billions of tiny whiskers create a thin cushion of air above the cotton fabric, smoothing out wrinkles and allowing liquids to bead up and roll off without wetting the fabric.

According to William Atkinson in his Book - Nanocosm: Nanotech and the big changes coming from the inconceivably small.

List of products and applications that are coming short-term - 2 to 5 years:

- Car tyres that require air just once a year

- Self-assembly of small electronic parts
- Artificial semiconductors based on proteins
- Instant, error-proof pregnancy tests
- Medical diagnostics computer chips
- Portable concentrators that produce drinking water from air

On the horizon - 5-10 years:

- Erasable, re-writable paper for books and newspapers
- Bulletproof armor
- Ultra-light, ceramic car engines
- Voice-recognition hearing-aids
- AIDS and cancer treatments
- Smart buildings that resist earthquakes

Nanotechnology applications in Textiles

The textile and clothing industry, normally seen as a 'traditional industry' is an important part of the European manufacturing industry and gives employment to over two million people. Increased competition, specifically from Asia, and the proposed abolition of all import quotas for textiles and clothing in the EU, United States, Canada and Norway in 2005, is forcing the industry to restructure and modernize. Significant restructuring has taken place over the last decade, however, there is a general recognition that producing traditional apparel products may no longer be sufficient to sustain a viable business, and the EU textile industries may have to move towards more innovative, high quality products in order to differentiate themselves and compete. The key areas for increased competitiveness are seen to be in Information Technology, Biotechnology and the emerging Nanotechnology.

Already, Nanotechnology is being used to improve the function ability of many consumer products. Nanotechnology improved products rely on a change in the physical properties when the feature sizes are shrunk. One trend in the textile industry is that more and more clothes are manufactured in low-cost countries. High-cost countries like Western Europe can only compete in this industry if they produce high-tech clothes with additional benefits for users. This includes windproof and waterproof jackets, where Nanotechnology already plays a role. For the future, the buzzwords "smart clothes", "wearable electronics", etc. discuss clothes with additional electronic functionalities.

Nanotechnology, though still very early in its infancy, is already proving to be a useful tool in improving the performance of textiles. With increased performance comes added value and additional revenue. One company to realize this has been the Burlington Industries subsidiary, Nano-Tex. Branded as one of the 'coolest' products in 2003 by Time Magazine, Nano-Tex is providing clothing manufactures such as Levi's, Eddie Bauer, GAP and Old Navy the means to make their products more durable, water and oil repellent, stain resistant and having the reduced need for washing, all without altering the feel of the fabric. Their chemical formulation and application technology, which is easily adopted by existing textile mills, changes the fabric itself on a molecular level, embedding it with tiny, floppy, hair like fibers that themselves are attached to a common spine. The 'nano whiskers' in the chemical mix keeps stains away from soaking into clothing. Nano-Tex is said to have plans to expand its product range to include stain-proof mattresses, boat covers and hotel bedding markets.

Another company in the same field is Schoeller Textiles AG, a Swiss textile company and producer of Nano Sphere a finishing process that renders fabric water-repellent, dirt repellent and anti-adhesive. Using the technology a special three-dimensional structure is created, limiting the available contact surface for dirt particles.

Sensors To Monitor Body Functions

Modern technology, including Nanotechnology, could provide features like sensors (which could monitor body functions or release drugs in the required amounts), self-repairing mechanisms or access to the Internet. Simpler realisations are readily available, which make clothes water-repellent or wrinkle-free. Franz Ziener GmbH&Co produces a ski jacket based on nanotechnology. The windproof and waterproof properties are not obtained by a surface coating of the jacket but by the use of nanofibres.

Wrinkle Resistant Nanotechnology Fabrics

The company Nano-Tex produce wrinkle-resistant and stain-repellent fabrics by attaching molecular structures to cotton fibres. Textiles with a nanotechnological finish can be washed less frequently and at lower temperatures. High-performance functional clothing is an increasingly important feature of the workplace. For example Gore-Tex has developed an antistatic, weather-protective, outerwear fabric. Nanotechnology has been used to integrate tiny carbon particles membrane and guarantee full-surface protection from electrostatic charges for the wearer.

Nanotechnology in Sports Equipment

A high-performance ski wax, which produces a hard and fast-gliding surface, is already in use. The ultra thin coating lasts much longer than conventional waxing systems. The French tennis racket manufacturer Babolat introduced a racket with carbon nanotubes, which lead to an increased torsion and flex resistance. The rackets are more rigid than current carbon rackets and pack more power. Coating the inner core with clay polymer nanocomposites makes long-lasting tennis-balls. These tennis-balls, made by the company InMat have twice the lifetime of conventional balls.

Nanotechnology Involvement In Sunscreens

One field of application is in sunscreens. The traditional chemical UV protection approach suffers from its poor long-term stability. A sunscreen based on mineral Nanoparticles such as titanium dioxide offers several advantages. Titanium dioxide Nanoparticles have a comparable UV protection property as the bulk material, but lose the cosmetically undesirable whitening as the particle size is decreased. L´Oréal offers an anti wrinkle cream, where a polymer capsule (NanosomesTM) is used to transport active agents like vitamins and a hair conditioner “Aqua-Oleum” where nanotechnology leads to improved care power (Primary author: Nanoforum, Source: Benefits, Risks, Ethical, Legal and Social Aspects of Nanotechnology Report).

Multifunctional Textiles

The use of Nanotechnology is allowing textiles to become multifunctional. For instance, Plasma technology is being used to modify the top nanometer layers of textiles, allowing them to be made antibacterial, fungicidal and water repellent. Other areas of interest include heat resistant and mechanically resilient work wear, ballistic protection, sensors and camouflage.

Protective Work Wear

W.L. Gore & Associates ‘Gore-Tex Work wear’ which applies Nanotechnology and Dupont’s Teflon to produce an anti-static membrane for protective clothing against bad weather and electrostatic discharges.

Freshness you can wear

Nanoparticles have been used to provide the controlled release of fragrances, biocides and antifungals on textiles, leading to the expression, 'Freshness you can wear'. Ciba Specialty Chemicals (CSC) is modifying fibers on the basis of nanocontainer microcapsules that prevent bacterial growth by releasing antimicrobiotics. The same technology is used to absorb odors.

Improved Moisture Absorption

Kanebo Spinning Corp of Japan has produced a polyester yarn with thirty times the ability of normal polyester to absorb moisture. The yarn, suitable for use in undergarments, has twenty layers for containing moisture and oil content. The layers have a total thickness of fifty nanometers. Toray Industries, Inc. of Japan has developed a fabric containing bundles of ultra fine nanometer nylon threads that allow superior moisture absorption properties.

Increased Aesthetic Options

Teijin Fibers Ltd. of Japan has held trials in the production of luminescent polyester. A polyester substrate is covered with approximately sixty layers of polyester and nylon that have different refractive indices for light. The layers, which are only approximately sixty-nine nanometers thick, refract the light to create a 'mystical' hue that changes according the viewpoint of the observer and the angle the light hits the fabric.

Lighter and Stronger Materials

The development of nanofibres could lead to stronger and lighter fibre-polymer composites. EFPL (The Swiss Federal Institute of Technology) is already spinning Nanofibres and the University of Texas and Ireland's Trinity College are said to have spun carbon nanotube composite fibres with toughness in the order of seventeen times that of Kevlar. Nanocyl, a spin-off company from the University of Namur, Belgium is also in the stages of commercializing its carbon nanotube technology.

The potential application of these composite fibers not only includes lightweight polymer-fiber composites but, bulletproof vests and energy storage devices contained within a textile fabric that could be used to power an electronic device. General Motors are producing stronger bumpers using nano materials.

Investments

- The USA is leading the way by allocating over \$800million in funding to the 2004 National Nanotechnology Initiative (NNI). As a further sign of the technology's economic potential, in December of 2003, President Bush signed a bill authorizing \$3.7 billion in federal funding for Nanotechnology research at government labs, universities and private companies.
- Japan is the second largest spender in Nanotechnology research and development worldwide, and has being investing in the technology since the 1980s. In 2002, it provided roughly \$750million in funding.
- Germany, Switzerland and the UK lead the way in Europe, and the EU has assigned Nanotechnology special status in the Sixth Framework Programme. Germany, the most active EU country in Nanotechnology, provided over €110million in funding in 2003 and has set-up 'Nanonet' competence

networks in which research institutes, industries and SMEs collaborate. Switzerland has done much the same thing with its TOPNano21 programme and the French are setting up a similar structure.

In UK, the government is investing £90million over the next six years into the research, development and commercialization of Nanotechnology, with an additional £200million slated to come from industry and regional spending sources. The funding will help set-up a new network of micro and Nanotechnology facilities and aid collaborative research. A university Innovation Center in micro systems and Nanotechnology has been set-up at the Universities of Newcastle and Durham ('Future Needs and Challenges for Materials and Nanotechnology Research',European Commission Research Directorate General, DGRTD/G3).

Problems

There has been no awakening yet of civil society, or of governments, to the level of disruption that Nanotechnology will have on the poverty-stricken and the disabled, on human health and the environment, on trade, on security, on food systems and even on what it is to be human.

Impact on Health and Environment

- There are uncertainties regarding the effects and behavior of nano-particles. Studies have been scarce and there is virtually no monitoring. Nano-particles have been released to the environment that have never been there before. What reactions they might have on living organisms are unknown.
- Nano-particles go through immune system and through the brain blood barrier. They have broader, quicker catalytic effects. The cosmetics industry uses

these aspects of nano-particles to deliver substances to the body, which would normally be rejected by the immune system. For example, anti-ageing compounds, which would normally remain on the surface of the skin, now penetrate deeper. After the compounds are released, the nano-capsule material stays in the body.

- It is known that there is accumulation of nano-particles in organs and tissues – such as liver, brain and lungs. The lungs, for example, cannot detect these particles, and therefore take no action to expel them. This may lead to damage to the vital organs and there is a risk of cancer. In one experiment, it was found that in fish fed with nano-particulate food, there was damage to their brains within 48 hours in 40% of the fish.
- Another danger might be nano-capsules being utilized to promote the use of banned pesticides and other chemicals, the argument being that the chemicals would not damage any bodies apart from the target because of the capsules.
- Jim Thomas, an Oxford-based programme officer with the technology watchdog ETC, writing in *The Ecologist* in February 2004, revealed that US and other regulatory agencies are "privately admitting they have made a mistake in letting Nano products onto the market without safety studies, and are looking for ways to weak existing regulations. A July 2004 ETC report says only in recent months have governments on both sides of the Atlantic "reluctantly conceded that current safety and health regulations may not be adequate" for nano materials. "Ironically, they are talking about the need to be proactive, failing to admit that they are already at least one decade

late: Nanotech products are already commercially available and laboratory workers and consumers are already being exposed to Nanoparticles that could pose serious risks to people and the environment."

- In his May 2004 "Nanowatch" column in *The Ecologist*, Thomas points out that the first ever scientific conference on nano-toxicity, Nanotox 2004, only took place in January this year. He lists "Ten toxic warnings" including NASA research in 2003 showing nano-tubes produce a more toxic response in rats than quartz dust and claims by top UK toxicopathologist Vyvyan Howard that nano-particles can cross the blood-brain barrier in humans and gold nano-particles can move across the placenta from mother to fetus.

Economic Impact

The economic impacts of Nanotechnology are potentially enormous, greater than that of any other comparative new technology. They can be used to substitute for raw materials, the production of which gives employment to millions. For example, the rubber and mining industries may be destroyed. Textile fibers such as cotton and silk would not have to be grown and harvested. The effects will be far greater in the Third World, where most production of raw materials takes place.

The producers of nano-materials can achieve market monopolies through patents. Broader patents will be possible, and that can lead to broader monopolies, with all the adverse economic impacts of monopolies (Vinod Moonesinghe).

Other Impact

Using nano-technology sensors, control and surveillance will be facilitated. Governments will have greater control over their people. In May of 2004, Swiss Re, the world's second-largest reinsurance firm, issued a report calling for the Precautionary Principle to guide Nanotech development. Swiss Re itemized a host of potential problems that it says need to be resolved before Nanotech products are fully deployed, including :

- If they become airborne, nano particles can float for very long periods because -- unlike larger particles -- they do not readily settle onto surfaces. In water, nano particles spread unhindered and pass through most available filters. So, for example, current drinking water filters will not effectively remove nano particles. Even in soil, nano particles may move in unexpected ways, perhaps penetrating the roots of plants and thus entering the food chains of humans and animals.
- Once in the body, nano particles can enter the heart, bone marrow, ovaries, muscles, brain, liver, spleen and lymph nodes. During pregnancy, nano particles would likely cross the placenta and enter the fetus. The specific effects in any given organ would depend upon the surface chemistry of particular particles, which in turn would be determined by their size and surface coating. "It is likely that in the course of its entire evolution, humankind has never been exposed to such a wide variety of substances that can penetrate the human body apparently unhindered," Swiss Re says.
- Nano particles in disposable products will eventually enter the environment. In the environment, nano particles represent an entirely new class of pollutants with which scientists and nature have no experience. Swiss Re speculates that, "Via the water cycle, nano particles could spread rapidly all over the globe,

possibly also promoting the transport of pollutants." Swiss Re asks, "What would happen if certain Nanoparticles did exert a harmful influence on the environment? Would it be possible to withdraw them from circulation? Would there be any way of removing Nanoparticles from the water, earth, or air?"

Conclusions

The pressure for rapid development of Nanotech is enormous. The surprising properties of materials at the nano scale have opened up a new universe of industrial applications and entrepreneurial dreams. Largely unnoticed, hundreds of products containing nano-sized particles have already reached the market. The British Royal Society and the Royal Academy of Engineering issued a Nanotech report in July 2004 recommending a series of precautionary actions, with the following chain of reasoning:

The Royal Society puts the burden of producing information about safety on industry, not on the public: "A wide range of uses for nanotubes and Nanoparticles is envisaged that will fix them within products.... We believe that the onus should be on industry to assess ... releases [of nano particles from products] throughout a product's lifetime (including at the end-of-life) and to make that information available to the regulator."

The Royal Society recommended that the use of zinc oxide nano particles and iron oxide nano particles in cosmetics should "await a safety assessment" -- in other words a moratorium on these products is recommended. Likewise, "the release of free manufactured Nanoparticles into the environment for [pollution] remediation (which has been piloted in the USA) should be prohibited until there is sufficient information to allow the potential risks to be evaluated as well as the benefits."

References

'Future Needs and Challenges for Materials and Nanotechnology Research', European Commission Research Directorate General, DGRTD/G3.

Institute of Nanotechnology January 2004.

Jim Thomas (2004) "Nanotech". The Ecologist, February 2004.

Jim Thomas (2005) Nanowatch, "The Ecologist", May, 2005.

Louis Theodore and Robert G. Kunz, Nanotechnology: Environmental Implications and Solutions, ISBN: 0-471-69976-4.

Nanotechwire.com

Paul, Davies (2004) Managing the risks from Nanotechnology, HSE chief scientist, HSC, 22 March 2004. Paper to the 6 April Health and Safety Commission meeting.

Peter, Montague (2005) Nanotechnology and the Precautionary Principle. RACHEL'S ENVIRONMENT & HEALTH NEWS, http://www.rachel.org. April 28, Published May 5.

Royal Society and the Royal Academy of Engineering Report, 29 July 2004, and news release

Swiss, Re (2004) Nanotechnology: small matter, many unknowns, full report, 10 May 2004.

Vinod Moonesinghe, NANOTECHNOLOGY: The Fourth Technological Revolution? Information Officer at EFL and editor of *Biosphere*.

"Welcome to NanoWorld: Nanotechnology and the Precautionary Principle Imperative" (2004) The Multinational Monitor, 25, (9) : 16-19.

CHAPTER 5

MACROPHYTE DECOMPOSITION AND CHANGES IN WATER QUALITY

P.A. Azeez, N.R. Nadarajan and B.A.K. Prusty

Environmental Impact Assessment Division
Sálim Ali Centre for Ornithology and Natural History
Anaikatty (PO), Coimbatore- 641 108, Tamil Nadu, India.

ABSTRACT

The decomposition of select macrophytes and its implication on the water quality was studied using litter-bags of two different mesh-sizes (0.14 and 0.375 mm) in the wetland system of Keoladeo National Park. The study was also conducted in laboratory water tanks with the input water from the park. The rate of macrophyte decay and their half-life was estimated. Seven macrophyte species viz., *Paspalum distichum, Paspalidium punctatum, Cyperus alopecuroides, Pseudoraphis spinescens, Ipomoea aquatica, Neptunia oleracea and Hydrilla verticillata* were selected for the study, as they were dominant in the aquatic vegetation of the wetland system. The highest and lowest decay rate with corresponding lowest and highest half-life was seen in the case of *Hydrilla verticillata* and *Paspalidium punctatum* respectively. In general, the grass species had low decay rate and high half-life.

Key Words: macrophytes, decomposition, water quality

Introduction

Macrophytes occupy an important position in the structure and functioning of aquatic ecosystems (Boston and

Perkins, 1982). Detritus being an important component of wetland, exposition of the macrophyte decomposition has attracted wide attention from researchers. Decomposition, an intricate process, includes changes and loss of organic matter by senescence and breakdown, and interactions between detritus and decomposer organisms. In water, macrophytes are subject to physical breakdown, leaching and fragmentation, because of water movements and browsing by animals, and to biochemical breakdown, autolysis due to the activity of microbial enzymes (Brock, 1984). First two processes occur fairly simultaneously.

Present understanding of macrophyte decomposition is largely based on loss of particulate matter and nutrients from dead plant material enclosed in mesh bags and incubated in the field (Rogers and Breen, 1982; Brock, 1984; and Tupacz and Day, 1990) or incubated in the laboratory (Kok *et al.*, 1990). The quality of water in wetlands depends on a variety of aspects, an important one of which is the extent of input of allochthonous materials and availability of autochthonous materials. Allochthonous materials mostly comprise of nutrients and other biodegradable and non-biodegradable materials derived from outside the water body, where as autochthonous materials are that of detritus, phyto and zoo detritus, derived within the system. The decomposition of detritus and the surrounding water quality are mutually influential. The detritus in aquatic systems is largely phytodetritus. Consequently, the quality of detritus largely depends on the type of vegetation. Occurrence and growth of macrophytes is affected by abiotic conditions such as water quality, sediment properties, temperature conditions and water level fluctuation (Mäkelä *et al.*, 2004). Thus, water and sediment properties, vegetation structure, macrophyte decomposition, and detritus formation are mutually interactional and influence each other.

The present study was carried out to i) study the rate and pattern of decomposition of select aquatic macrophytes, ii) assess variations in rates of decomposition on a temporal scale, iii) chemically characterize the macrophytes and surrounding water column, and iv) find the major groups of organisms colonizing the decomposing macrophytes and likely to be involved in the decomposition process.

Study area

The present investigation was carried out in Keoladeo National Park (Fig. 1), Bharatpur, Rajasthan, India. This park is one of the most important waterfowl habitats with the existence of more than 250 years (Azeez *et al.,* 1992) and one of the early Ramsar sites (Mathur *et al.*, 2005). The Park is one of the most important and popular havens of birds, both during migratory seasons and otherwise. The most unique feature of the park is the range of habitats (Prusty *et al.*, 2006), clearly distinguished by the vegetation types (Davis and van der Valk, 1988) and hydrological parameters (Prusty *et al.* In Press), available in the 2900 ha. The total area of this park (about 29 km^2), out of which the central submersible area (the central dotted area in the Fig. 1), the wetlands, cover about 8.5 km^2 and the rest is covered by woodland and grassland (Azeez *et al.*, 2000). The park is split into several blocks or compartments that are separated from each other, by earthen dykes or mud trails, for the ease of management (Azeez *et al.,* 1992; Vijayan, 1991).

The Park location falls under arid or semi-arid zone of India (Pal *et al.,* 2000). The temperature here ranges from about 1°C to 49°C, i.e. chilly winter and scorching summer. Drastic variations in temperature are seen on diurnal basis as well as seasonally. The climate of the area encompass four distinct seasons: summer / premonsoon (April to June), rainy / monsoon (July to Mid-September), post monsoon

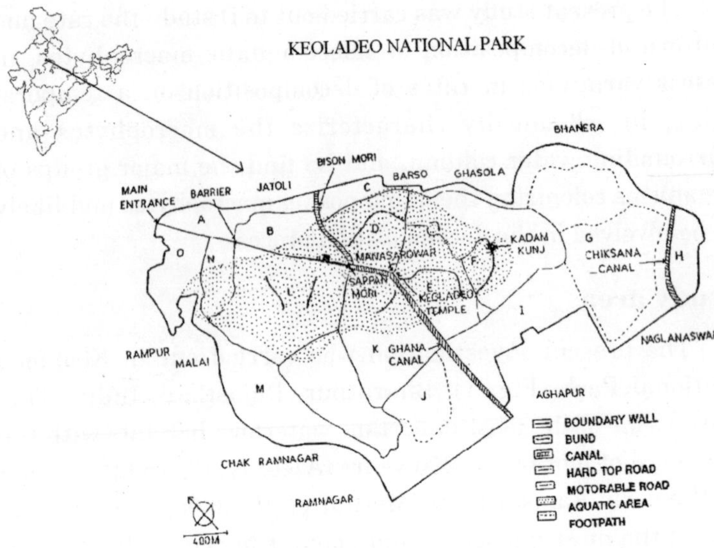

Fig. 1: Map of study area

(mid-September to mid-November) and winter (mid-November to March, Prusty and Azeez, 2004; Prusty *et al.*, 2006).

Materials and Methods

Macrophyte selection and processing

Seven macrophyte species viz., *Paspalum distichum* (PLM), *Paspalidium punctatum* (PDM), *Cyperus alopecuroides, Pseudoraphis spinescens, Ipomoea aquatica, Neptunia oleracea and Hydrilla verticillata* were selected for the study among the dominant aquatic species (Table 1 and 2). The plants were harvested after their peak growth just before the flowering, air-dried and cut into 3 to 4 cm long pieces. The decomposition of these species was studied both in the field and in the laboratory with the litter-bag (mesh bag) technique. The bags were (20 cm × 30 cm) of two different mesh-sizes (0.14 mm and 0.375 mm). Twenty-five grams of each species were enclosed in nylon litterbags.

Table 1 : Average grade of aquatic plants in the wetland

Species	Grade	Species	Grade
Paspalum	14.18	*Eleocharis*	0.266
Pseudoraphis	9.375	*Sporobolus*	0.244
C. alopecuroides	6.138	*Ceratophyllum*	0.218
Panicum	5.788	*Nymphaea pubescens*	0.164
Nymphoides cristata	4.532	*Cynodon*	0.156
Paspalidium	4.211	*Nitella*	0.145
Azolla	3.974	*U. stellaris*	0.113
Ipomoea aquatica	3.025	*Lemna*	0.109
Algae	2.124	*Typha*	0.091
Scripus littoralis	1.864	*Hygrophila*	0.069
Hydrilla	1.799	*Melochia*	0.058
Najas	1.463	*I. carnia*	0.054
Utricularia exoleta	1.273	*Marsilea*	0.047
U. flexuosa	1.229	*Wolfia*	0.036
S. tuberosus	0.901	*Echinocloa*	0.036
Oryza	0.810	*Limnophyla*	0.018
Spinrodela	0.675	*Commelina*	0.018
Limnophyton	0.514	*Eichornia*	0.018
Vetiveria	0.408	*Aeschynomene indica*	0.010
Chara	0.408	*Alternanthera sessilis*	0.007
Nymphoides indica	0.343	*C. rotundus*	0.003
Vallisneria	0.332	*Iseilema*	0.003
Neptunia	0.288	-	-

Average water depth = 41.22 cm, Grade is in % cover in 0.5 × 0.5m quadrat measured in winter 1988

Table 2 : Macrophyte species used in the study

Macrophyte species	Code
Paspalum distichum	PLM
Paspalidium punctatum	PDM
Cyperus alopecuroides	CYP
Pseudoraphis spinescens	PSU
Ipomoea aquatica	IPO
Neptunia oleracea	NEP
Hydrilla verticillata	HYD

In the field, samples of each plant enclosed in bags of both mesh sizes in duplicates were kept submerged in water almost lying at the bottom. The bags were placed at D, E and L blocks and the canal in the Park. All the seven plant species in different bags were secured with a long plastic rope to a pole planted in water. Six of such poles were planted in the field, each for one sampling. One each of the poles were removed from water on 10, 30, 60, 90 120 and 150th day, and taken to the laboratory. In the laboratory, the study was conducted in cement tanks of size 70 × 50 × 50 cm with a capacity of 80 L. Before beginning the study, the tanks were thoroughly washed and filled with 60 L of freshly collected filtered water from the wetland. Six bags of one mesh size (0.14 mm) with one plant species were kept immersed in a tank and six bags of the second mesh size (0.375 mm) in a separate one. The water in each tank was aerated approximately for 5 to 6 hrs daily to avoid development of an anaerobic condition and formation of reduced condition. The water level in each tank was maintained by adding required quantity of filtered Park water, a sample of which was taken for laboratory analysis. One bag each was removed from each tank on 10, 30, 60, 90, 120 and 150th day and prepared for further analysis. Along with the litterbags, water samples were also collected from each tank.

The bags collected from both the field and the tanks were drained of water and wet weights were determined. A weighed sample of decomposing plant matter in each bag was taken for dry weight determination after oven drying at approximately 60°C for 24 hrs till constant weight. The other portion of the contents in each bag was divided into two portions (75 and 25 %), the first for biological analysis and the second for chemical analysis. To identify the organisms in the samples a portion was weighed, suspended in water and each organism was hand picked with a fine brush and put in Lugol's solution (60g potassium iodide and 40g iodine crystals dissolved in 1000 ml distilled water), identified up to genera and counted. The portion meant for chemical analysis was oven dried, weighed, and analyzed for organic carbon (OC) and phosphate (PO_4) by titrimetric or spectrophotometric methods (Allen *et al.*, 1989). Milton Roy Spectronic 20 D Spectrophotometer (Bausch and Lomb) was employed for spectrophotometric analysis. Samples were also analyzed for Sodium, Potassium, Calcium, Magnesium, Iron, Manganese, Zinc, Copper, Nickel, Chromium, Lead and Cadmium. A Perkin Elmer Atomic Absorption Spectrophotometer (model AA 1100) was used for estimating metal in the samples digested with nitric acid-perchloric acid mixture. Detailed analysis of water samples from laboratory tanks were done for the above chemical parameters apart from pH, phenolphthalein and methyl orange alkalinity, total hardness, sulfate (SO_4) and chloride (Cl) following APHA / AWWA / WPCF (1985), where as in the case of study in the field, only decomposing plant matter was analyzed. Water analysis was excluded in the field condition as water quality is influenced not only by the decomposition of the macrophytes in the bag but also others in the environment.

Results and Discussion

Laboratory studies

Physico chemical characteristics of the water used in the study

The study was conducted in concrete tank, kept filled with water for more than a month with frequent change of water to remove the leachable chemicals, with filtered water from the Park. The chemical properties of water used in the laboratory study are given in Table 3. The pH of the water varied

Table 3 : Chemical properties of water used in the laboratory study*

Parameter	Maximum	Minimum	Average
pH	8.8	7	7.7
Phenolphthalein alkalinity	19	0	8.9
Total alkalinity	317.3	218.5	266.5
Total Hardness	226.2	116.7	182.4
Chloride	266	44.2	137.5
Chemical oxygen demand	294.6	16.3	62.2
PO_4	3.5	0.1	1.3
SO_4	2167.1	299.4	752.1
Ca	153.8	52.3	80.6
Mg	38.8	5.8	24.8
Na	88.49	28.51	58.78
K	97.1	3.5	53.97
Fe	11.89	0.54	3.97
Mn	0.17	0.02	0.08
Cr	0.02	0	0.01
Cu	0.02	0	0.01
Ni	0.04	0	0.02
Pb	0.08	0	0.02
Zn	0.2	0	0.03

* All concentrations are in milligrams per liter

between 7.0 and 8.8 with the average being 7.7. The Phenolphthalein alkalinity ranged up to 19 mg L^{-1} from the lowest 0.0 mg L^{-1}. The total alkalinity varied between 218.5 mg L^{-1} and 317.3 mg L^{-1} with the average of 266.5 mg L^{-1}. Average hardness of the water samples was 182.4 mg L^{-1}. The average chemical oxygen demands (COD) of the samples were 2.2 mg L^{-1}. The maximum and the minimum sulfate concentrations were 2167.1 and 299.4 mg L^{-1}, respectively. The chloride content varied between 266.0 and 44.2 mg L^{-1}. Highest phosphate concentration was 3.5 mg L^{-1} and the lowest 0.01 mg L^{-1}. Concentration of Sodium ranged between 28.5 and 88.5 mg L^{-1}, that of Calcium between 52.3 and 153.8 mg L^{-1}. The average concentration of Magnesium recorded was 97.1 mg L^{-1}. Average concentration of iron was 3.97 mg L^{-1} and that of Manganese 0.08 mg L^{-1}. Chromium was recorded in least number of samples and in low concentration. The average concentrations of Copper, Chromium, Nickel, Lead and Zinc were 0.01, 0.01, 0.02, 0.02 and 0.03 mg L^{-1}, respectively.

Physicochemical changes of the plant material

The different plant species differed notably in the loss of weight. The weight loss followed in almost all the cases an exponential decay tending towards a lower asymptote level. *Hydrilla* almost disappeared from the bag completely between 60 to 90 days. In the case of other species about 25 to 45 % of the plant material remained in the bag of mesh size (0.14mm) even after 150 days. In bags of higher mesh size, the remainder of vegetal matter was 32 to 42 %. Chiefly fibrous matter may constitute the remainder of the matter. In smaller mesh sized bag after *Hydrilla*, *Cyperus* disappeared the most. There was no substantial difference in the decomposition of plants between the bags of two different mesh sizes. It was noted that a significant quantity of clay and silt settling on the bags and entering inside might also significantly contribute to the remainder weight.

The exponential decay rate of the macrophytes were estimated using as d = Ln (w_{t2} / w_{t1}) / t. The half-life (the time required for half of the biomass to get disappear) was estimated as $t^{1/2}$ = Ln (0.5) / d., where, $t^{1/2}$ = half-life, d = exponential decay rate, w_{t1} = initial dry weight of the plant matter, w_{t2} = final dry weight of the plant matter and t = total duration of the experiment, i.e. $t_2 - t_1$.

The exponential decay rates in the case of both types of bags were similar. Though, the rates were always higher in the bags of higher mesh size than in the lower ones (Table 4),

Table 4: The exponential decay rate and half-life of decomposing macrophytes.

Species	Treatment	Decay rate	Half life
PDM	0.14 mm mesh bag in the lab	-0.0018	385.08
PSU	"	-0.0019	364.81
CYP	"	-0.0020	346.57
PLM	"	-0.0020	346.57
IPO	"	-0.0025	277.26
NEP	"	-0.0031	226.52
HYD	"	-0.0228	30.40
PDM	0.375 mm mesh bag in the lab	-0.0019	364.81
PSU	"	-0.0019	364.81
PLM	"	-0.0024	288.81
IPO	"	-0.0029	239.02
CYP	"	-0.0047	147.48
NEP	"	-0.0051	135.38
HYD	"	-0.0350	19.80

the differences were not statistically significant. *Hydrilla* showed the highest decay rate of –0.0228 in the small sized bags and –0.0350 in the large mesh sized bags. These rates correspond to half-lives of 30.40 days and 19.80 days. *Paspalidium* in both type of bags decomposed the lowest with the corresponding half-lives being 385.1 and 364.8 days in the small and the large meshed bag respectively. The plants in the decreasing order of decay rate and increasing order of half life were *Hydrilla, Neptunia, Ipomoea, Paspalum, Cyperus, Pseudoraphis* and *Paspalidium* in the 0.14 mm mesh sized bags while the order was *Hydrilla, Neptunia, Cyperus, Ipomoea, Paspalum, Pseudoraphis and Paspalidium* in the 0.375 mm mesh sized bags. Even, if there is considerable difference in the order, generally the grass species had lower decay rate and high half-life.

Phosphate

The plant species vary in the phosphate contents. The variations in the phosphate contents in the plant matter in the tanks are given in Table 5. The highest phosphate content was recorded in *Hydrilla* (0.69 %) and the lowest in *Paspalidium* (0.32 %). The pattern of phosphate loss was similar to that of weight loss; exponential phosphate loss was

Table 5 : Phosphate in decomposing plant matter in the tank after the experiment

	CYP	HYD*	IPO	NEP	PDM	PLM	PSU
Initial#	0.44	0.69	0.45	0.46	0.32	0.41	0.39
Mesh1@	39.43	82.02	79.63	92.40	86.36	31.91	84.84
Mesh2@	48.77	60.89	76.42	79.04	64.64	21.29	89.25

@ % of the initial concentration, *Hydrilla after 60 days. # Concentration % dry weight, Mesh1=Bag with mesh size 0.14mm, Mesh2 = Bag with mesh size 0.375 mm

always lower than that in the small mesh sized ones. The loss of Phosphate content varied much between the plants. The highest removal of phosphate was seen in the case of *Paspalum* where in only 31.9 and 21.3 % was remaining after 150 days in the small and the large mesh size bags respectively.

Organic carbon

The plants in the decreasing order of initial carbon content were *Pseudoraphis, Paspalidium, Paspalum, Ipomoea, Cyperus* and *Neptunia*. *Pseudoraphis* contained 50 % of dry weight as carbon content and *Neptunia* 43.9 %. The reduction in carbon content did not show an initial high rate gradually getting lower with duration as in the case of phosphate or weight. The carbon content in the decomposing plant matter after 150 days varied between 38.97 % (in *Hydrilla* in mesh 2 bags) and 97.3 % (in *Paspalum* in mesh 1 bags) (Table 6). The carbon content was always lower in the large mesh size bags than in the small mesh sized ones. The difference between the two was the minimum in case of *Pseudoraphis* (3.4%) and the highest in case of *Hydrilla* (35.6 %).

Table 6 : Organic carbon content of the decomposing plant matter in the tank after the experiment

	CYP	HYD*	IPO	NEP	PDM	PLM	PSU
Initial#	44.39	49.84	44.89	43.95	47.50	46.64	50.00
Mesh1@	86.48	74.61	62.47	81.63	82.38	97.30	63.60
Mesh2@	75.99	38.97	59.12	77.14	74.39	85.55	60.22

@ % of the initial concentration, # Concentration % dry weight, * *Hydrilla* after 60 days, Mesh1=Bag with mesh size 0.14mm, Mesh2 = Bag with mesh size 0.375 mm

Physicochemical changes of water

pH

The initial pH of the water in the laboratory experiment was 8.25. The pH of water in all the tanks including the control increased considerably from the starting day of the experiment towards the end. In the control tank, pH increased up to 9.08 by the 120th day. By the 10th day of the experiment, the pH showed a slight decrease in both the control and experimental tanks. The fall in pH was the maximum in the tank with *Ipomoea* (pH 6.82). The pattern was same in both tanks with small and large mesh bags (Table 7). During the study, however the pH was not allowed

Table 7 : pH of water in the tank during decomposition of macrophytes

Bags	Day	CON*	CYP	HYD	IPO	NEP	PDM	PLM	PSU
Mesh1	0	8.25	8.25	8.25	8.25	8.25	8.25	8.25	8.25
	10	8.20	7.42	7.17	6.82	7.35	7.42	6.98	7.07
	30	8.34	7.60	7.80	7.60	7.75	7.73	7.75	7.10
	60	9.02	8.34	8.95	8.64	8.51	8.39	8.47	8.43
	90	9.13	8.55	9.12	8.66	8.69	8.55	8.34	8.80
	120	9.08	9.48	9.19	8.63	8.95	9.04	8.96	8.43
	150	8.30	8.93	8.87	8.88	8.95	8.96	9.02	8.73
Mesh2	0	8.25	8.25	8.25	8.25	8.25	8.25	8.25	8.25
	10	8.20	7.38	7.20	7.20	7.30	7.18	7.14	7.42
	30	8.34	7.78	7.99	8.00	7.84	7.66	7.80	7.70
	60	9.02	8.46	8.60	8.93	9.04	8.41	8.45	8.68
	90	9.13	8.90	8.70	8.62	8.64	8.66	8.58	8.79
	120	9.08	9.14	8.96	8.95	8.92	8.97	9.33	8.80
	150	8.30	8.91	8.89	8.72	8.85	9.10	8.78	9.14

*CON = Water in the tank without any plant matter for decomposition

to change widely since, it is likely to alter the decomposition processes. Hence, frequently the tank water was supplemented with fixed amount of wetland water. The wetland water had lower pH. This helps in (i) maintaining the volume of water in the tank (ii) keeping control over the pH changes.

Alkalinity

The phenolphthalein alkalinity of the water used in the study before the beginning of the study was approximately 4.5 mg L^{-1} as $CaCO_3$ (Table 8). During the first two samplings (10 and 30th days), the alkalinity due to hydroxides and carbonates was nil. Nevertheless, later on the phenolphthalein alkalinity showed rise. This trend continued till the 120th day. In the samples of 150th day, the phenolphthalein alkalinity dropped down to zero. This may be due to the freshly added water from the sanctuary, which has comparatively lower pH than the tank water. The increase (up to 120th day) in the phenolphthalein alkalinity was 164 % than the alkalinity (on the initial day) of water in the control tank while the increase was more than 400 % with decomposing plants except in the case of tanks with *Paspalidium* and *Paspalum* (in small mesh bags). With *Paspalidium* the increase was 191 % and with *Paspalum* 179 %. Similar was the increase in phenolphthalein alkalinity in the water with the large mesh bags also. The total alkalinity of water on the first day of the study was 234 mg L^{-1} as $CaCO_3$ and by the end of the study (150th day), it increased up to 342 mg L^{-1} as $CaCO_3$. Except for a slight peak by the 30th day, the trend was of rise all through. In the tanks with the macrophytes rise in the total alkalinity was in the range of 116.1 to 193.2 %, the lowest being with *Paspalidium* and the highest with *Pseudoraphis* both in small and large mesh bags.

Table 8 : Alkalinity of the water in the tank during plant decomposition*

Bags	Day	CON**	CYP	HYD	IPO	NEP	PDM	PLM	PSU
Phenolphthalein Alkalinity									
Mesh1	0	4.5	4.5	4.5	4.5	4.5	4.5	4.5	4.5
	10	0.0	0.0	0.0	0.0	0.0	0.0	0.0	0.0
	30	0.0	0.0	0.0	28.5	0.0	0.0	0.0	0.0
	70	31.6	17.2	27.7	27.7	8.3	7.2	26.4	8.3
	90	20.4	22.0	27.7	23.9	22.7	11.2	34.2	38.2
	120	7.4	19.1	18.8	21.2	19.8	8.6	8.1	20.4
	150	0.0	0.0	0.0	0.0	0.0	0.0	0.0	0.0
Mesh2	0	4.5	4.5	4.5	4.5	4.5	4.5	4.5	4.5
	10	0.0	0.0	0.0	0.0	0.0	0.0	0.0	0.0
	30	0.0	19.0	0.0	0.0	0.0	19.0	19.0	0.0
	70	31.6	17.0	7.2	17.0	7.5	7.4	17.0	26.5
	90	20.4	40.9	12.0	12.2	13.1	40.8	31.4	21.8
	120	7.4	20.0	9.7	19.6	10.9	19.6	25.6	19.6
	150	0.0	0.0	0.0	0.0	0.0	0.0	0.0	0.0
Total alkalinity									
Mesh1	0	234.0	234.0	234.0	234.0	234.0	234.0	234.0	234.0
	10	247.0	338.2	437.0	408.5	298.3	370.5	357.2	298.3
	30	423.7	364.8	541.5	513.0	361.0	404.7	370.5	383.8
	70	228.0	408.5	380.0	518.7	389.5	421.8	461.7	404.7
	90	319.2	461.7	399.0	465.5	437.0	357.2	469.3	459.8
	120	357.2	465.5	408.5	427.5	427.5	313.5	393.3	465.5
	150	342.0	326.8	399.0	389.5	361.0	271.7	366.7	452.2
Mesh 2	0	234.0	234.0	234.0	234.0	234.0	234.0	234.0	234.0
	10	247.0	361.0	499.7	465.5	323.0	370.5	385.7	357.2
	30	423.7	385.7	522.5	556.7	342.0	399.0	452.2	423.7
	70	228.0	459.8	374.3	357.2	347.7	414.2	490.2	437.0
	90	319.2	484.5	370.5	361.0	366.7	427.5	437.0	446.5
	120	357.2	421.8	342.0	374.3	332.5	389.5	385.7	389.5
	150	342.0	399.0	304.0	336.3	332.5	361.0	357.2	342.0

* in mg L^{-1} as $CaCO_3$, **CON = water in the tank without any plant material for decomposition

Hardness

At the launch of the experiment, the total hardness of the experimental water was 177.5 mg L^{-1} as $CaCO_3$. Hardness increased slightly (9.9 %) by the 10th day in the control tank. This was the case in the tanks with plant matter too. The highest increase noted with *Ipomoea* (approximately 230 % higher than the initial). Latter, the trend reversed and hardness declined gradually till the end of the experiment (Table 9). By 120th day, hardness was the lowest in all the tanks; with values ranging from 15.0 (with *Paspalum)* to 90.8 % (with *Pseudoraphis*) of the initial concentration in small mesh bags. In the case of bags of larger mesh the situation was that the water with *Hydrilla* had the lowest hardness and with *Pseudoraphis*, the highest. In contrast to the control, all the tanks with plants had high hardness. The highest on

Table 9: Hardness of the water in the tank during plant decomposition *

Bags	DAY	CON**	CYP	HYD	IPO	NEP	PDM	PLM	PSU
Mesh 1	0	177.5	177.5	177.5	177.5	177.5	177.5	177.5	177.5
	10	195.1	259.4	364.8	587.4	300.2	315.1	296.9	264.6
	30	174.7	258.6	366.4	374.9	284.8	337.3	316.3	267.9
	70	87.6	255.1	259.5	380.2	264.4	235.2	284.1	270.5
	90	67.9	225.2	196.9	260.7	227.1	118.2	208.1	250.3
	120	5.6	47.8	90.1	123.5	118.5	-	26.6	161.2
	150	-	-	37.9	29.2	-	-	-	94.7
Mesh 2	0	177.5	177.5	177.5	177.5	177.5	177.5	177.5	177.5
	10	195.1	265.4	430.3	403.2	305.0	309.1	322.0	278.0
	30	174.7	267.2	407.0	304.2	300.0	295.1	336.5	292.9
	70	87.6	269.0	205.5	179.9	201.8	229.0	291.1	269.8
	90	67.9	211.5	121.3	102.1	161.5	159.4	171.2	176.8
	120	5.6	70.3	36.5	57.5	64.0	52.8	47.8	84.0
	150	-	8.1	-	-	-	-	-	-

* in mg L^{-1} as $CaCO_3$, ** CON = water in the tank without any plant matter for decomposition

the 10th day was 220.55 % of control with *Hydrilla*. On the 120th day hardness of water with plants were 651.8 to 1500 % of the controls, the lowest and the highest being with *Hydrilla* and *Pseudoraphis* respectively.

Chemical oxygen demand

The chemical oxygen demand of the experimental water on the first day of the study was 35.7 mg L^{-1} (Table 10). The COD gradually decreased in the case of the control down to 3.5 mg l^{-1} on the 120th day. The patterns of change of COD in the experimental tanks were different. Here, the pattern was an initial rise followed by a gradual decline. The peak in concentration was seen in most of the cases on the 10th day, the exceptions being the cases of *Cyperus* and *Paspalum* (in small mesh bags), *Neptunia* (in large mesh bags). In these cases, the peaks were on the 30th day (Table 10). Highest COD

Table 10 : Chemical Oxygen Demand (mg L^{-1}) of the water in the tank during plant decomposition*

BAGS	DAY	CON*	CYP	HYD	IPO	NEP	PDM	PLM	PSU
Mesh 1	0	35.7	35.7	35.7	35.7	35.7	35.7	35.7	35.7
	10	16.1	38.5	91.8	122.4	96.9	51.0	45.9	77.8
	30	16.0	74.4	72.6	95.3	54.5	73.4	68.9	57.2
	60	22.1	50.8	48.2	28.1	17.2	33.8	69.4	27.2
	90	22.0	45.2	49.8	26.2	26.8	31.5	18.5	24.3
	120	3.5	61.4	51.2	35.3	27.6	18.8	27.2	23.5
	150	—	61.2	41.3	—	25.2	4.3	—	—
Mesh 2	0	35.7	35.7	35.7	35.7	35.7	35.7	35.7	35.7
	10	16.1	71.4	117.3	134.6	53.0	66.3	71.4	275.4
	30	16.0	64.6	78.9	39.7	88.9	48.9	44.5	44.6
	60	22.1	45.3	29.4	50.3	35.1	44.4	45.3	38.6
	90	22.0	44.8	36.1	41.4	37.5	36.5	49.9	37.4
	120	3.5	49.8	41.9	33.3	44.6	42.5	89.6	38.3
	150	0.0	45.6	27.3	26.1	47.5	—	128.0	—

* CON = water in the tank without any plant matter for decomposition

(with both the small mesh bags and large mesh bags) caused by *Ipomoea* on the 10th day. With small mesh size bags, COD on the day was 122.4 mg l^{-1} i.e., 760.2 % of the control tank. With respect to COD of the same tank on the 0th day, the value was 342.4 % in small mesh bags. With large mesh bags, the COD was 134.6 mgl^{-1}, 836 % of the control and 377.03 % of the initial concentration. By 120th day, the COD load in almost all of the experimental tanks was more than 1000 % than the control tanks.

Chloride

The initial chloride content in the tank water was 44.2 mg L^{-1} (Table 11). Towards the end of the experiment, chloride in the control tank showed a slight increase; the highest concentration of chloride recorded was 84.8 mg L^{-1} (on 120th day). In the presence of decomposing plant matter, the

Table 11 : Chloride content (mg L^{-1}) of the water in the tank during plant decomposition*

BAGS	DAY	CON*	CYP	HYD	IPO	NEP	PDM	PLM	PSU
Mesh 1	0	44.2	44.2	44.2	44.2	44.2	44.2	44.2	44.2
	10	59.6	74.7	69.5	90.9	89.0	68.8	86.6	59.4
	30	64.7	75.4	69.9	91.9	91.3	76.5	93.9	62.5
	70	69.9	75.6	77.6	96.5	93.7	79.8	91.6	63.9
	90	75.5	76.0	71.3	96.7	90.2	81.8	85.7	63.4
	120	84.8	85.1	77.5	105.2	97.3	108.5	83.9	71.4
	150	51.6	78.7	85.1	110.5	104.2	99.4	71.4	79.4
Mesh 1	0	44.2	44.2	42.2	44.2	44.2	44.2	44.2	44.2
	10	59.6	80.8	76.4	97.3	84.8	72.1	87.3	65.5
	30	64.7	37.8	75.9	94.3	99.8	67.0	82.4	63.5
	70	69.9	76.5	71.4	88.3	76.9	64.8	79.0	62.8
	90	75.5	80.0	72.4	86.9	82.0	68.1	85.7	68.1
	120	84.8	87.7	94.1	108.0	104.6	95.1	92.8	88.8
	150	51.6	94.9	91.5	110.7	108.7	132.9	98.2	93.4

* CON = water in the tank without any plant matter for decomposition

chloride content gradually improved. Thus, by 150th day (in the small mesh bags) chloride was in the range 71.4 to 110.5 mg L^{-1} (161.5 to 250 % of the corresponding initial value). The lowest value was in the water in which *Paspalum* was decomposing and the highest was with *Ipomoea*. With reference to the corresponding controls, these values were 138.3 and 214.1 % respectively. With the large mesh bags, the lowest and highest chloride concentrations were 91.5 mg L^{-1} (with *Hydrilla*) and 132.9 mg L^{-1} (with *Paspalidium*) respectively corresponding to 216.8 and 300.6 % of the initial values. These values were 177.3 and 257.5 % respectively with respect to the corresponding chloride concentrations of the controls.

Phosphate

The water at the start of the experiment had 0.40 mg L^{-1} phosphate content (Table 12). Phosphate concentration increased to 1.70 mg L^{-1} by the 10th day in case of control tank. However, afterwards the concentration declined reaching down to 0.30 mg L^{-1} by the end of experiment. In water with the plants enclosed in small mesh bags, the concentration increased by the 10th day, similar to that of control, but the trend continued upto the 30th day. After 60th day the trend reversed. While on 30th day when the concentration was at the peak, it was almost 38 to 160 times of the initial concentration (0th day). When the concentration was at the peak, the highest and the lowest levels were 15.3 and 64.3 mg L^{-1}, the former with *Paspalidium* and the latter with *Pseudoraphis*, both in small mesh bags. In case of large mesh bags, in contrast to the other ones, the increase in concentration by the second sampling (10th day) was very high, almost double of that in the experiment with small mesh bags. With the small mesh bags while the rise continued, the rate was much lesser than that with large

Table 12 : Phosphate content of the water in the tank during plant decomposition *

BAGS	DAY	CON**	CYP	HYD	IPO	NEP	PDM	PLM	PSU
Mesh 1	0	0.4	0.4	0.4	0.4	0.4	0.4	0.4	0.4
	10	1.7	19.4	20.7	12.6	17.3	6.1	15.9	28.0
	30	0.4	48.1	53.3	54.2	56.6	15.3	41.7	64.3
	60	0.2	26.1	11.6	16.5	21.7	2.3	19.2	33.3
	90	0.2	10.9	7.3	10.0	14.4	0.4	8.6	17.7
	120	0.2	2.7	6.5	13.3	10.1	0.4	3.4	14.9
	150	0.3	-	1.0	7.8	4.4	0.9	2.6	6.6
Mesh 1	0	0.4	0.4	0.4	0.4	0.4	0.4	0.4	0.4
	10	1.7	45.2	47.7	33.3	35.5	17.6	40.1	40.5
	30	0.4	49.9	38.7	32.6	40.8	18.0	37.5	44.7
	60	0.2	23.1	5.6	-	4.6	3.1	14.5	9.7
	90	0.2	6.5	2.6	0.3	12.4	1.3	4.7	3.5
	120	0.2	0.7	2.1	2.2	0.8	-	2.9	3.6
	150	0.3	2.4	4.5	5.4	0.3	-	-	5.5

* mg L^{-1}, **CON = water in the control tank

mesh bags until the next sampling (30th day) with *Cyperus, Neptunia* and *Pseudoraphis*. The samples with other species showed a decline than the previous sampling.

Organisms present in the bag during decomposition

In the decomposing plant matter, the variety of organisms was low: only Chironomus, Ostracods and Psychodids were seen. In both small and large mesh bags from the 60th day onwards macro invertebrates were encountered. Chironomus constituted the major portion of the organisms seen in the mesh bags. In the case of small mesh bags Chironomus was seen with all the seven plant species while Ostracods were seen in 5 out of 7 plants species, Psychodids in 3 out of 7 and Leech in only one (Table 13). In the case of large mesh bags Chironomus was seen with all the plants, Psychodids with 3,

Table 13 : Organisms (per litre) in the decomposing plant material in small mesh bags at different days of submergence

Plant	Organisms	Days of submergence					
		10	30	60	90	120	150
Cyperus	Chironomus	-	-	55	76	14	1
	Ostracod	-	-	-	-	3	2
	Total	**-**	**-**	**55**	**76**	**17**	**3**
Hydrilla	Chironomus	-	-	-	119	25	2
	Ostracod	-	-	-	-	27	-
	Psycodid	-	-	-	1	-	-
	Total	**-**	**-**	**-**	**120**	**52**	**2**
Ipomoea	Chironomus	-	-	25	22	7	4
	Ostracod	-	-	-	-	10	5
	Psycodid	-	-	8	-	-	-
	Total			**33**	**22**	**7**	**9**
Neptunia	Chironomus	-	-	6	82	22	8
	Ostracod	-	-	-	-	5	6
	Total	**-**	**-**	**6**	**82**	**27**	**14**
Paspalidium	Chironomus	-	-	176	72	30	-
	Total	**-**	**-**	**176**	**72**	**30**	**-**
Paspalum	Chironomus	-	-	5	66	20	3
	Leech	-	-	-	1	-	-
	Ostracod	-	-	1	-	-	-
	Psycodid	-	-	3	1	-	-
	Total	**-**	**-**	**9**	**68**	**20**	**3**
Pseudoraphis	Chironomus	-	-	16	86	31	12
	Ostracod	-	-	-	2	25	200
	Psycodid	-	-	-	2	-	-
	Total	**0**	**0**	**16**	**90**	**56**	**212**

Ostracods with 2 and leech with one (Table 14). The highest number of organisms were seen on either the 60th or the 90th day. Afterwards, the number of organisms decreased drastically and by 150th day, it was negligibly lower or absent. Only exception to this pattern was the bags with *Pseudoraphis*. With *Pseudoraphis*, of the total number (212) of

Table 14 : Organisms (per liter) in the decomposing plant material in large mesh bags at different days of submergence

Plant	Organisms	Days of submergence					
		10	30	60	90	120	150
Cyperus	Chironomus	-	-	50	34	-	-
	Psycodid	-	-	3	-	-	-
	Total	-	-	**53**	**34**	-	-
Hydrilla	Chironomus	-	-	5	323	62	12
	Ostracod	-	-	-	-	1	-
	Psycodid	-	-	3	-	-	-
	Total	-	-	**8**	**323**	**63**	**12**
Ipomoea	Chironomus	-	-	9	57	36	-
	Psycodid	-	-	1	-	-	-
	Total	-	-	**10**	**57**	**36**	-
Neptunia	Chironomus	-	-	126	154	11	-
	Total	-	-	**126**	**154**	**11**	-
Paspalidium	Chironomus	-	-	32	158	3	70
	Leech	-	-	-	1	-	-
	Total	-	-	**32**	**159**	**3**	**70**
Paspalum	Chironomus	-	-	68	125	14	13
	Total	-	-	**68**	**125**	**14**	**13**
Pseudoraphis	Chironomus	-	-	173	52	10	14
	Ostracod	-	-	-	-	27	12
	Total	-	-	**173**	**52**	**37**	**26**

organisms encountered, 200 were Ostracods. In all other cases, Ostracods were only second in number or negligibly higher than chironomids.

Organisms present in water during decomposition

Water contained numerous and varied species of organisms than obtained in bags (Table 15 and Table 16). The major groups of organisms were chironomids, Ostracods, Cladocerans, Rotifers, Copepods, Psychodids, Calanoids and some algal forms. The organisms were recorded in the bags 60th day onwards. The number of these macro invertebrates

Table 15 : Organisms (per liter) in water with decomposing plant matter in small mesh bags at different days of submergence

Plant	Organisms	Days of submergence					
		10	30	60	90	120	150
Control	Ostracod	-	-	-	-	-	800
	Rotifer	-	50	-	150	-	-
	Cladocera	-	-	50	58	1650	-
	Mosquito larva	-	-	1	-	-	-
	Chironomus	-	-	-	1	-	1
	Copepod	-	-	-	100	300	-
	Calanoid	-	50	-	-	100	-
	Total	**-**	**50**	**51**	**309**	**2050**	**801**
Cyperus	Chironomus	-	-	3	1	3	3
	Cladocera	-	-	5150	400	156	200
	Caladophora	-	-	-	-	12	-
	Copepod	-	-	-	300	50	-
	Ostracod	-	-	-	-	-	850
	Psycodid	-	-	3	-	-	-
	Rotifer	-	-	450	-	-	50
	Watermite	-	-	-	-	-	50
	Total	**-**	**-**	**5606**	**701**	**221**	**1153**
Hydrilla	Anacystis	-	-	250	-	-	-
	Chironomus	-	-	3	-	-	-
	Cladocera	-	-	1	300	100	500
	Copepod	-	-	-	250	-	50
	Ostracod	-	-	-	-	11	950
	Psycodid	-	-	-	2	-	-
	Rotifer	-	-	1650	100	150	250
	Tipulid	-	-	-	1	-	-
	Total	**-**	**-**	**1904**	**653**	**261**	**1750**

Contd.

Table 15 Contd...

Ipomoea	Chironomus	-	-	11	3	-	-
	Cladocera	-	-	-	102	200	1100
	Cladophora	-	-	-	-	1500	-
	Copepod	-	-	-	50	-	50
	Mosquito larva	-	2	-	-	-	-
	Oligochaeta	-	-	-	2	-	-
	Ostracod	-	-	-	-	76	-
	Pediastrum	-	-	50	-	-	-
	Psycodid	-	-	1	-	-	-
	Rotifer	-	-	200	50	50	200
	Wolfia	-	-	-	-	-	17400
	Total	**-**	**2**	**262**	**207**	**1826**	**18750**
Neptunia	Cladocera	-	-	74	119	100	300
	Cladophora	-	-	-	-	50	11650
	Cliates	-	-	250	-	-	-
	Closterium	-	-	150	-	-	-
	Copepod	-	-	-	-	100	250
	Ostracod	-	-	-	-	50	150
	Total	**-**	**-**	**474**	**119**	**300**	**12350**
Paspalidium	Cladocera	-	-	350	111	400	600
	Cladophora	-	-	-	-	-	6800
	Copepod	-	-	100	-	400	50
	Ostracod	-	-	-	-	50	850
	Rotifer	-	-	-	-	-	100
	Total	**-**	**-**	**450**	**111**	**850**	**8400**
Paspalum	Anacystis	-	-	150	-	-	-
	Chironomus	-	-	-	3	-	-
	Cladocera	-	-	66	141	200	-
	Cladophora	-	-	-	-	-	450
	Copepod	-	-	50	-	200	800
	Ostracod	-	-	-	-	12	1150
	Rotifer	-	-	200	-	50	150
	Total	**-**	**-**	**466**	**144**	**462**	**2550**

Contd.

Table 15 Contd...

Pseudoraphis	Chironomus	-	-	-	4	-	-
	Cladocera	-	-	-	-	100	1250
	Copepod	-	-	-	150	-	50
	Mosquito larva	-	-	7	-	-	-
	Ostracod	-	-	-	-	43	5
	Psycodid	-	-	-	2	-	-
	Rotifer	-	-	-	-	100	50
	Total	**-**	**-**	**7**	**156**	**243**	**1355**

Table 16 : Organisms (per liter) in water with de-composing plant material in large mesh bags at different days of submergence

Plant	**Organisms**	**Days of submergence**					
		10	**30**	**60**	**90**	**120**	**150**
Control	Ostracod	-	-	-	-	-	800
	Rotifer	-	50	-	150	-	-
	Cladocera	-	-	50	58	1650	-
	Mosquito larva	-	-	1	-	-	-
	Chironomus	-	-	-	1	-	1
	Copepod	-	-	-	100	300	-
	Calanoid	-	50	-	-	100	-
	Total	**-**	**100**	**51**	**309**	**2050**	**801**
Cyperus	Chironomus	-	-	1	-	2	-
	Cladocera	-	-	2300	3	50	-
	Copepod	-	-	150	100	350	50
	Ostracod	-	-	-	-	24	2900
	Psycodid	-	-	1	-	-	-
	Rotifer	-	551	50	-	-	-
	Total	**-**	**551**	**2502**	**103**	**426**	**2950**
Hydrilla	Chironomus	-	-	-	2	3	-
	Cladocera	-	-	-	46	500	-
	Caladophora	-	-	-	-	-	12
	Copepod	-	-	350	200	50	50
	Ostracod	-	-	-	-	50	950
	Psycodid	-	-	6	-	-	-
	Rotifer	-	-	400	-	-	50
	Total	**-**	**-**	**756**	**248**	**603**	**1062**

Contd.

Table 16 Contd...

Ipomoea	Cladocera	-	-	-	200	550	150
	Copepod	-	-	-	150	200	50
	Ostracod	-	-	-	400	150	950
	Psycodid	-	-	3	-	-	-
	Rotifer	-	-	300	-	150	-
	Total	**-**	**-**	**303**	**750**	**1050**	**1150**
Neptunia	Chironomus	-	-	3	-	-	-
	Cladocera	-	-	-	-	-	100
	Copepod	-	-	1	150	50	50
	Ostracod	-	-	-	-	46	1000
	Total	**-**	**-**	**4**	**150**	**96**	**1150**
Paspalidium	Calanoid	-	-	-	-	50	-
	Chironomus	-	-	-	1	-	-
	Cladocera	-	-	650	76	10	2450
	Cladophora	-	-	-	-	-	450
	Copepod	-	-	50	60	350	150
	Ostracod	-	-	-	-	-	150
	Rotifer	-	200	-	-	-	2100
	Total	**-**	**200**	**700**	**137**	**410**	**5300**
Paspalum	Caenid	-	-	-	-	-	1
	Chironomus	-	-	-	1	-	4
	Cladocera	-	-	-	-	50	-
	Copepod	-	-	200	150	-	-
	Mosquito larva	-	-	2	-	-	-
	Ostracod	-	-	-	-	-	1050
	Psycodid	-	-	1	-	-	-
	Rotifer	-	-	-	-	-	200
	Total	**-**	**-**	**203**	**151**	**50**	**1255**
Pseudoraphis	Chironomus	-	-	-	-	100	-
	Cladocera	-	-	-	-	50	-
	Cladophora	-	-	1	1350	350	1500
	Closterium	-	-	-	-	-	1300
	Calanoid	-	-	100	-	-	-
	Copepod	-	-	50	150	-	100
	Ostracod	-	-	-	-	250	350
	Psycodid	-	-	-	1	-	-
	Rotifer	-	-	-	-	50	-
	Total	**-**	**-**	**151**	**1501**	**800**	**3250**

increased towards the end of the study. Except in very rare cases such as that of *Cyperus* in small mesh bags and the control in all others, the number of macro invertebrates was very high by the 150th day. The maximum number of organisms (18750 L^{-1}) recorded were of *Ipomoea* in small mesh bags (Table 15). Highest number of species of macro organisms was also recorded in small mesh bags with *Ipomoea* species on 150th day. Of the 18750 organisms (total of both faunal and floral forms) per litre that was seen with *Ipomoea*, 17400 were *Wolfia*, smallest flowering plant. The species is not likely to be related with the actual process of decomposition. The species must have established because of nutrient enrichment, absence of no other competing macrophytes and it might have got unintended access to the tank. Among animals in water, Cladocerans were very common followed by Ostracods.

Field studies

Physicochemical changes of the plant material

The results obtained in field studies were similar to that of the laboratory. During the initial period, the loss of weight was high, but it got lower with time. The rate of exponential decay in the field was almost in the same range as obtained in the laboratory studies. Most of the *Hydrilla* species disappeared between 30 to 60 days of submergence in the field. In both the small mesh-sized as well as in the large mesh sized bags the plants decomposed of completely within the same period. *Pseudoraphis* and *Paspalidium* had the highest quantity of remainder in the bags after 150 days in the 0.14 mm mesh size bags. Considerable differences were noted in the decomposition between plants enclosed in smaller pored and larger pored bags. In the bigger pored bags (0.375 mm), only 37 % of *Paspalum* was remaining after 150 days of submergence.

As in the case of laboratory experiment in the field, the rate of decomposition was high in the large mesh sized bags.

Hydrilla was the fastest decomposing plant with the rate of decay, –0.0496 in the small sized bags and –0.0548 in the large mesh sized bags. These rates correspond to half-lives of 13.97 days and 12.65 days. *Cyperus* and *Pseudoraphis* had the lowest decay rates and corresponding highest half-life periods in small mesh bags, where as in the case of larger mesh bags, it was *Paspalidium*. In *Cyperus* and *Pseudoraphis*, the decay rate was –0.0019 with corresponding half-life of 364.81 days where as in *Paspalidium*, it was –0.0018 and 385.08 respectively (Table 17).

Table 17 : The exponential decay rate and half-life of decomposing macrophytes in the field

Species	Treatment	Decay rate	Half life
CYP	0.14 mm mesh bag in the field	-0.0019	364.81
PSU		-0.0019	364.81
PDM		-0.0020	346.57
PLM		-0.0027	256.72
IPO		-0.0028	247.55
NEP		-0.0038	182.41
HYD		-0.0496	13.97
PDM	0.375 mm mesh bag in the field	-0.0018	385.08
PSU		-0.0019	364.81
PLM		-0.0027	256.72
IPO		-0.0029	239.01
CYP		-0.0043	161.20
NEP		-0.0060	115.52
HYD		-0.0548	12.65

Phosphate

The phosphate content in the macrophyte reduced with decomposition. In general, the plant matter in the large mesh bags lost more phosphate than those in the small mesh bags.

The phosphate content in the species studied ranged between 0.69 (*Hydrilla*) and 0.32 % (*Paspalidium*) of the dry weight. After the 150 days of submergence in block E, wetland of the Park, the phosphate concentration in plants, in small mesh bags ranged between 0.13 (*Paspalidium*) and 0.17 % (*Paspalum*), both approximately 42% of the initial concentration. In the large mesh bags, phosphate ranged between 0.04 (*Pseudoraphis*) and 0.13 % (*Neptunia*); 10 and 29.5 % respectively of the initial concentrations. In the plants submerged in block D wetland of the Park the pattern of change was more or less similar to that of block E. Reduction, by the end of the experiment, in small mesh bags ranged between 52.4 (*Neptunia*) and 78.9 % (*Paspalidium*) and in large mesh bags 56.7 (*Neptunia*) and 78.9 % (*Paspalidium*) and in large mesh bags 56.7 (*Neptunia*) and 89.1 % (*Paspalum*).

Organic carbon

The organic carbon content in the plants decreased considerably in the field during decomposition. In wetland block E, the reduction was higher than that in wetland block D. Likewise, the reduction was much higher in larger mesh bags than the smaller ones. For example in the case of *Pseudoraphis* in block D, the reduction was 18.64 and 29.33 % of the initial concentration, in smaller and larger mesh bags respectively. The reduction in the similar bags in block E was between 24.55 and 49.11 %, in *Paspalum* and *Ipomoea* respectively.

Organisms present in the bag during decomposition

Similar to the results of the laboratory tank study only Chironomus, Caenis, Planorbis and leeches were seen initially in the decomposing plant matter in the field. Other macro invertebrates were recorded 60th day onwards in block D water and 90th day onwards in block E water as is seen in Table 18 and Table 19.

Table 18 : Organisms (per liter) in decomposing plant material at different days of submergence in block D water

Plant	Mesh	Organisms	Days of submergence					
			10	30	60	90	120	150
Cyperus	1	Caeni	--	-	-	-	1	-
		Chironomus	-	-	2	2	1	57
		Leech	-	-	-	-	1	-
		Oligochaeta	-	-	72	2	-	-
		Ostracod	-	-	-	4	2	6
		Planorbis	-	-	-	-	2	1
		Total		**-**	**74**	**8**	**7**	**64**
Cyperus	2	Caenis	-	-	-	2	-	9
		Chironomus	-	2	4	1	13	4
		Cladocera	-	-	1	6	-	-
		Limnea	-	-	-	-	1	-
		Oligochaeta	-	-	8	4	-	2
		Ostracod	-	-	5	4	2	18
		Planorbis	-	-	5	1	21	5
		Total	**-**	**2**	**23**	**18**	**37**	**38**
Hydrilla	1	Caenis	-	-	-	-	1	-
		Chironomus	-	-	7	11	7	13
		Caladocera	-	-	1	-	-	-
		Leech	-	-	-	2	-	1
		Oligochaeta	-	-	45	5	6	-
		Ostracod	-	-	-	-	8	33
		Planorbis	-	-	-	35	2	3
		Total	**-**	**-**	**53**	**53**	**24**	**50**
	2	Caenis	-	-	-	2	-	1
		Chironomus	-	7	24	17	-	3
		Caladocera	-	-	4	2	-	-
		Gyrinid	-	-	-	-	2	4
		Limnea	-	-	-	1	-	-
		Oligochaeta	-	-	33	-	-	11
		Ostracod	-	-	6	12	51	13
		Planorbis	-	-	-	10	12	76
		Total	**-**	**7**	**67**	**44**	**65**	**108**

Contd.

Table 18 Contd...

Ipomoea	1	Caenis	-	-	-	-	-	1
		Chironomus	-	-	3	4	-	11
		Leech	-	-	-	-	1	1
		Limnea	-	-	-	-	1	-
		Oligochaeta	-	-	117	3	23	-
		Ostracod	-	-	-	6	-	11
		Planorbis	-	-	-	3	7	-
		Total	**-**	**-**	**120**	**16**	**32**	**24**
	2	Caenis	-	-	-	2	1	19
		Chironomus	-	-	6	16	1	3
		Caladocera	-	-	3	2	-	-
		Gyrinid	-	-	-	-	1	-
		Leech	-	-	1	-	-	-
		Oligochaeta	-	-	20	7	1	-
		Ostracod	-	-	13	24	18	29
		Planorbis	-	-	1	2	8	8
		Total	**-**	**-**	**44**	**53**	**30**	**59**
Neptunia	1	Chironomus	-	1	1	-	37	11
		Odonata	-	-	-	-	1	-
		Oligochaeta	-	-	26	-	2	-
		Ostracod	-	-	2	31	12	29
		Planorbis	-	-	-	20	-	1
		Total	**-**	**1**	**29**	**51**	**52**	**41**
	2	Caenis	-	-	-	-	-	9
		Chironomus	-	9	10	2	1	6
		Caladocera	-	-	3	-	-	-
		Gyrinid	-	-	-	-	-	1
		Leech	-	-	-	1	-	-
		Oligochaeta	-	-	1	7	4	-
		Ostracod	-	-	11	11	-	36
		Planorbis	-	-	-	7	9	3
		Total	**-**	**9**	**25**	**28**	**14**	**55**
Paspalidium	1	Chironomus	-	1	3	13	6	32
		Leech	-	-	-	-	6	1
		Oligochaeta	-	-	7	12	3	-
		Ostracod	-	-	-	11	-	5
		Planorbis	-	-	-	-	3	1
		Total	**-**	**1**	**10**	**36**	**18**	**39**

Contd.

Table 18 Contd...

	2	Chironomus	-	9	5	16	-	9
		Caladocera	-	-	2	-	-	-
		Gyrinid	-	-	-	-	-	1
		Leech	-	-	-	1	-	-
		Odonata	-	-	-	1	-	-
		Oligochaeta	-	-	70	31	11	-
		Ostracod	-	-	9	7	3	37
		Planorbis	-	-	5	5	6	8
		Total	**-**	**9**	**91**	**61**	**20**	**55**
Paspalum	1	Caenid	-	-	-	-	2	-
		Chironomus	-	-	22	54	4	9
		Leech	-	-	-	3	-	-
		Oligochaeta	-	-	71	104	14	-
		Ostracod	-	-	2	-	-	13
		Planorbis	-	-	-	-	1	7
		Total	**-**	**-**	**95**	**161**	**21**	**29**
	2	Caenis	-	-	-	-	-	1
		Chironomus	-	1	52	63	11	4
		Caladocera	-	-	2	-	-	-
		Gyrinid	-		-	-	1	-
		Leech	-	-	-	1	-	2
		Limnea	-	-	-	-	1	-
		Oligochaeta	-	-	9	-	14	-
		Ostracod	-	-	4	11	1	34
		Planorbis	-	-	2	1	6	6
		Total	**-**	**1**	**69**	**76**	**34**	**47**
Pseudoraphis	1	Caenis	-	-	-	-	2	1
		Chironomus	-	1	8	13	1	13
		Caladocera	-	-	-	1	-	-
		Leech	-	-	-	2	-	-
		Oligochaeta	-	-	4	2	27	-
		Ostracod	-	-	-	3	-	4
		Planorbis	-	-	-	2	13	2
		Total	**-**	**1**	**12**	**23**	**43**	**20**
	2	Caenis	-	-	1	-	2	8
		Chironomus	-	7	39	86	-	3
		Leech	-	-	1	-	1	-
		Oligochaeta	-	-	-	11	56	-
		Ostracod	-	-	17	25	-	32
		Planorbis	-	-	29	5	7	9
		Total	**-**	**7**	**87**	**127**	**66**	**52**

Table 19 : Organisms (per liter) in decomposing plant material at different days of submergence in block E water

Plant	Mesh	Organisms	Days of submergence					
			10	30	60	90	120	150
Cyperus	1	Caenis	-	-	-	1	-	1
		Chironomus	-	3	-	1	8	20
		Leech	-	-	-	5	7	6
		Limnea	-	-	-	1	-	-
		Oligochaeta	-	-	-	29	-	2
		Ostracod	-	-	-	-	3	2
		Planorbis	-	-	-	5	3	4
		Total	**-**	**3**	**-**	**42**	**21**	**35**
	2	Caenis	-	5	-	1	1	35
		Chironomus	-	-	-	1	1	18
		Gyrinid	-	-	-	2	-	67
		Leech	-	-	-	3	5	2
		Mosquito Larva	-	-	-	1	-	8
		Oligochaeta	-	-	-	9	29	-
		Ostracod	-	-	-	-	5	-
		Planorbis	-	-	-	5	5	8
		Total	**-**	**5**	**-**	**22**	**46**	**138**
Hydrilla	1	Caenis	-	-	-	-	-	2
		Chironomus	-	2	-	-	-	68
		Ephemeroptera	-	-	-	8	-	-
		Gyrinid	-	-	-	-	1	-
		Leech	-	-	-	2	5	3
		Odonata	-	-	-	3	-	-
		Oligochaeta	-	-	-	-	1	-
		Ostracod	-	-	-	11	-	16
		Planorbis	-	1	-	31	4	2
		Total	**-**	**3**	**-**	**55**	**11**	**91**
	2	Caenis	-	-	-	4	2	17
		Chironomus	-	8	-	2	-	25
		Gyrinid	-	-	-	3	-	1
		Leech	-	-	-	9	3	2
		Limnea	-	-	-	1	2	-
		Oligochaeta	-	-	-	5	-	5
		Planorbis	-	-	-	9	27	2
		Polycentropidae	-	-	-	-	-	1
		Total	**-**	**8**	**-**	**33**	**34**	**53**

Contd.

Table 19 Contd...

Ipomoea	1	Chironomus	-	1	-	1	4	23
		Ephemeroptera	-	-	-	1	-	-
		Hygrobatidae	-	-	-	-	2	-
		Leech	-	-	-	4	5	5
		Odonata	-	-	-	1	-	-
		Oligochaeta	-	-	-	16	-	-
		Ostracod	-	-	-	2	-	11
		Planorbis	-	1	-	3	-	2
		Total	**-**	**2**	**-**	**28**	**11**	**41**
	2	Caenis	-	-	-	1	1	1
		Chironomus	-	-	-	-	2	11
		Gyrinid	-	-	-	2	1	1
		Leech	-	-	-	16	6	7
		Oligochaeta	-	-	-	38	17	-
		Ostracod	-	-	-	-	-	10
		Planorbis	-	-	-	12	-	10
		Total	**-**	**-**	**-**	**69**	**27**	**40**
Neptunia	1	Caenis	-	-	-	-	2	-
		Chironomus	-	1	-	1	-	47
		Coleoptera	-	-	-	-	-	3
		Leech	-	-	-	8	1	8
		Limnea	-	-	-	2	-	-
		Oligochaeta	-	-	-	6	1	-
		Ostracod	-	-	-	-	-	8
		Planorbis	-	1	-	10	-	5
		Total	**-**	**2**	**-**	**27**	**4**	**71**
	2	Caenis	-	-	-	1	1	7
		Chironomus	-	8	-	10	-	15
		Gyrinid	-	-	-	-	-	2
		Leech	-	-	-	10	6	6
		Oligochaeta	-	-	-	28	21	4
		Ostracod	-	-	-	9	1	26
		Planorbis	-	2	-	13	2	-
		Total	**-**	**10**	**-**	**71**	**31**	**60**

Contd.

Table 19 Contd...

Paspalidium	1	Caenis	-	-	-	-	1	-
		Chironomus	-	3	-	1	8	34
		Leech	-	-	-	2	-	8
		Limnea	-	-	-	4	-	-
		Oligochaeta	-	-	-	6	2	-
		Ostracod	-	-	-	-	2	5
		Planorbis	-	-	-	4	1	-
		Total	**-**	**3**	**-**	**17**	**14**	**47**
	2	Caenis	-	-	-	-	-	21
		Chironomus	-	8	-	-	22	71
		Gyrinid	-	-	-	1	-	-
		Leech	-	-	-	-	13	9
		Limnea	-	-	-	1	-	-
		Oligochaeta	-	-	-	55	28	3
		Ostracod	-	-	-	3	5	10
		Planorbis	-	1	-	4	1	2
		Polycentropidae	-	-	-	-	-	1
		Total	**-**	**9**	**-**	**64**	**69**	**117**
Paspalum	1	Caenis	-	-	-	4	-	1
		Chironomus	-	4	-	-	8	17
		Caladocera	-	-	-	-	-	1
		Hygrobatidae	-	-	-	-	-	1
		Leech	-	-	-	10	3	6
		Limnea	-	-	-	-	-	1
		Oligochaeta	-	-	-	4	20	-
		Ostracod	-	-	-	1	-	11
		Planorbis	-	3	-	12	1	-
		Total	**-**	**7**	**-**	**31**	**32**	**38**
	2	Caenis	-	-	-	2	-	16
		Chironomus	-	10	-	-	2	39
		Gyrinid	-	-	-	-	-	2
		Leech	-	-	-	8	3	8
		Oligochaeta	-	-	-	40	5	12
		Ostracod	-	-	-	3	1	13
		Planorbis	-	5	-	11	4	4
		Total	**-**	**15**	**-**	**64**	**15**	**94**

Contd.

Table 19 Contd...

Pseudoraphis	1	Chironomus	-	2	-	-	15	11
		Ephimeroptera	-	-	-	2	-	-
		Hygrobatidae	-	-	-	-	-	1
		Leech	-	-	-	9	5	8
		Limnea	-	-	-	1	-	-
		Oligochaeta	-	-	-	3	-	1
		Ostracod	-	-	-	-	1	21
		Planorbis	-	-	-	6	-	6
		Total	**-**	**2**	**-**	**21**	**21**	**48**
	2	Caenis	-	-	-	1	-	24
		Chironomus	-	6	-	-	1	52
		Gyrinid	-	-	-	1	-	-
		Leech	-	1	-	4	7	10
		Limnea	-	-	-	1	-	-
		Oligochaeta	-	-	-	19	27	9
		Ostracod	-	-	-	-	1	44
		Planorbis	-	4	-	3	13	-
		Total	**-**	**11**	**-**	**29**	**49**	**139**

Discussion

The rate of breakdown of macrophyte species varied among themselves on a temporal scale. The variability of reported decay rates of different macrophyte species may be because of the composition of the plant material as lignin-type substances and structural fiber content which were relatively resistant to degradation in addition to the micro environmental conditions (Wahbeh and Mahasneh, 1985; Kok *et al.*, 1990 and Wrubleski *et al.*, 1997). The pattern of loss was described as occurring in three phases (Valiela *et al.*, 1984; Murkin *et al.*, 1991 and Wrubleski *et al.*, 1997). The first phase was a periodic rapid mass loss, attributed to physical leaching. The second phase was a period of sustained, but reduced mass loss attributed to active microbial decomposition and the third phase was characterized by considerable slowdown of mass loss.

However, in the present experiment, a gradual reduction in weight was recorded which varied from 25 to 45% at the end of the experiment. Mainly fibrous matter, which is generally resistant to degradation, might constitute the remainder of the plant matter. Moreover, in field condition clay and silt deposition may also contribute to the remainder weight. van der Valk and Attiwill (1984) has also reported the low decay rate of fibrous matter decomposition and its contribution to the remainder weight in litter bags after the normal decomposition study. Similar findings were reported by Briggs *et al.,* (1985) on *Vallisneria spiralis* L. for 60 days. In the present study, the organic carbon as well as phosphate content in the decomposing plant material were low in the larger mesh size bags than the smaller ones. This was in pace with the decay rate in both the mesh bags. The loss of organic carbon can be attributed to the loss of the plant material in the mesh bags. However, the situation with phosphate is somewhat more complex. Macrophytes may accumulate phosphorus in excess of their metabolic needs; however; a large proportion of this internal phosphorus content may be leached upon death (Tupacz and Day, 1990). Van der Valk and Attiwill (1984) have also reported the leaching losses of phosphorus to the tune of 67% for the leaf and root litter of mangrove species *Avicennia marina*.

The quality of water in the tanks with decomposing plant material varied notably. The COD was fluctuating with an initial increase up to 10th day, followed by a decrease and subsequent increase. In water, the COD is dependent upon the quantum of organic material already present, those entering in unit time and the extent of microbial activity. In the present study, the weight loss from the decomposing plant matter had a gradual declining trend. However, the fluctuation in the COD, which differed from a corresponding trend, can be attributed to the quantum of microbes in the system and their processing ability. The probable physical leaching of organic materials and the micro detritus that flow through the pores of the litterbags may add on to the COD level considerably. It might also be because of the gradual addition of organic wastes in the form of microbial excrements, as in due course of time microbes start colonizing. The macroinvertebrates and other organisms also may add on to the COD load.

Chloride in the tank water was gradually increasing throughout the study period. Probably the concentrating effect due to evaporation and replenishment of water in the tank to maintain a fixed level would have contributed to this. Unlike chloride, the phosphate content of tank water showed fluctuating trend, with an initial increase up to 10th – 30th day followed by a decrease in both the mesh bags. The initial increasing trend might be because of the leaching of phosphorus in the form of phosphates from the decaying plant matter. However, under oxidizing conditions, created by the periodic aeration of tank water, phosphates precipitated and settled in the sediments resulting in the depletion of phosphorus in water (Saxena, 1987). It is not clear why in certain cases P concentrations increased in the decomposing plant matter. Kok *et al.* (1990) hypothesized that such increase may be because of the microbial uptake of P from the surrounding water into the detritus.

Of the two types of alkalinity examined in the present experiment, the trends of phenolphthalein and total alkalinity were different. The zero value for phenolphthalein alkalinity was an indication of the presence of free carbon dioxide and absence of hydroxide and carbonate ions. As in due course of time decomposition process speeds up releasing CO_2 in addition to the contribution from microbial respiration, the value showed an increasing trend. However, the sudden decline during the end of the experiment might be because of the addition of park water afresh. Whereas, the continuous increase in total alkalinity may be due to the gradual release of ions such as carbonates, bicarbonates, hydroxides, borates, phosphates and sulphates in the course of decomposition. In the case of total hardness, the trend was almost similar for both the mesh bags, i.e., an initial increase followed by a gradual decrease till the end of the experiment. The initial increase on 10th day might be because of the availability of Ca and Mg ions, which normally complexed with humic substances. Moreover, the pH of water was low than the initial day, which suppressed the production of humic compounds (Kok *et al.*, 1990). Hence, the contribution of these cations might be more towards hardness.

Conclusions

Experiments were performed in the laboratory and in field enclosures, in order to evaluate the magnitude of effect of the macrophyte decomposition on the water quality. In both field and laboratory conditions, the trend in the decay rate of all the macrophyte species was similar. It was also found that the exponential decay rate was always higher in the bags of higher mesh size than the lower ones. Irrespective of the mesh bag and incubating condition, it was found that among all the selected macrophytes, *Hydrilla* and *Paspalidium* had the highest and the lowest decay rate respectively, except in lower mesh bags in field, whereas *Cyperus* had the lowest decay rate. The low decay rate obtained for some of the macrophyte species here may be attributed partly to the quality and composition of leaves, partly to the fact that incubations were made submerged in water (in field and in laboratory water tanks) where the effect of water movement is very less to have a considerable influence on the process of decomposition and partly to ambient conditions where in litterbags were incubated. In the case of phosphates, it decreased in the water column with an increasing concentration in the plant matter, though both cannot be related directly. The trend in COD was more or less related to the macrophyte decay rate, though microbes must have also been involved. The laboratory water tank study demonstrates that water quality is influenced by the decomposition of macrophytes. However, other factors such as, soil characteristics may have important role in determining the water quality.

Acknowledgements

The U.S. Fish and Wildlife Service through the Ministry of Environment and Forest, Govt. of India provided support for this study. Bombay Natural History Society (BNHS), India, provided facilities for the experiments and SACON, for data analysis and manuscript preparation.

References

Allen, S.E. (1989) *Chemical Analysis of Ecological Materials.* Blackwell Scientific Publications, London, pp. 368.

APHA / AWWA / WPCF (1985) *Standard Methods for the Examination of Water and Wastewater.* 16th edition, American Public Health Association, Washington DC.

Azeez, P.A., Nadarajan, N.R. and Mittal, D.D. (2000) The impact of a monsoonal wetland on ground water chemistry. Pollution Resarch, 19 (2): 249-255.

Azeez, P.A., Ramachandran, N. K. and Vijayan, V.S. (1992) The socioeconomics of the villagers around Keoladeo National Park, Bharatpur, Rajasthan. Int. J. Ecol. Environ. Sci., 18: 1-15.

Boston, H.L. and Perkins, M.A. (1982) Water column impacts of macrophyte decomposition beneath fibreglass screens. Aquat. Botany, 14: 15-27.

Briggs, S.V., Maher, M.T. and Tongway, D.J. (1985) Dry matter and nutrient loss from decomposing *Vallisneria spiralis* L. Aquat. Botany, 22: 387-392.

Brock, T.C.M. 91984) Aspects of the decomposition of *Nymphoides peltata* (Gmel.) O. Kuntze (Menyanthaceae). Aquat. Botany, 19: 131-156.

Davis, C. B. and van der Valk, A. (1988) Ecology of a semitropical monsoonal wetland in India. The Keoladeo National Park, Bharatpur, Rajasthan. Final Report, September 1988. Ohio State University, pp. 104.

Kok, C.J., Meesters, H.W.G. and Kempers, A.J. (1990) Decomposition rate, Chemical composition and nutrient cycling of *Nymphaea alba* L. floating leaf detritus as influenced by pH, alkalinity and aluminium in laboratory experiments. Aquat. Botany, 37: 215-227.

Mäkelä, S., Huitu, E. and Arvola, L. (2004) Spatial patterns in aquatic vegetation composition and environmental covariates chains of lakes in the Kokemaenjoki watershed (S. Finland). Aquat. Botany, 80: 253-269.

Mathur, V. B., Sinha, P. R. and Mishra, M. (2005) Keoladeo National Park World Heritage Site. Technical Report No. 5, UNESCO-IUCN-Wild Life Institute of India, Dehradun, India.

Murkin, H.R., van der Valk, A.G. and Davis, C.B. (1989) Decomposition of four dominant macrophytes in the Delta marsh, Manitoba. Wildl. Soc. Bull., 17: 215-221.

Pal, D. K., Bhattacharyya, T., Deshpande, S. B., Sarma, V. A. K. and Velayutham, M. (2000) Significance of minerals in soil environment of India. NBSS Review Series 1. Nagpur, India: National Bureau of Soil Survey & Land Use Planning, pp. 68

Prusty, B. A. K., Azeez, P, A., Vasanthakumar, R. and Jayalakshmi, V. (2006) Carbon and nitrogen dynamics in the soil system of a wetland-terrestrial ecosystem complex. *In* : The Proceedings of National Conference on Environment and Sustainable Development. Bharathidasan University, Trichirappalli, Tamil Nadu, (19-17 February), pp. 12.

Prusty, B. A. K., Azeez, P. A. and Jagadeesh, E. P.(2006) Select Alkali and Transition Metals in Macrophytes of a Wetland System. Bull. Environ. Contam. Toxicol. (In Press).

Prusty, B.A.K. and Azeez, P.A. (2004) Seasonal variation in water chemistry of a monsoonal wetland. In: The National Conference on Water Vision-2004. PSGR Krishnamal College for Women, Coimbatore, (6th – 8th October), pp. 47.

Rogers, K.H. and Breen, C.M. (1982) Decomposition of *Potamogeton crispus* L.: The effects of drying on the pattern of mass and nutrient loss. Aquat. Botany, 12: 1-12.

Saxena, M.M. (1987) Environmental Analysis of water, soil and air. Agro Botanical Publishers, Bikaner, India, pp. 74-77.

Tupacz, E.G. and Day, F.P. (1990) Decomposition of roots in a seasonally flooded swamp ecosystems. Aquat. Botany, 37: 199-214.

Valiela, I., Wilson, J., Buchsbaum, R., Rietsma, C., Bryant, D., Foreman, K. and Teal, J. (1984) Importance of chemical composition of salt marsh litter on decay rate and feeding by detritivores. Bull. Mar. Sci., 35: 261-269.

van der Valk, A.G and Attiwill, P.M. (1984) Decomposition of leaf and root litter of *Avicennia Marina* at Westernport Bay, Victoria, Australia. Aquat. Botany, Vol. 18: 205-221.

Vijayan, V.S. (1991) Keoladeo National Park Ecology Study (1980 – 1990), Final report. Bombay Natural History Society, India, pp. 337.

Wahbeh, M.I. and Mahasneh, A.M. (1985) Some aspects of decomposition of leaf litter of the seagrass *Halophila stipulacea* from the gulf of Aqaba (Jordan). Aquat. Botany, 21: 237-244.

Wrubleski, D.A., Murkin, H.R., van der Valk, A.G. and Nelson, J.W. (1997) Decomposition of emergent macrophyte roots and rhizomes in a northern prairie marsh. Aquat. Botany, 58: 121-134.

CHAPTER 6

OZONE LAYER DEPLETION AND ITS EFFECTS ON HUMAN HEALTH

Basudeo Prasad

Environment Monitoring Instrument Division, CSIO, Chandigarh.

ABSTRACT

An article on depletion of ozone layer is presented, which focuses light on various causes of its depletion, its ill effects on human beings and environment at Chandigarh. The measurements were done by equipment developed by CSIO, Chandigarh. Some ozone friendly products as alternatives of CFCs are given in the chapter.

Key Words : Ozone layer, human health.

Introduction

A Scientific statement **Ozone Good at High but Bad Nearby** stands true in our present scenario of changing climate and pollution episode. Ozone occurs in two layers of atmosphere as shown in Fig. 1.

Ozone (O_3) is available in natural form and omni present at all altitudes in atmosphere but its concentration is very high in stratosphere and ozonosphere in particular.

Ozone is a molecule of three oxygen atoms bound together (0_3). It is unstable and highly reactive. Ozone is used as bleach, a deodorizing agent, and a sterilization agent for air and drinking water. Ozone is a bluish gas that is harmful to breath and even at low concentrations, it is toxic.

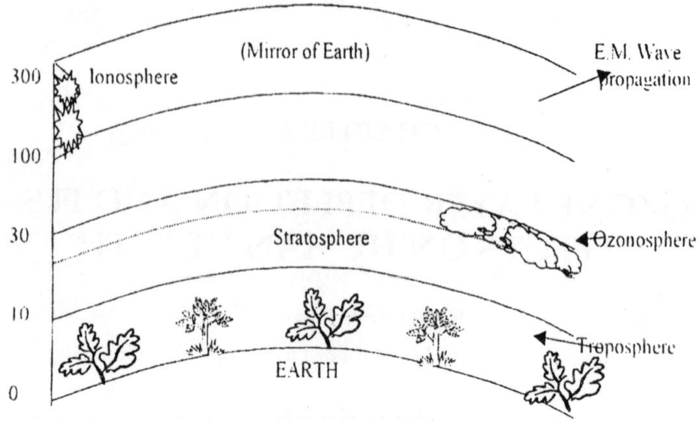

Fig. 1 : Ozone in Earth's Atmosphere

The troposphere begins at the Earth's surface and extends up to 18 km height. This is where we live. As we climb higher in this layer, the temperature drops from about 17°C to –51°C. Ozone found in this layer is known as ground-level ozone or "bad" ozone and is regarded as an air pollutant that damages human health and vegetation and also forms a key ingredient of urban smog.

The stratosphere extends from the troposphere up to 50 km above the Earth's surface. This layer holds 19% of the atmosphere's gases. The temperature rises from – 60°C at the bottom to a maximum of about – 15°C. Nearly 90% of the Earth's ozone is in the stratosphere and is referred to as the ozone layer. Ozone found in this layer is also known as stratospheric ozone or "good" ozone. It protects life on Earth by filtering the sun's harmful ultraviolet rays (UV-B).

Formation Mechanism of "bad" Ozone

Ozone is not emitted directly into the air, but at ground level, it is created by a chemical reaction between oxides of nitrogen (NO_x)*, and volatile organic compounds (VOC)** in the presence of sunlight. Motor vehicle exhaust, industrial emissions, gasoline vapors and chemical solvents are some of the major sources of NO_x and VOC, also known as "ozone precursors".

* NO_x = nitrogen oxide compounds.

** VOC = volatile organic compounds.

Some areas are also subject to high ozone levels as winds carry NOx emissions, hundreds of miles away from their original sources (like the Sierra Nevada due to traffic in the Central Valley. Source : EPA, USA website). Significant levels of ozone pollution can be detected in rural areas as far as 250 miles (150 km) downwind from urban industrial zones.

Strong sunlight and hot weather cause ground-level ozone to form in harmful concentrations in the air. Changing weather patterns (especially the number of hot, sunny days), periods of air stagnation, and other factors that contribute to ozone formation make long-term predictions difficult. Under some meteorological conditions, such as thunderstorm convection, which displaces much air vertically, down as well as up, ozone from the stratosphere can be brought to the surface.

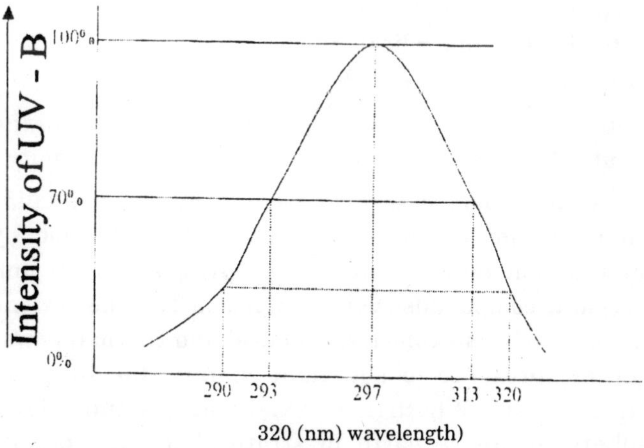

Fig. 2 : Effects of sun's harmful ultraviolet rays (UV-B)

The layer surrounding the earth's surface is the troposphere. Here, the Ozone level at ground is found to be in higher concentration above 120 ppbv, which causes damage to human health. It is a key ingredient of urban smog (smoke + fog). Where as stratospheric ozone layer is beneficial which extends from 10 to 30 km above earth's surface and it protects biosphere from sun's harmful ultraviolet rays (UV-B). Effects of UV-B has been shown in Fig. 2, which causes diseases like skin cancer, eye cataract, loss of eye sight and reduction in crops yield Asian continent, and growth of red pigments on body skin mostly in Australian continent (Sydney, Melbourne and Perth) where also material. Its concentration varies from 0·05—10 ppm.

Various sources of ozone at ground levels are :

(*i*) Release of ozone during water purification from water ozonofication plant during bacteriological treatment of potable mineral water

(*ii*) Our photo copier machines

(*iii*) Arc welding machines

(*iv*) Potato field-soil (due to high use of nitrates as fertilizer and our age old farming practices)

(*v*) Sterilization of medical appliances

(*vi*) Bleaching plants in Textile Industries

(*vii*) During electrodialysis cum ozonolysis of drinking water (Tsunami disaster and other natural calamity)

Apart from above, it is also created due to vehicular pollution in all metro cities and towns. It is formed by chemical reaction between oxides of Nitrogen (NOx) and volatile organic compounds (VOC) - Benzene Toluene, Xylene and PAN released from vehicles, chemical and thermal power plants in the presence of sun light mainly due to photo chemical reaction. Whether it exists at ground level (Troposphere) or above earth in stratosphere, as per its presence, it can be either harmful or harmless.

But definitely at ground level, the rising level of ozone due to increase in NO_x as revealed from increasing number of petroleum vehicles, it has caused higher damage to human health. Its hazardous effect has been depicted in Table 1 below. The maximum concentration of ozone level has been monitored at Aroma Chowk Sector 22 in Chandigarh, which is in correlation with rising number in vehicular moment at this junction point and is in coherence with the fact noted by Prasad *et al.* undersigned earlier from 1999 - 2004. Motor vehicle exhaust and industrial emissions, gasoline vapours and chemical solvents are some of the major sources of Ozone. VOC is also known as ozone precursors. Climatic change and climatological effect in Chandigarh and worldwide, strong sunlight and hot weather on most occasions and rising trend of day and night temperature have enhanced ground level ozone to form harmful concentration in the air. Ozone concentration of course varies from year to year as evident from our survey report but changing weather pattern (especially increasing number of hot sunny days, air stagnation period) and other factors have contributed to ozone formation at ground level and thereby rising trend of smog nowadays in Delhi, Patiala, Ludhiana and similar other polluted cities of India. Status of O_3 concentration during 90-92 and its rising trend during 2004-05 have been depicted in Fig. 3-6.

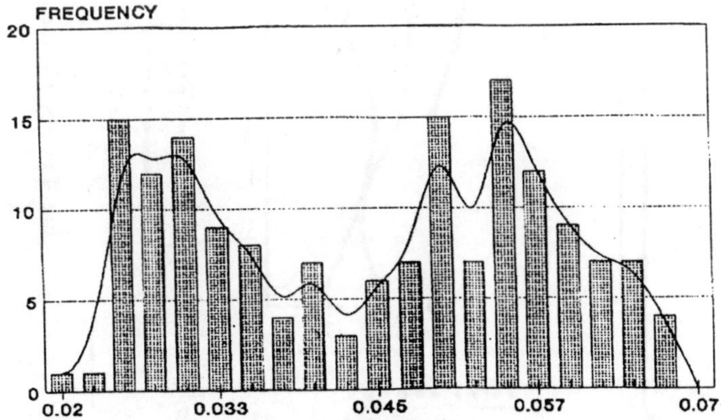

Fig. 3 : Frequency distribution of daily ozone levels during 1990s

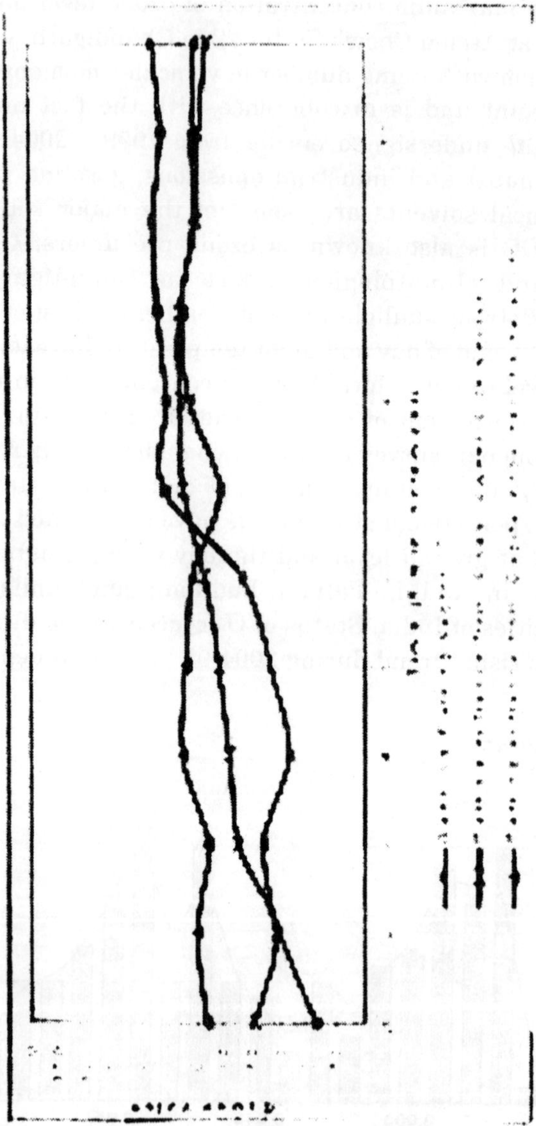

Fig. 4 : Ozone Values from morning at Sector — 17 (Commercial location)

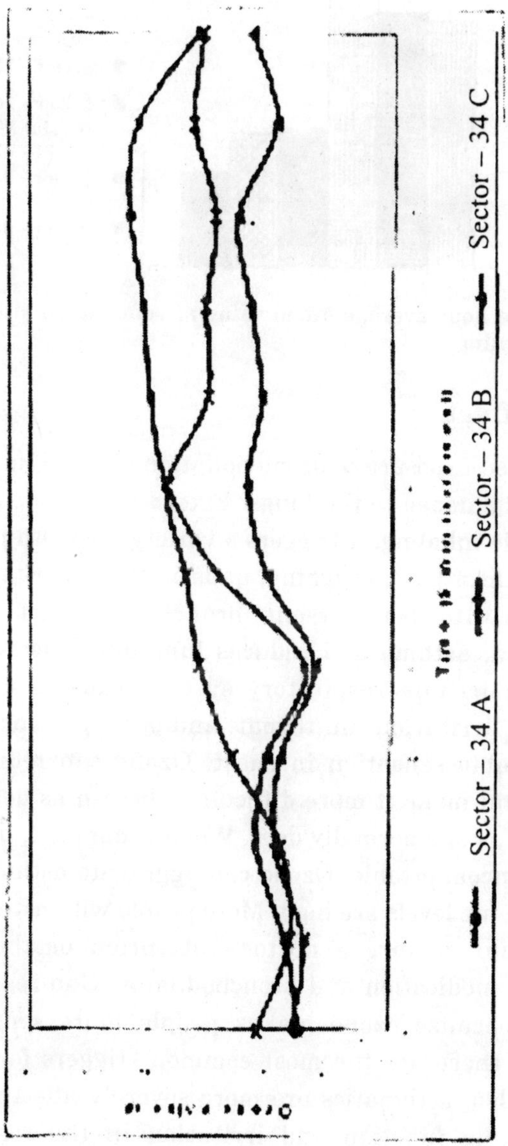

Fig. 5 : Ozone values for morning at Sector—34 (Commercial location)

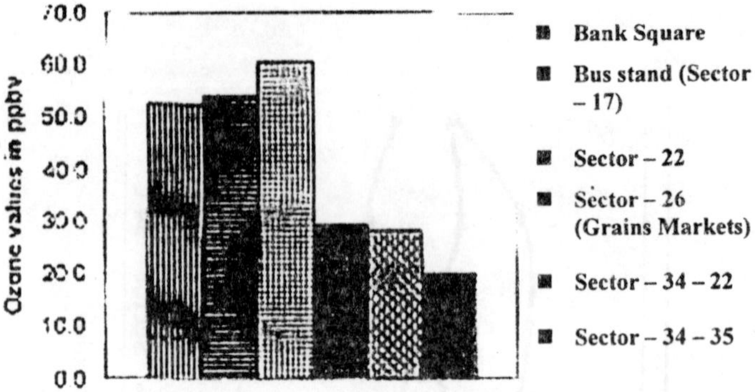

Fig. 6 : One hour average ozone value at commercial sites during morning

Health Effect

Repeated exposure to ozone pollution (Table 1) may cause permanent damage to the lungs. Even when Ozone is in low levels, while inhaling, it triggers a variety of health problems including chest pain, coughing, nausea, throat irritation and congestion. It also worsens bronchitis, heart disease, emphysema, asthma and reduces lung-inhalation capacity. Ozone can irritate respiratory system, causing coughing, feeling of irritation in throat and/or experience of an uncomfortable sensation in chest. Ozone can reduce lung function and make it more difficult to breath as deeply and vigorously as one normally does. When it happens, breathing becomes uncomfortable. Ozone can aggravate asthma, when ambient ozone levels are high. More people with asthma have attacks that require a doctor's attention or the use of additional medication and bronchodilator. One reason, this happens because ozone makes people more sensitive to allergens; these are the most common triggers for asthma attacks. Also, asthmatics are more severely affected by the reduced lung function and irritation in the respiratory system. Ozone can inflame and damage lung cells. Within few days of ozone exposure, the damaged cells are replaced and the old cells are shed. Ozone may aggravate chronic lung diseases such as emphysema and bronchitis and reduce the immune system's ability to fight off bacterial infections in the respiratory system. Because ozone pollution usually forms in hot weather, anyone who spends time outdoors in the summer may be affected.

Table 1 : Human population affected by repeated exposure to ozone

Ozone Exposure		**Population affected**	**Response**
Time	**Concentration**		
1-2 hours	120	10-20% of population	12% decline FEVI*
6.6 hours	80	Few Individuals	38% decline FEVI*
8 hours	120	Population average	20% decline FEVI*
6.6 hours	120	Asthmatics and non-asthmatic	Non-specific bronchial hyper responsiveness
1 hour	120	Asthmatic	Specific bronchial hyper responsiveness
3 hours	250-400	Asthmatic	Specific bronchial hyper responsiveness

Ozone Monitoring Equipment

Central Scientific Instruments Organisation (CSIO) has recently developed a real time computer based ozone monitoring instrument to monitor the status of ozone gas concentration in horizontal profile and also engaged in the preparation of status report of ozone gas in Chandigarh. This will be highly useful for Department of Environment, Chandigarh Administration to adopt suitable control strategies at certain junctions in city beautiful to provide relief to all residents from this culprit gas (Fig. 7).

$I = Ioe^{-alc}$

$$C = \text{Log}_e \frac{I_o\, P_o\, T}{L_a\, LPT_o} \times 10^{-6} \text{ ppm}$$

$C = O_3$ concentration in ppm.

T_o = incident light without 0_3 in gas sample.

P = Absorption co-efficient 308 cm^{-1} at 1 Atm. (It is abbreviation of atmosphere) (Po).

P = ~ Pressure of gas sample.

L = absorption cell (71 cm) length

T_o = 273° K.

T = Temp. of gas in absorption cell.

Here :

UV light sources absorbs O_3 at 254 nm.

We have used Cesium telluride detector in our electronic circuit.

In 1998 - 1999 using Dobson spectrophotometer. Less than 100 D.U. in Antarctica was measured having layer thickness of 1 mm at 273° K and 1 Atm. pressure.

With Micro Top II UV - β radiation was measured at 305, 312.5 and 320.5 nm wave length.

The Memory has Data, time, solar angle, height from sea level, P & Temperature measurement facilities also.

CSIO's hand held 0_3 & radiation meter - (DOEn) sponsored, Microcontroller based ozone monitor has data logging facility. It is compatible with IC RS - 232.

Fig. 7 : Micro controller bared ozone monitoring instrument

Methodology / Experimental Set up :

As stated above our instrument operates on the principle of absorption of UV rays by ozone. It absorbs UV rays in the range of 250 – 260 nm. The standards suggested by the Environment Protection agency (EPA), USA have been used as follows :

Pollutant	Averaging Period	Standard	Primary NAAQS	Secondary NAAQS
OZONE	1-hr	Not to be at or above this level on more than three days over three years.	125 ppb	125 ppb
	8-hr	The average of the annual fourth highest daily eight-hour maximum over a three-year period is not to be at or above this level.	85 ppb	85 ppb

Primary NAAQS : * the levels of air quality that the EPA judges necessary, with an adequate margin of safety, to protect the public health.

* National Ambient Air Quality Standard.

Secondary NAAQS : the levels of air quality that the EPA judges necessary to protect the public welfare from any known or anticipated adverse effects.

Damage to Humans

Repeated exposure to ozone pollution may cause permanent damage to the lungs. Even when ozone is present in low levels, inhaling it triggers a variety of health problems including : chest pains, coughing, nausea, throat irritation, and congestion and worsen bronchitis, heart disease, emphysema, and asthma, and reduce lung capacity.

Formation of Ozone Layer

(*a*) Nearly 3 billion years ago atmosphere was mainly comprising of CH_4, N_2, CO_2, NH_3, H_2, water vapor and devoid of O_2. Photosynthesis with blue green algae & anaerobic unicellular organisms/microbes helped in building of O_2 level.

(*b*) When O_2 level rose to 0.6% > multicellular microbes formed. The building up of oxygen level in atmosphere helped in retaining of deadly UV radiation of Sun in upper atmosphere which led to formation of ozone layer in stratosphere (16 – 40 kms).

(*c*) During natural process in the lower mesosphere the atmospheric oxygen absorbs UV radiation < 240 nm and photodissociates into two oxygen atoms. These atoms subsequently combine with molecular O_2 at upper atmosphere producing O_3.

(*d*) $NO_2 \rightarrow NO + O$; $O_2 + O \rightarrow O_3$. Thickness of Ozone Layer is measured in D.U. (Dobson Unit). {1 D.U. = 0.01mm of compressed Gas at 1 Atm. pressure and 273° K temperature}

It protects the bio-diversity from UV radiations coming from solar systems. Due to decrease in O_3 concentration, UV-B radiation (280 > λ < 320 nm) will cause following ill effects :

(*a*) Biological furnace of biosphere will become blast furnace.

(*b*) Mutation in DNA, Death, Cancer, and will affect foetus and cause birth of mentally retarded children.

(*c*) Reduction in crop yield.

(*d*) Affects immune system of our body.

(*e*) Imbalance in ecological system, eye-cataract, increase in natural disasters.

- 10% decrease in Ozone concentration in stratosphere will increase 30% skin cancer due to formation of ozone layer holes.
- 7000 deaths due to skin cancer in USA.
- 10% increase in cancer patients in Australia and Newzealand have been reported due to ozone layer depletion.

So, we should be scared of ozone layer depletion and also protect the same sometimes. Only we have to identity the status and type of precursors.

Precursors of O_3 on regional level and its control

A basic and obvious requirement for determining air quality is the collection and archival of relevant data from a stable air monitoring network using instrument methods that are uniformly comparable and are well characterized with standards and operation. Demerjian reviews national air monitoring networks in North America for O_3, its precursors and other air pollutants. In the US, of the approximately 4000 monitoring stations operated by the state and local authorities about 25% provide continuous monitoring of ambient O_3 concentrations, mostly in urban, suburban and multi-source influence locations. In Canada, the National Air Pollution Surveillance Network (NAPS) consists of 173 stations located primarily in urban areas. In Mexico, there are 93 stations among seven urban monitoring networks. These have provided reasonable service for measurement of urban ambient O_3 concentrations over time. There are, however, very few analogous rural monitoring stations tracking changes over a long period of time. Furthermore, there are virtually no data available that provide reliable long-term trends for O_3 precursors though some believe that the monitoring of elevated concentrations of NO_3 in urban areas reflect at least semi-quantitatively trends in these gases.

Trend analysis of ambient data indicate that urban and rural O_3 concentrations do not necessarily follow the same spatial and temporal patterns, and that rural patterns may be a good indication of regional pollution and interurban transport. It is recognized that additional O_3 monitoring stations outside the urban and precursor source areas are needed in all areas of North America.

Rao *et al.* (1999), discussed the current picture of O_3 trends in North America. Most urban and sub urban locations in the US show a downward trend in concentrations during the last decade. The largest improvements in O_3 air quality appear to have occurred in Los Angels and the New York metropolitan area. Conversely, urban trends in Canadian cities over the last decade have shown small increases. While Mexico city conditions tended to become worse in the 1980s, recent data suggest that O_3 concentration have levelled off there.

Monitoring of the precursors of O_3 (NO, NO_2, VOC, and CO) is required to track the effectiveness of emissions control programs targeted at reducing the ambient concentration of these compounds. Moreover, trends of the O_3 precursors are required to understand and interpret the effectiveness of the emission control programs in reducing ambient O_3 concentrations. Despite the importance of observing the precursors there is almost universally inadequate historical data collected from monitoring efforts, especially for VOC and NO_2. This is the result in part, of the greater difficulty in making quantitative measurements of the precursors and the lack of availability of robust instrumental methods capable of reliable, sustained operation with minimal operator attention. In recent years, however, methods have improved significantly. For example, the US launched the Photochemical Assessment Monitoring Stations (PAMS) network in 1993. The PAMS consists of 65 sites in and around urban areas with the most serious O_3 problems. Operating from mid-May through mid-September each year. These stations provide for measurements of O_3, NO, NO_x, speciated VOC aldehydes and surface meteorological parameters. Despite problems in the first few years of operation and data collection the PAMS has the potential to provide the data required to help assess emission trends and provide the linkage with O_3 concentration trends. Also, NO_x and CO are measured at many central urban sites operated by state and local monitoring networks. In Canada. NO_x and CO are also measured routinely at many urban NAPS sites and VOC samples are obtained at a subset of these sites. In Mexico City, O_3 and NO_x are measured routinely, and occasional samples of VOC are obtained as part of their program. Monitoring for O_3 has been initiated in Monterrey and Vera Cruz to add to their national programs.

Rao *et al.* (1999) indicate that very few studies of long term trends in ambient VOC and NO_x concentrations have been reported. Principally because of the shortness and unreliability of the data record. The studies that have been performed have all been in urban and urban-influenced sites. The Los Angeles area has the longest data record for O_3 precursors. The data over the past decade indicate declines in both VOC and NO_x concentrations concurrent with O_3 decreases. During the period between 1986 and 1991 VOC concentrations in the north-eastern US cities appear to have decreased faster than Nox concentrations, at the same time O_3 concentrations have been decreasing. At Canadian urban sites, NO_x concentrations decreased from 1980 to 1993 and VOC concentrations have decreased slightly, while O_3 concentrations have generally increased over the same period.

The documentation of ambient concentration trends needs to be linked with emissions trends. Systematic changes in real world emissions are poorly documented in North America, but there is reasonable circumstantial evidence that (light duty) motor vehicle emissions have been reduced for both VOC's and NO_x as the vehicle fleets have evolved since the 1970s. In the US, for example, studies suggest that most of the emissions are associated with a small fraction of the on-road fleet of light duty vehicles, which are older and not well maintained (Sawyer *et al.*). Operating records suggest that many large point sources have significantly reduced their NO_x emissions in accordance with permitting requirements. Perhaps, the least well documented and most difficult to assess categories are the small sources of industrial, commercial and residential activity (Placet *et al*). To insure reliable interpretation of ambient O_3 trends, systematic efforts will be needed in most urban areas to document the changes in these source emissions as well as transportation sources not covered by light duty vehicle emission standards.

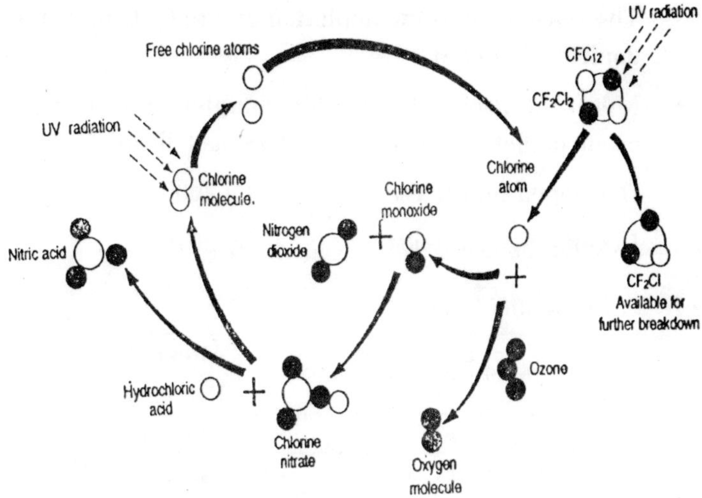

Fig. 8 : How breakdown products of CFCs attack atmospheric ozone molecules

Depletion of Ozone Layer

- Ozone occurs in stratosphere at a height of 16-40 km from earth surface with maximum concentration around 25 km. This ozone-rich band near 25 km is referred to as ozone layer.
- Protects living organisms from harmful UV radiations (could even affect genetic material - DNA).
- Man made chemicals (chlorofluoro carbons (CFCs) and halons) deplete ozone.
- CFCs have long residency period ranging from 55-400 years.
- Ozone hole has been regularly recorded in Antarctica (South Pole) during August to October every year at a height ranging from 13.5 to 19 km (Ozone depletion was upto 44%).

The reasons of ozone depletion due to CFC have been depicted in Fig. 8

- Montreal Protocol calls for complete phase out of ozone depleting substances (ODS) as follows :

  Developed countries — by 2000

  Developing countries — by 2010

Table 2 : CFCs and Alternatives

Use	CFC Used	Alternatives
Refrigeration	CFC—11	Helium, Ammonia,
	CFC—12	HFC—134 A
	CFC—114	HCFC—142 B
		HCFC—22
Air-conditioning	CFC—11	HCFC—22 + HCFC—142B
		HFC—134A
Foam-blowing	CHF—11	Water-blown foam
	CFC—12	HCFC—141 B
		HCFC—22, HCFC—123, Alternative insulation vaccum Insulation, etc.
Sterilization	CFC—12	Carbon Dioxide, HCFC—22.
Fire Suppression	Halons	Carbon Dioxide, no known Adequate substitutes for some Uses.
Solvents	CFC—123	aqueous cleaning terpenes No clean technologies.
Aerosol	CFC—11	Carbon Dioxide, nitrous oxide, Pump spray, etc.

Table 3 : US Ambient Air Quality Criteria for Ozone

Ozone Concentration in Air (ppm)	Human Symptoms and Vegetation Injury Threshold ....
10.0	Severe pulmonary odema, possible acute broncholitic, decreased blood pressure, rapid weak pulse.
1.0	Coughing, extreme fatigue, lack of coordination, increased airway resistance, decreased forced expiratory volume.
0.5	Chest constriction impaired carbon monoxide diffusion capacity, decrease in lung function without exercise.
0.3	Headache, chest discomfort, prevent completion of exercise, decease in lung function in exercising subject.
0.25	Increase in incidence and severity of asthma attacks, moderate eye irritation. For sensitive individuals, reduction in pulmonary lung function, chest discomforts, irritation of the respiratory tract, coughing and wheezing. Threshold for injury to vegetation.
0.12	USEPA National Primary and Secondary Ambient Air Quality Standard, attained when the expected number of days per calendar year with maximum hourly average concentration above 0.12 ppm is equal to or less than 1, as determined in a specified manner.

DAMAGES TO PLANTS

It interferes with the ability of plants to produce and store food, making them more susceptible to disease, insects, other pollutants, and harsh weather. "Bad" ozone damages the foliage of trees and other plants, ruining the landscape of cities, national parks and forests, and recreation areas. Ground-level ozone damages plant life and is responsible for 500 million dollars in reduced crop production in the United States each year.

Objectives

As the "City Beautiful" is a relatively young city and one with a high inflow of people due to a developed service sector and due to it is being tagged as the most livable city. Due to all this, the vehicular traffic is increasing day by day in Chandigarh. So, it makes all the sense to measure the level of ozone being formed majority because of this motor vehicle pollution.

- To measure the level of ozone at the points identified and earmarked for measurement purposes. (These points have been identified on the basis of the heavy traffic rush that exists at these points during the rush hours.)
- To try to analyze and form strategies in general and for the observed points in particular.
- Suggesting ways to reduce and control ozone pollution.

As discussed above, ozone at stratospheric level in ozonosphere (Fig. 1) is a blessing to protect us from UV-B radiation. So, we must adhere to following nine sermons. The nine pledged attempts along with our sincere efforts will protect our ozone layer and make the life blissful.

Be an Ozone-friendly consumer

Buy products (aerosol spray cans, refrigerators, fire extinguishers, etc.) that are labeled "ozone friendly" or "CFC free" . The product labels should indicate that they do not contain ozone-depleting substances such as CFCs or halons. Ask for more information from the seller to ensure that the product is ozone friendly. Tell your neighbour that you are the proud owner of "ozone friendly" products.

Be an ozone-friendly homeowner

Dispose off old refrigerators and appliances responsibly. CFC and HCFC refrigerants should be removed from an appliance before it is discarded. Portable halon fire extinguishers that are no longer needed should be returned to your fire protection authority for recycling. Consider purchasing new fire extinguishers that do not contain halon (e.g., dry power) as recommended by your fire protection authority.

Be an ozone-friendly farmer

If you use methyl bromide for soil fumigation, consider switching over to effective and safe alternatives that are currently being used in many countries to replace this ozone damaging pesticide. Consider options such as integrated pest management that do not rely on costly chemical inputs. If you don't currently use methyl bromide, don't begin to use it now (you will have to get rid of it in the future).

Be an ozone-friendly refrigeration servicing technician

Ensure that the refrigerant you recover from air conditioner, refrigerators or freezer during servicing is not "vented" or released to the atmosphere. Regularly check and fix leaks before they become a problem. Help start a refrigerant recovery and recycling programme in your area.

Be an ozone-friendly worker

Help your company identify its existing equipments (e.g., water coolers, air conditioners, cleaning solvents, fire extinguishers), and the products it buys (aerosol sprays, foam cushions/mattresses) and whether it uses ozone depleting substances, and develop a plan for replacing them with cost-effective alternatives. Become an environmental leader within your office.

Be an ozone-friendly company

Replace ozone-depleting substances used on your premises and in your manufacturing processes (contact your National Ozone Unit to see if you are eligible for financial and technical assistance from the Multilateral Fund). If you products contain ozone-depleting substances, change your product formulation to use alternative substances that do not destroy the ozone layer.

Be an ozone-friendly teacher

Inform your students about the importance of protecting the environment and in particular, the ozone layer. Teach students about the damaging impact of ozone depleting substances on the atmosphere, health impacts and what steps are being taken internationally and nationally to solve this problem. Encourage your students to spread the message to their families.

Be an ozone-friendly community organizer

Inform your family, neighbours and friends about the need to protect the ozone layer and help them get involved. Work with Non-Governmental Organisations to help start information campaigns and technical assistance projects to phase out ozone depleting substances in your city, town or village.

Be an ozone-friendly citizen

Read and learn more about the effects of ozone depletion on people, animals and the environment; your national strategy and policies to implement the Montreal protocol, and what the phase out of ozone depleting substances means to your country. Get in touch with your country's National Ozone Unit and learn how you can get involved on an individual level.

Results : Observation shows 23% increase in D (Erythemal Dose) → 10% rise in skin cancer.

The total impact on human health, crop production & aquatic organisms is largely unknown in developing countries. So, the use of available information and indigenous R & D with recommended action programmes are needed for sound policy decisions to protect biological systems from deleterious effects of ozone depletion. At national Chemical Laboratory, Pune, a lot of R & D programmes to find out alternatives of CFC are in active consideration. The CSIR scientists have found suitable substitutes of CFCs.

Global Policy for Ozone protection

Industrialised countries currently emit 85% of ozone depleting chemicals. However, the lack of Third World participation in Montreal Protocol 1987, is the single largest obstacle to the long-term reduction of atmospheric chlorine level. If India & China were to use the same quantities of ozone depleting chemicals per person (around 1.5 kg. / person) emission of ozone depleting compounds would increase three fold. If they were to produce these chemicals at the limits currently envisaged in the protocol for developing countries, its use will increase by 50%.

At the same time, phasing out the use of CFCs and other ozone depleting substances will have direct effect on industries. Funding for technology transfer has been the greatest issue of contention between 3rd World & Industrialised Countries. There is a vital need for these funds as the costs of substitute chemicals are five times more than those of currently available. If India does not leap forward; it is likely to be at a far greater technological & economic disadvantage ten years hence.

It is, therefore, immensely needed that India and 3rd World Countries get into forefront of the effort to reverse ozone depletion, both to promote their own technological leadership and to save ozone layer simultaneously. The list of alternatives and CFCs has been given in (Table 2).

Acknowledgement

I am grateful to Dr. Pawan Kapur, Director, CSIO who allowed me to publish this paper. I also owe so much to Mr. Mohan Kumar and Mr. Ashok Kumar, my colleague, who have provided me all kinds of support to complete this chapter.

Reference

CPCB, New Delhi, Parivesh Report (2003) Phase out of ozone layer — A status report 2004, pp., 11—14.

Dreher, K.L., Jaskot, R.H. and Lehmann, J.R. *et al.* (1997) J. Toxicol Environmental Health, 50 : 285—305.

Hitsfeld, B, Friedrichs, K.H., Ring, J., and Behrendt, H. (1997) Toxicol Environment Health, 120 : 185—195.

NARSTO (1999), An Assessment of Troposheric Ozone Pollution, Draft report (ftp://ftp.cgenv.com) NARSTO—1997.

Watson, J.G., Chow, J. and Fujita, C. (1999) Review of Volatile organic compound atmospheric environment, Sept. 1999, pp., 200—203.

Danict—J. Jacob, (2000) Hetrogeneous chemistry and tropospheric ozone. Atmospheric Environment, 34 pp., 2131—2158.

CHAPTER 7

EVALUATION OF THE PERFORMANCE OF COMBINING NATURAL LAGOONING AND USE OF TWO SAND FILTERS IN THE TREATMENT OF LANDFILL LEACHATES

ALEYA Lotfi[1], KHATTABI Hicham[1], Jean-Louis Morel[2].

[1]Laboratoire de Biologie Environnementale, Université de Franche-Comté, 1, Place Leclerc, 25030 Besançon cedex (France)

[2]Laboratoire Sols et Environnement, 2, Avenue Foret de Haye 54505 Vandoeuvre Nancy (France)

ABSTRACT

A study in the Etueffont landfill, located in Belfort (France), was conducted to evaluate the performance of combining natural lagooning and use of two sand filters for treating leachates through the coupling estimation of several abiotic and biotic parameters. Two gravel filters were installed in the upstream of the first basin which communicates with the remaing 2, 3 and 4 basins. The distribution of physical-chemical (Temp., T, pH, Eh, EC, O_2, SM, SO_4^{2-}, Cl^-, Zn, Fe, Mg, Ni, Al, As, Ba, Cu, Sn, Zn, BOD, COD, KN, NH_4^+, NO_2^- ,TP, AOX: absorbable organic halides, VFA: volatile fatty acids, ,and atrazine) and biological (bacteria, protozoa, phytoplankton) parameters was assessed in the leachate entering in basin 1, and downstream of the filters. The results showed slight variations in the physical-chemical composition of the leachate between 2000 and 2001, most likely ascribed to the maturation of the landfill but a very significant removal of SM (suspended matter) by the sand filters. This, applied to the majority of the studied parameters. Thus, the sand filter treatment of the leachates combined to natural lagooning was efficient in the improvement of water clarification.

Keywords: Landfill leachate; Sand filters; Metals; Bacteria; Protozoa; Phytoplankton.

Introduction

Landfill leachate generated by the biodegradation of solid wastes migrate away from a landfill and may pollute ground as well as surface waters (Diels *et al.*, 2002; Ikem *et al.*, 2002; Vrijheid *et al.*, 2002; Rushton, 2003; Jensen *et al.*, 2004; Silva *et al.*, 2004). While landfilling is the most attractive option for waste disposal, it may be a source of large quantities of organic and inorganic matters and heavy metals (Kabata-Pendias and Pendias, 2001; Schwarzbauer *et al.*, 2002; Baun *et al.*, 2004). In particular, heavy metals that accumulate in the body with long biological half-lives (Radha *et al.*, 1997), have been shown to cause several health hazards (Omura *et al.*, 1991; Thacker *et al.*, 1992; Harrison, 2000; Harrison, 2003). Thus, understanding the mechanisms fueling leachate generation may be a clue to reduce efficiently their unfavourable impacts on the surrounding environments (Baccini *et al.*, 1987; Jokela and Rintala, 2003). Furthermore, leachate composition has been shown from laboratory experiments (Bookter and Ham, 1982; Blaky, 1992) and *in situ* (Kjeldsen *et al.*, 2002) to be closely linked to climate, hydrology and waste-hiding techniques. The stabilization ponds, that are generally designed to treat only an average quality of the leachate, are commonly put under extreme pressure-induced organic matter overload. Therefore, the process of leachate treatment, when it is conceived must take into account 'worse case scenario', i.e., intense increase in the concentration of polluting compounds.

In the Etueffont landfill (Belfort, France), leachate components are treated by 4 stabilization ponds. However, in periods of high concentrations of organic matter in the basins, this option of leachate treatment showed low performance as it seemed unable to fulfill European standards (ISO 14000) to discharge into the surface and ground waters (Christensen *et al.*, 2001). This study thus aimed at improving the performance of leachate treatment by combining natural lagooning and use of two sand filters upstream from the first basin. The capability for removing metals and other pollutants, together with microbial populations, was assessed through the measurement of several abiotic (major elements, metals and organics AOX: absorbable organic halides, VFA: volatile fatty acids and atrazine) and biotic parameters (bacteria, protozoa and phytoplankton).

Materials and methods

Study site

The Etueffont municipal solid waste landfill was opened in 1974. It is located in the North-East of Belfort France, (Fig. 1) and extends on 2.2 hectares from impermeable schistous layers. The width, length and depth are respectively 110, 200 and 5m. The landfill contains 200000 tons of crushed household refuse, and operates in the open air without cover after grinding the waste before landfilling. The site has been exploited until July 2002 and was covered by a layer of vegetal soil coming from the old crushed organic wastes (wood, residues of lawn shearings, straws, fabrics). The leachates were collected downstream by a draining system and treated by a four-basin lagooning system. Two sand filters, with perforated drains, were placed upstream from the first basin (Fig. 2). Geotextiles consisted of synthetic fibers (polymeric materials) which are made of flexible porous fabrics by standard weaving machinery (woven geotextile).

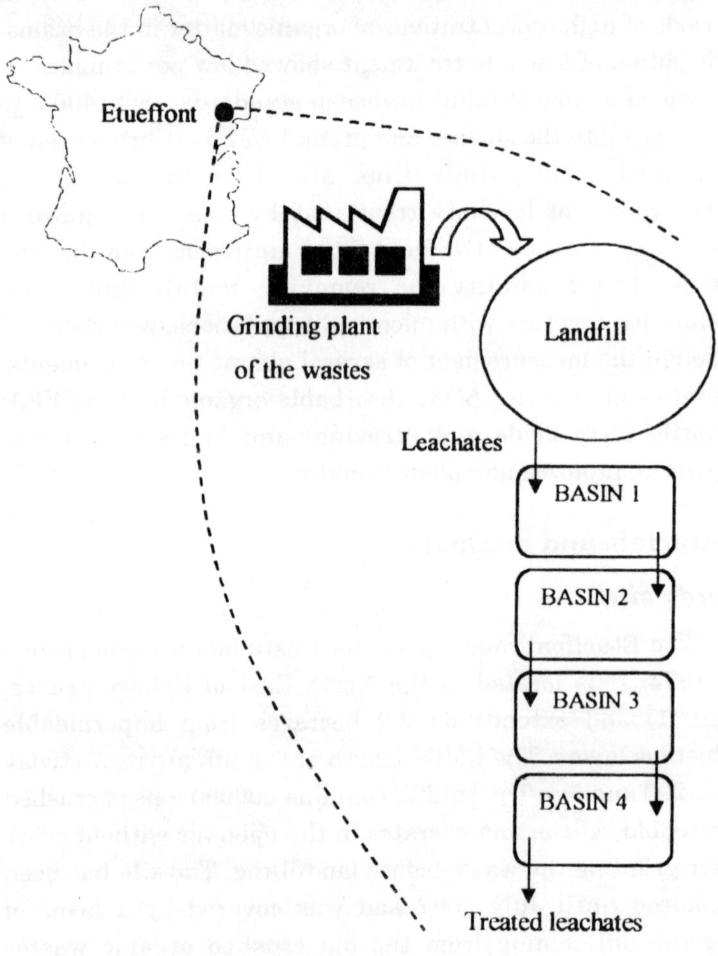

Fig. 1 : Map of the Etueffont station

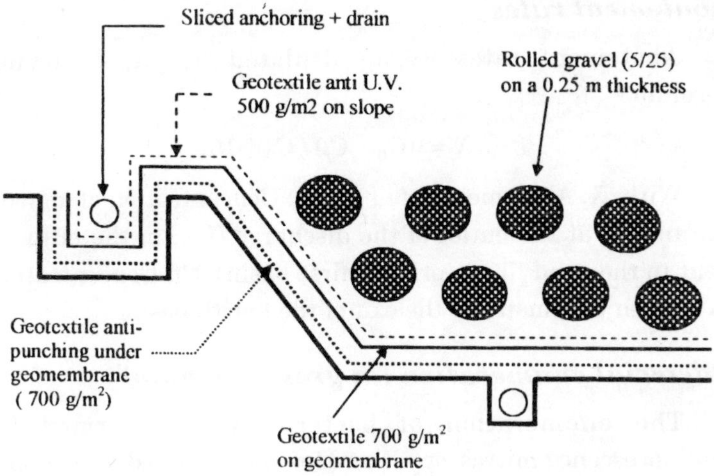

Fig. 2 : Simplified diagram of the used sand filter

Samplings and analysis procedures

Leachate samples were collected at the input and output of the sand filter, in the four basins and at the output of the last basin in 1999 and 2000 (4 samplings/year) in pyrex glass containers pre-rinsed with bidistilled water. Temperature, pH, dissolved oxygen and electric conductivity were assessed *in situ* by a multiparameter probe (WTW, Multiline P3 PH/LF-SET). Concentrations of Cl^- were analysed by an ion chromatograph (Dionex DX-100) and those of iron (Fe), zinc (Zn), nickel (Ni), copper (Cu) and magnesium (Mg) determined by UV/vis spectrophotometry (WTW Photolab). Total nitrogen (TN) was estimated by distillation, after mineralization in N-NH_4 (Rodier, 1984) and (NH_4) by spectrophotometry, following a sodium nitroprussiate alkaline reaction. Total phosphorus (TP) was assessed by colorimetry (Rodier, 1984). Concentrations in fatty volatile acids (FVA), absorbable organic halides (AOX), and atrazine were estimated according to Eisenreich *et al.* (1994) and Rodier (1996).

Abatement rates

Abatement rates were calculated by the following formula:

$$X = ((C_0 - C_f) / C_0)^* \ 100$$

With: X: Abatement rate (%), C_0: Concentration of a given parameter at the outlet of the discharge (i.e., in the effluent sent to the sand filters prior to first basin), Cf: Concentration of a given parameter at the exit of the fourth basin.

Bacterial enumeration (in gross leachate)

The enumeration of bacteria was performed by epifluorescence microscopy. Samples were stained with DAPI (4-6-diamino-2-phenylindol), (Porter and Feig, 1980) and filtered on a polycarbonate filter (Millipore, pore size: 0.2 μm, GTBP type) at low vacuum (<13 KPa). 1500 to 2000 cells were counted on 20 fields (measurement error not exceeding 7%, Overbeck, 1974; Marvalin *et al.*, 1989) with a Leica DM IRB inverted microscope.

Protozoa (in gross leachate)

Autotrophic and heterotrophic flagellated protozoa were fixed (25 μL) with glutaraldehyde, stained with primuline and counted by epifluorescence microscopy. Ciliated protozoa and amoebae were fixed with mercuric chloride ($HgCI_2$) and counted with a Leica DM IRB inverted microscope. Ciliates abundance was estimated from three replicates (Madoni, 1988).

Phytoplankton (in basins)

Phytoplankton enumeration were made with an inverted microscope by Uthermöl's method (1958), modified by Legendre and Whatt (1971-1972) after fixation with a Lugol's (4%) iodine solution (Bourrelly, 1985).

Results and discussions

Leachate characterization

Organic components

The organic matter contained in leachates have been demonstrated to consist of valuable amounts of humic substances (Chian and DeWalle, 1977; Tatsi and Zouboulis, 2002). These substances can be compared to those encountered in the normal organic matter (NOM) in aquatic environments. Humic substances in leachates contain aromatic and aliphatic compounds with mainly carboxylic and phenolic functional groups. The carboxylic functional groups explained between 60 and 90% of the functional groups (Ehrig, 1978). The dissolved organic matter in leachates is crucial in the study of landfill leachates from domestic wastes covering a variety of organic by degradation, extending from low volatile acids to refractory fulvic and humic acids (Chian and DeWalle, 1977). However, few studies targeted the characterization of the organic matter of leachates generated from household wastes (Navarro *et al.*, 1988), and the contents of organic matter are very dependent on physical factors such as temperature. Harmsen (1983) highlighted a predominance of the VFA in the young leachate (more than 95% of the COD). Weis *et al.* (1989), by comparing the various fulvic acids from leachates with those from lake and marsh waters, pointed out that fulvic acids extracted from the leachate contained high rates of C, H, and S, but low levels of phenolic groups that presented low Cu binding potentials and decreased weight. The organic component of the leachate in Etueffont that has been characterized previously by BOD and COD (Khattabi *et al.*, 2002) was approached in this study through FVA. The results summarized in Table 1 showed a low FVA average (about 450 mgL^{-1}) which has commonly been quoted from old landfills undergoing a full stabilization phase

(Christensen, 2001). Moreover, the temporal distribution of the organic load in the leachate between 1999 and 2000 (Khattabi *et al.*, 2002), pointed out a clear decrease in the two descriptors of organic pollution (BOD and COD) most likely attributable to degradation by micro-organisms. This translated into a decrease (from 0.09 to 0.05) in BOD/COD ratio and a slight increase in pH. Our findings are in agreement with those of Ehrig (1978) and Barkowski *et al.* (1987) who demonstrated that a BOD/COD ratio close to zero means the landfill is old with a fermentation-inducing alkaline leachate production.

Table 1: Biological and physical-chemical composition of the Etueffont landfill leachates (1999 and 2000)

	Etueffont leachate 1999		***Etueffont leachate 2000***	
	Average	**Ecartype**	**Average**	**Ecartype**
T°C	13.4	5.81	18.8	2.61
pH	7.76	0.42	7.8	0.11
EC νScm^{-1}	5343	1344	4673	1371
SM μg 1^{-1}	157	160	32	19
BOD	98	79	46	15
COD	1085	587	892	597
NO_2	0.00	0	7.11	3.08
NO_3	47	77	254	353
SO_4	163	64	139	38
Ng	34	6	42	8
NH_4	178	43	178	94
NK	188	74	174	68

Contd.

TP	1.36	0.49	1.58	1.41
Cu	0.73	0.9	0.22	0.05
Fe	2.93	2.21	3.61	0.96
Ni	3.23	4.69	0.13	0.07
Sn	0.51	0.48	0.11	0.08
Zn	0.61	0.28	0.4	0.32
AGV	—	—	73	0.04
Atrazine ng/l	—	—	268	31.13
AOX μg/;	—	—	950	0.6
Bacteria 10^6* ind. ml^{-1}	0.20	64	0.19	39
Ciliates 10^6* ind. ml^{-1}	9320	51	8840	43

Biological components

Bacteria: the bacterial numbers recorded in the gross leachate varied from 0.04 x 10^6, in 1999 to 0.35 x 10^6 cellmL^{-1}, in 2000. Overall, this abundance was lower than that reported from other aquatic systems (Jordan and Likens, 1980; Porter and Feig, 1980; Albright and Mac Crae, 1987; Scavia and Laird, 1987; Nagata,1988; Marvalin *et al.*, 1989; Krstulovic *et al.*, 1995; Ochs *et al.*, 1995; Carrias, 1996). This may be ascribed to lower levels in oxygen concentrations in the Etueffont leachate, and competition between autochthonous and allochthonous micro-organisms with the need, for the latters, to adapt to both new environmental conditions and leachate toxicity (Plotkin and Ram, 1984; Deneuvy, 1987; Ernst *et al.*, 1994; Devare and Bahadir, 1994; Clement *et al.*, 1996; Ferrari *et al.*, 1999; Marnie *et al.*, 2002; Mackenzie *et al.*, 2003; El-Masry *et al.*, 2004; Svensson *et al.*, 2005).

The enumeration of the protozoan community in the Etueffont leachate showed that flagellated protozoa were the main contributors to the total protozoan abundance (98% and

94%), followed by ciliated protozoa (1.7 and 3%) and naked amoebae (0.3 and 3%), in 1999 and 2000, respectively. These heterotrophs, through grazing on bacteria, may have contributed to the control of bacterial populations, which number was reduced in 2000. Our suggestions are in line with several studies showing the significance of protozoa in biological wastewater treatment plants (Bomo *et al.*, 2005). In addition to removing a fraction of bacteria, protozoan communities can be involved in primary removal of organic matter in polluted waters and suspended matter (Curds and Hawkes, 1983; Aleya *et al.*, 1992; Salvado *et al.*, 1995).

AOX and atrazine

In order to go further in characterizing Etueffont leachates, we estimated AOX and atrazine since little is known on their concentrations in landfill leachates (Table 1). The (AOX) that are poorly prone to biodegradation, were high on average (950 μgL^{-1}) and most likely due to specific wastes in the landfill. Triazinic atrazine (2-chloro-4-ethylamino-6-isopylamino-1,3,5-triazine) which is commonly used in agriculture (chiefly in corn fields), showed low concentrations (268 ngL^{-1}), likely ascribed to atrazine-treated and landfilled plant detritus. Moreover, the levels of triazinic atrazine detected were lower than those reported by Schultz and Kjeldsen (1986), Gintautas *et al.* (1992) and Lyngkilde and Christensen (1992).

Inorganic components

Contrary to organic compounds, the distribution of leachate inorganic substances between 1999 and 2000 was relatively stable (Table 1), except a slight increase in Mg (from 34 to 42 mgL^{-1}) and Fe (from 2.93 to 3.61 mgL^{-1}) concentrations, attributable to the low-autumnal precipitations registered in 2000. Sulfates concentrations were also lower over this year than those measured in 1999, due to microbial reduction of SO_4^{--} and S^{--}. The NH_4^+ concentrations observed did not show any temporal decrease going along with the results reported by others (Muhammad *et al.*, 1998; Mulamoottil *et al.*, 1999). These overall stable distribution patterns also applied to heavy metals, putting our findings in line with those of Mæhlum *et al.* (1999) and Christensen *et al.* (2001). Fluctuations of the SO_4^{--}/Cl^- ratio may be informative on both oxygenation status and solubility of metallic cations. Indeed, the rapid decrease in SO_4^{--}/Cl^- from 0.36 in 1999 to 0.23 in 2000 was likely linked to the prevailing anaerobic conditions, inducing a decrease in initial sulfate concentrations. Ions resulting from sulfides will further react with metallic cations to form insoluble metallic sulfide precipitates. These latters may also co-precipitate with iron and other metals. The collapse of SO_4^{--}/Cl^- ratios in the leachate is symptomatic of the strong anaerobic activity within the Etueffont landfill. Our results go along with those reported by others (Pohland *et al.*, 1985; Tatsi and Zouboulis, 2002).

Sand filter performance (2000)

The BOD and COD estimated in the leachate entering in the sand filter, were clearly higher than those measured at the outlet of basin 1 (Fig. 3). They decreased from 141 to 81 and 1293 to 932, respectively, concomitantly to a drop in SM (Fig. 3). This suggests that a large fraction of organic matter was particulate-based. In addition, the downstream waning of BOD (Fig. 3) correlated with a drop in bacterial numbers (0.19 x 10^6 cellmL^{-1} to 0.079 x 10^6 cellmL^{-1}, before and after filter installation, respectively, and protozoans as reported by others (Lee *et al.*, 2002). Also, the sand filtration has been shown to significantly contribute to bacterial removal capacity of hydroponics (60-87%) in wastewater treatment experiments (Ottoson *et al.*, 2005) and surface waters (84-100%) (El-Taweel and Ali, 2000). One should note Hassani *et al.* (1999)'s observations pointing out that 84% of bacteria treated by an experimental sand filter from the effluent were resistant to antibiotics.

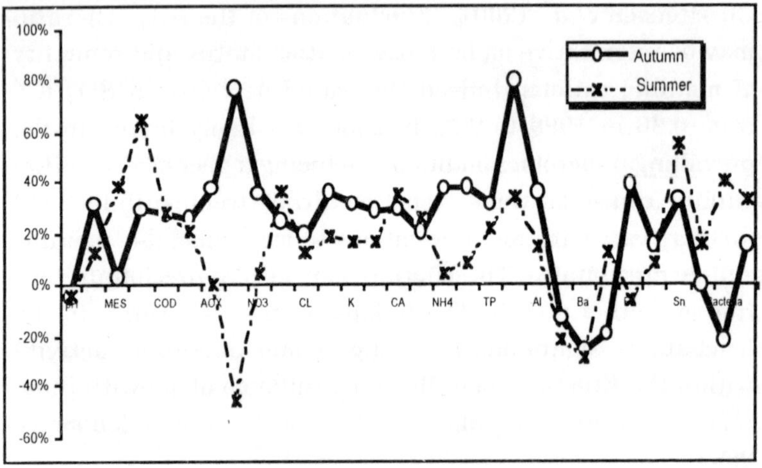

Fig. 3: Abatement rate (%) by the sand filters of several parameters

The temporal distribution of the abatement rates of several chemical species reflected a quasi-similar filter removal abilities except for BOD. Indeed, because the abatement rate of this descriptor was closed related to temperature, any increase of the latter will induce a bacterial proliferation-inducing a drop in BOD. The mean removal rates of the remaining studied parameters were good (between 20 and 80%) except the negative values recorded for AOX, NO_2^-, Ba and Cu. This dysfunctioning is most likely linked to resuspension of elements from clays, induced by water turbulence in the first basin.

Lagooning performance

In summer 2000, the abatement rates of several parameters were high (Fig. 4) except for BOD and SM (suspended matter) which showed negative values (-146 and -57). This dysfunctioning may be ascribed to the summer spectacular proliferation of the Euglenophyta, *Phacus* sp. and *Euglena* sp., the metabolic activity of which through primary production and excretion (Riemann and Sondergaard, 1986; Aleya *et al.*, 1988; Feuillade *et al.*,1988) strongly masked the removal efficiency of the sand filters. The removal performance of bacteria and protozoa in the Etueffont station was high and close to that reported in literature (Shuval *et al.*, 1986; Rose *et al.*, 1996; Bouhoum and Schwartzbrod, 1998). The abatement rate of the COD is about 58% which seems satisfactory since biological treatment of landfill leachate usually yielded low treatment efficiencies because of high chemical oxygen demand (COD) (Kargi and Pamukoglu, 2003; Kylefors *et al.*, 2003). Moreover, an encouraging result was the removal rate obtained for atrazine (80%), due to its degradation when the leachate transits from onc basin to another, and/or its complexation with bottom muds. These two processes are supported by the rise in the oxidizing capacity of the leachate (Tuxen *et al.*, 2000) which is induced by the mechanical mixing of the passing from basin to basin-water and by phytoplankton primary production-inducing increase in oxygen concentrations in water of the last basins. Also, bacteria may have contributed to overall oxidating potential of the leachate (Lovley, 1991; Shen *et al.*, 1996; Boon *et al.*, 1998; Fowler and Crundwell, 1998). It would be thus useful further to estimate, from both leachate and mud samples, the concentration of the different molecules resulting from atrazine based-wastes. The removal rate of Zn (90%) is in line with that reported by Maehlum (1995).

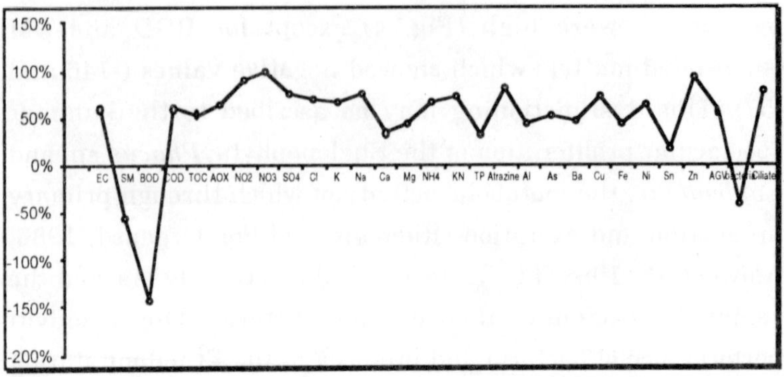

Fig. 4: Abatement rate (%) by the sand filters and natural lagooning of several parameters

Conclusions

Our work demonstrated that the sand filter treatment of Etueffont leachates was overall efficient in removing valuable amounts of organic loads and microbial populations. The protozoan community optimized this performance. The changes in bacterial abundance were linked to the amount of available inorganic and organic elements, to temperature and grazing by protozoa. Viral lysis might also have decreased bacterial numbers (Fuhrman and Noble, 1995). The treated effluent, which is of good quality, may be discharged, with no risk, to the receiving river after lagooning.

References

Aleya, L., Devaux, J., and Marvalin, O., (1988). Primary production and bacterial heterotrophic activity potential in a eutrophic lake (Lake Aydat, Puy-de-Dôme, France). Rev. Sci. Eau., 1 : 23–35.

Aleya, L., Hartmann, H.J., and Devaux, J., (1992). Evidence for the contribution of ciliates to denitrification in a eutrophic lake. Europ. J. Protistol., 28, 316–321.

Albright, L.J., and Mac Crae, S.K., (1987). Annual cycle of bacterial specific biovolumes in Howe sound, a Canadian West Coast Fjord Sound. Appl. Environ. Microbiol., 12 : 2739–2744.

Baccini, G., Henseler, R., Figi, and Belevi, H., (1987). Water and element balances of municipal solid waste landfills. Waste Manage. Res., 5 : 483–499.

Barkowski, D., Gunther P., Rochert R., (1987). Atlasten. Edition C.F. Muller, Karlsruhe, pp., 87–93.

Blaky, N.C. (1992). Model prediction of landfill leachate production. Elsevier. Appl. Sci., London, England, pp. 17–34.

Bookter, T.J.B., Ham, R., (1982). Decomposition of solid waste in test lysimeters. J. Environ. Engin. Div. ASSCE., 108 : 1147–1170.

Boon, M., Snijder, M., Hansford, G.S., Heijnen, J.J., (1998). The oxidation kinetics of zinc sulphide with *Thiobacillus ferrooxidans*. Hydrometallurgy, 33: 137–152.

Bourrelly, P., (1985). Les algues d'eau douce, les algues bleues et rouges, Paris, France, Boubée et Cie, pp., 606.

Carrias, J.F., (1996). *La boucle microbienne en milieu lacustre: structure et fonctionnement des communautés picoplanctoniques et des protistes flagellés et ciliés.* Thèse de doctorat de 3ème Cycle, Université de Blaise Pascal.

Chian, E.S.K., DeWalle, F.B., (1977). Characterization of soluble organic matter in leachate. Environ. Sci. Technol., 11 : 158–163.

Christensen, T.H., Kjeldsen, P., Bjerg, P.L., Jensen, D.L., Christensen, J.B., Baun, A., Albrechtsen, H.J., and Heron G., (2001). Biogeochemistry of landfill leachate plumes. Appl. Geochemistry, 16 : 659–718.

Clement, B., Persoone, G., Janssen, C. and Le Dù-Delpierre, A., (1996). Estimation of the hazard of landfills through toxicity testing of leachates. Chemosphere, 11 : 2203–2320.

Curds, C.R. and Hawkes, H.A., (1983). Biological activities and treatment processes. Chapter 2, *In: Ecological Aspects of Used-Water Treatment*, Academic Press, London.

Deneuvy, J.P. (1987). *Les lixiviats de décharges, approche méthodologique de leur toxicité aiguë en fonction des différents modes de traitement.* Thèse de 3ème cycle, INSA Lyon.

Devare, M. and Bahadir, M., (1994). Biological monitoring of landfill leachate using plants and luminescent bacteria. Chemosphere, 28 : 261–271.

Ehrig, A., (1978). *Beitrag zum quantitativen und qualitativen Wasserhaushalt von Mulldeponien.* Veroffentlichungen des institut fûr Stadtbauwesen, Technischen Universitât Braunschweig, Germany.

Eisenreich, S., Schottler, S. and Hines, N. (1994). Standard Operating Procedure for Isolation, Extraction and Analysis of Atrazine. DEA and DIA, Dep. Environ. Sci., Rutgers Univ. pp. 245–251.

Ernst, W.R.P., Hennigar, K., Doe, S., and Wade, Julien, G., (1994). Characterization of the chemical constituents and toxicity to aquatic organisms of a municipal landfill leachate. Water Poll. Res. J. Can, 29 : 89–101.

Ferrari, B., Radetski, C.M., Veber, A.M. and Ferard, J.F., (1999). Ecotoxicological assessment of solid wastes: a combined liquid- and solid-phase testing approach using a battery of bioassays and biomarkers. Environ. Toxicol. Chem., 18 : 1195–1202.

Feuillade, M., Dufour, P. and Feuillade, J., (1988). Organic carbon release by phytoplankton and bacterial reassimilation. Schweiz. Z. Hydrol, 50 : 115–135.

Fowler, T.A. and Crundwell, F.K., (1998). Leaching of zinc sulfide by *Thiobacillus ferrooxidans*: Experiments with a controlled redox potential indicate no direct bacterial mechanism. Appl. Environ. Microbiol., 64 : 3570–3575.

Fuhrman, J. and Noble, R.T., (1995). Viruses and protests cause similar bacterial mortality in coastal seawater. Limnol. Oceanogr., 40 : 1236–1242.

Gintautas, P.A., Daniel, S.R., and Macalady, D.L. (1992). Phenoxyalkanoic acid herbicides in municipal landfill leachates. Environ. Sci. Technol., 26 : 517–521.

Harmsen, J. (1983). Identification of organic compounds in leachate from a waste tip. Water Res., 17 : 699–705.

Jordan, M.J. and Likens, G.E., (1980). Measurement of planktonic bacterial production in an oligotrophic lake. Limnol. Oceanogr., 25 : 719–732.

Kabata-Pendias, A. and Pendias, H., (2001). Trace elements in soils and plants, CRC Press LLC, Boca Raton, Florida, USA.

Khattabi, H., Lotfi, A. and Mania, J., (2001). Evolution temporelle de la composition du lixiviat d'une décharge à ciel ouvert: effet des précipitations. *Dechets-Sciences et Techniques*, 21 : 7–10.

Kjeldsen, P., Barlaz, M.A., Rooker, A.P., Baun, A., Ledin A. and Christensen, T.H., (2001). Present and long term composition of MSW landfill leachate. Crit. Rev. Environ. Sci. Technol., 32 : 297–336.

Krstulovic, N., Pucher-Petrovic, T. and Solic, M. (1995). The relation between bacterioplankton and phytoplankton production in the mid adriatic sea. Aquat. Microb. Ecol., 9 : 41–45.

Lee, S., Basu, S., Tyler, C.W and Wei, I.W. (2002). Ciliate populations as bio-indicators at Deer Island Treatment Plant. Adv. Environ. Res., 8 : 371–378.

Legendre, L. and Watt, W.D., (1971-1972). On rapid technic for plankton enumeration. Ann. Inst. Oceanogr., Paris WLVIII, pp., 173–177.

Lovley, D.R., (1991). Dissimilatory Fe(II) and Mn(IV) reduction. Microbiol. Rev., 55 : 59–28.

Lyngkilde, J. and Christensen, T.H. (1992) Redox zones of landfill leachate pollution plume (Vejen, Danemark). J. Contam. Hydrol., 10 : 273–289.

Madoni, P., (1988). *I protozoi ciliati nel controllo di efficienza dei fanghi attivi.* Centro Italiano Studi di Biologia Ambientale, Reggio Emilia, pp. 82.

Maehlum, T., Warner, W.S., Stalnacke, P. Jenssen, P.D., (1999). Leachate treatment in extended aeration lagoons and constructed wetlands in Norway. *In :* (Eds., G. Mulamoottil, E.A. McBean and F. Rovers) *Constructed wetlands for the treatment of landfill leachates*, Lewis Publishers, Boca Raton, pp. 151–163.

Maehlum, T., (1995). Treatment of landfill leachate in on–site lagoons and constructed wetlands. Water Sci. Tech., 32 : 129–135.

Marnie, L., Ward, G., Bitton, T., Townsend, T. and Booth, M., (2002). Determining toxicity of leachates from Florida municipal solid waste landfills using a battery-of-tests approach. Environ. Toxicol., 17 : 258–266.

Marvalin, O., Aleya, L., Hartmann, H.J., and Lazarek, S. (1989). Coupling of the seasonal patterns of bacterioplankton and phytoplankton in a eutrophic lake. Can. J. Microbiol., 35 : 706–712.

Muhammad, N., Parr, J., Smith, M.D., and Wheatley, A.D. (1998). Adsorption of heavy metals in slow sand filters. Sanitation and water for all. 24th WEDC Conference, Islamabad, Pakistan, pp. 346–349.

Nagata, T. (1988). The microflagellate-picoplankton food linkage in the water column of lake Biwa. Limnol. Oceanogr., 33 : 504–517.

Navarro, A., Bernard, D. and Millot, N. (1988). Les problèmes de pollution par les lixiviats de décharges. TSM., 3 : 541–545.

Ochs, C.A., Cole J.J. and Likens, G.E. (1995). Population dynamics of bacterioplankton in an oligotrophic lake. J. Plankton Res., 17 : 365–391.

Overbeck, J. (1974) Microbiology and biochemistry. Mih. Internat. Verein. Limnol., 20 : 198–228.

Omura, M., Inamasu, T. and Ishinishi, N. (1991). Mutagenicity assays of leachate from domestic waste landfills in Japan: the establishment of a protocol for measuring levels of leachate. Bull. Environ. Contam. Toxicol., 46 : 561–568.

Plotkin, S. and Ram, N.M. (1984) Multiple bioassays to assess the toxicity of a sanitary landfill leachate. Arch. Environ. Contam. Toxicol., 13 : 197–206.

Pohland, F.G., Harper, S.R., Chang, K.C., Dertien, J.T. and Chian, E.S.K. (1985) Leachate generation and control of landfill disposal sites. Water Pollut. Res. J. Can., 3 : 10–25.

Porter, K.G. and Feig, Y.S. (1980) The use of DAPI for identifying and counting aquatic microflora. Limnol. Oceanogr., 25 : 943–948.

Radha, R., Tripathi, R.M., Vinod, K.A., Sathe, A.P., Khandekar, R.N. and Nambi, K.S.V. (1997) Assessment of Pb, Cd, Cu, and Zn exposures of 6- to 10-year-old children in Mumbai. Environ. Res., 80 : 215–221.

Riemann, B. and Sondergaard, M., Eds., (1986) Carbon dynamics in eutrophic temperate lakes. Eds Elsevier, pp., 284.

Rodier, J. (1984) *L'analyse de l'eau.* 7ème édition Dunod, Paris.

Rodier, J. (1996) *L'analyse de l'eau: eaux naturelles, eaux résiduaires, eaux de mer.* 8ème édition Dunod, Paris.

Salvado, H., Gracia, M.P. and Amigo, J.M. (1995). Capability of ciliated protozoa as indicators of effluent quality in activated sludge plants. Water Res., 29 : 1041–1050.

Scavia, D. and Laird, G.A. (1987). Bacterioplankton in lake Michigan: dynamics, controls, and significance to carbon flux. Limnol. Oceanogr., 32 : 1017–1033.

Schultz, B. and Kjeldsen, P. (1986). Screening of organic matter in leachates from sanitary landfills using gas chromatography combined with mass spectrometry. Water Res., 20 : 965–970.

Shen, H., Pritchard, P.H., Sewell, G.W. (1996). Microbial reduction of Cr(VI) during anaerobic degradation of benzoate. Environ. Sci. Technol., 30 : 1667–1674.

Silva, A.C., Dezotti, M. and Sant'Anna, G.L. (2004). Treatment and detoxification of a sanitary landfill leachate. Chemosphere, 55 : 207–214.

Schwarzbauer, J., Heim, S., Brinker, S. and Littke, R., (2002). Occurrence and alteration of organic contaminants in seepage and leakage water from a waste deposit landfill. Water Res., 36 : 2275–2287.

Shuval, H.I., Adin, A., Fattal, B., Rawitz, E. and Yekutiel, P., (1986). Wastewater irrigation in developing countries: Health effects and technical solutions. World Bank Technical Paper, No. 51.

Svensson, B.M., Mathiasson, L. and Martensson L., Bergstrom (2005). *Artemia salina* as Test organism for assessment of acute toxicity of leachate water from landfills. Environ. Monitor. Assess., 102 : 309–321.

Tatsi, A.A. and Zouboulis, A.I. (2002). A field investigation of the quantity and quality of leachate from a municipal solid waste landfill in a Mediterranean climate (Thessaloniki, Greece). Adv. Environ. Res., 6 : 207–219.

Thacker, S.B., Hoffman, A., Steinberg, K., Zack, M. and Smith, J., (1992). Effect of low-level body burdens of lead on the mental development of children: limitations of metal-analysis in a review of longitudinal data. Arch. Environ. Health., 47 : 336–347.

Tuxen, N., Peter L., Tüchsen, P.L., Rügge, K., Albrechtsen, H.J. and Bjerg, P.L. (2000). Fate of seven pesticides in an aerobic aquifer studied in column experiments. Chemosphere, 41 : 1485–1494.

Vrijheid, M., Dolk, H. and Armstrong, B. (2002). Hazard potential ranking of hazardous waste landfill sites and risk of congenital anomalies. Occup. Environ. Med., 59 : 768–776.

Utermöhl, H. (1958). Zur Vervollkommung der quantitative Phytoplankton-Methodik. Mitt. Intern. Ver. Limnol., 9 : 1–38.

Weis, M., Abbt-Braun, G. and Frimmel, F.H. (1989). Humic-like substances from landfill leachates-characterization and comparison with terrestrial and aquatic humic substances. Sci. Total Environ., 81/82 : 343–352.

CHAPTER 8

COMMUNITY HEALTH STUDIES AND POLLUTION MONITORING INSTRUMENTS

Basudeo Prasad

Scientist, Environmental Monitoring Instruments Division,

C.S.I.O., Chandigarh-160030

ABSTRACT

These days, scientists and environmentalists consider the particles of size equal to and less than 2.5 micrometers ($PM_{2.5}$) as potential health hazard. In the paper community health and respiratory symptoms in relation to fine particulate effects ($PM_{2.5}$ and PM_{10}), and cyclone based personal fine dust monitor designed by CSIO to collect data, have been discussed. A case study of monitored data in two industrial towns of Punjab with their environmental monitored data with the designed instrument, has also been presented to lay emphasis on the design and development of the micro controller, PC based, low cost, high volume, self diagnostic, and self repairing instrument in terms of devising a network facility for rapid environmental monitoring and pollution mapping.

Key words: Particulates, blood plasma, cardio-vascular, coefficient of haze, network.

Introduction

The slogan of World Environment Day for the year 2001 was "Connect with the World Wide Web of Life", a choice that reflects the need for each and every one of us to recognize our role in preserving our fragile planet and the ecosystems, resources and natural processes that bind us all together. Literally this slogan is nothing but "Vasudhiav KutumbKam" i.e., life on earth requires of us a sense of universal responsibility - nation to nation, person to person, human to all other forms of life. We need knowledge about world's major ecosystems and the complex interplay between environment and development, since it is impossible to devise an effective policy unless it is based on sound scientific information. Based on this thinking, United Nations and World Resources Institute have launched a programme called Millennium Ecosystem Assessment System. It is an international collaborative effort to fill important gaps in our knowledge and to map the health of our planet and communities living thereon.

Effects of Particulate Matter on Health and Environment

Particulate matter is a term used for a mixture of solid particles and liquid droplets found in the air. Particulates originate from a variety of sources, including diesel trucks, agriculture fields, power plants, wood stoves, pesticides, husk, and road etc. Its chemical and physical composition varies widely. Particulate matter is divided into coarse and fine varieties. Coarse particles are of size above 10 micrometers and (PM 2.5 and PMIO) are fine. Individual fine particles cannot be seen with the naked eye, but collectively they appear as black soot, dust cloud or grey haze. Particulate matter creates series of significant health problems including (1) premature death, (2) aggravated asthma, (3) acute respiratory symptoms, (4) decreased lung function in the form of shortness of breath, (5) office and school absence, and (6) chronic bronchitis etc. Particulate matter is also a major cause of visibility impairment enhancing coefficient of haze (COH) in many parts of Asian countries and United States, because these particles can scatter and absorb light. Further, fine particles can remain suspended in air and travel long distance across regional and international borders without sinking and settling.

Coarse particles come from sources such as wind blown from dust-laden land, deserts, agricultural fields, and from unpaved roads due to vehicular traffic. Fine particles are generally emitted from activities, such as, industrial and residential combustion and from vehicular exhaust. Due to the use of CNG (Compressed Natural Gas), fine particles are also found in the atmosphere from excessive emissions of SO_2, NO_2, and volatile compounds. Recently, conducted community studies at Mandi Gobindgarh and Morinda towns (Punjab), reveal the adverse public health effects associated with exposure to fine particles for both short term (for one day to 5 days) and long term (for one year to several years). They have also been seen to contribute to alterations in the structure of lung tissues and respiratory track defence mechanisms.

Community Health Studies and Respiratory Symptoms

Numerous epidemiological studies (Vedal, 1997) indicate that an increase in PM concentration is associated with increased mortality, increased hospitalization for respiratory and cardiac vascular diseases, increased respiratory symptoms and decreased lung functions. A 10 microgram per cubic meter increase in PM10 concentration was found to be associated with 1% increase in daily mortality and a 3% increase in asthma attacks, broncodilator use and lower respiratory symptoms (Dockery and Pope, (1994). A graph between the various respiratory diseases and particle size surveyed by the Prasad (1996) exhibited in Fig. 1, depicts the effect on community health in and around Chandigarh. Elsewhere, Schwart *et al.,* had found that a 10 microgram per m^3 increase in PM25 (for the previous two days) was associated with a 1.5% (1.15 to 1.9%) increase in total mortality in the six U.S. cities studied by him. Pope *et al.,* (1995) using data from surveys of 15 U.S. metropolitan areas conducted by American Cancer Society have found a relative risk ratio of 1.17 (1.091 to 1.26) for mortality due to long-term exposure to PM2.5.

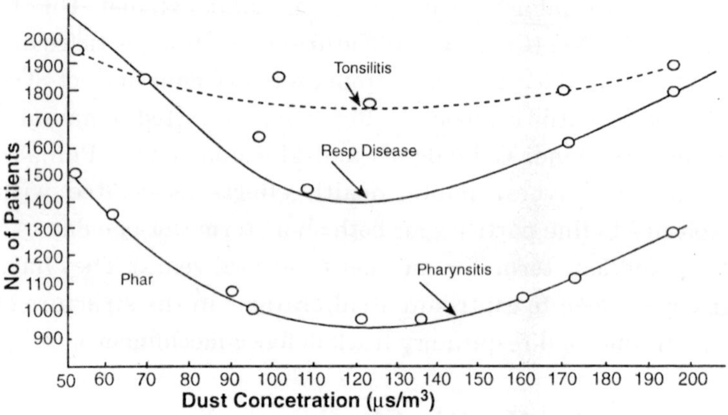

Fig. 1 : Dust Concentration and Disease

A recent report suggests that increased mortality among infants is also associated with increased exposure to PM. This result was obtained from data on almost four million infants from 86 US metropolitan areas exposed to PM10 in the range 11.9 to 68.8 μg m^{-3} during the first two months of life in normal birth-weight infants. High PM10 exposure was associated with death from respiratory causes and sudden infant death syndrome. An increase in death from respiratory causes was also found in low birth-weight infants, though the increase was not statistically significant (Delfino *et al.,* 1997a)

Researchers in California have reported a significant increase in inhaler use with a 10 μgm^{-3} increase in PM10. In Mexico city, lower respiratory illness in children (Romieu *et al.,* 1996) was found to increase with both a 20 microgram per m3 increase in PM10 and a 10 μgm^{-3} increase in PM2.5. In Amsterdam, with decrease in the morning and evening peak flow rate of 4% respectively, a significant increase in 3 or the 4 categories of subjects were found for exposure over the range 4 to 40 μgm^{-3}. A recent report from a large Swiss study (nearly 10,000 adjust subjects indicates that a 3.4% decrease in FVC (a lung function measure) is associated with a 10 μgm^{-3} increase in PM10. In Beijing, a study of approximately 75,000 first child-births, indicates an association between low birth-weight attributable to air pollution is 13%. (Delfino *et al., 1997b*)

The PM standards recently established by US EPA (Environmental Protection Agency) are 15 microgram per m3 for the annual mean and 65 μgm^{-3} for daily concentration of PM25. For PM10, the level of 15 μgm^{-3} (annual mean) and 150 μgm^{-3} (24 hours) remain in place. For each standard there are different averaging times or some other parameters to be used in determining compliance.

Hospital Admissions

Many but not all studies have found association between PM exposure and hospitalization. In England, 10 μgm^{-3} increase in PM10 has been found associated with 2 to 6 % increase in hospital admissions for asthma, bronchitis, and pneumonia, all respiratory causes and cerebro-vascular diseases Schwartz *et al.,* A recent study in Arizona by Pope *et al.* (1995) showed an increase in admissions for cardio vascular diseases (2.75%) for a change in PM10 from 28 to 51 $\mu g\ m^{-3}$. Biological Mechanics for PM Effects

Numerous toxicological studies and several clinical studies offer insight into biological means by which PM exposure would result in adverse respiratory or cardio vascular effects. Researchers (Drecher *et al.*, 1997) have found that components of both metals and solvents (poly nuclear aromatic hydro-carbons) can exacerbate inflammatory reactions. The aqueous component of particles was found associated with increased immune chemical levels reactions. The aqueous component of particles was found associated with organic PM components. Studies have further suggested that PM exposures may also exacerbate allergic responses. A recent study (Hitsfield *et al., 1997*) reports that parthenium grass pollen allergen is found with diesel exhaust particles. This allows allergen to become concentrated in polluted air resulting in triggering attacks of allergic asthma. German researchers (Peters *et al.,* 1997) have reported significant increase in plasma viscosity in men during the air pollution episode of the last decade. An increase was found associated with three measured pollutants, TSP, SO_2 and CO_2 but among women the association was only statistically significant for SO_2 and CO.

Design and Development of Personal Dust Monitors

To have clean and green environment, sustainable development and ecological balance, environmental pollution control is required. This can be assessed only through environmental monitoring, which is highly useful for integrated monitoring programme like stationary source monitoring, mobile source monitoring, personal monitoring and occupational monitoring.

A cyclone based PM10 Personal Dust Monitor designed and developed at Central Scientific Instruments Organisation, is shown in Fig.2. In this instrument the cyclone has been so mechanically designed that the cut off size of respirable particles is restricted to 75% of the respirable dust range.

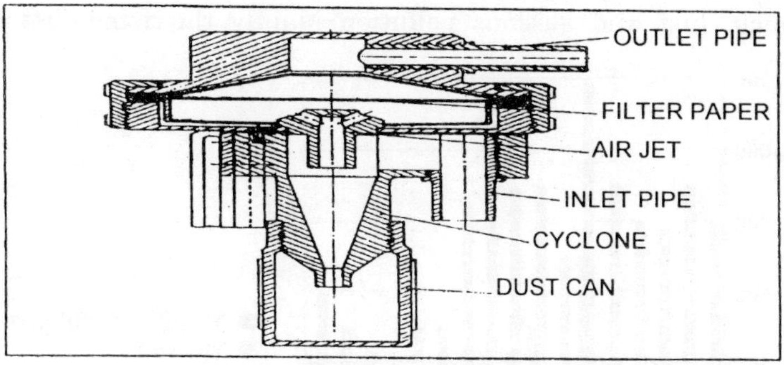

Fig. 2: Cyclone for Personal Dust Monitor CSIO Chandigarh

Due to cyclone motion and centripetal force acting upon dust particles, particle larger than 11 micrometers get settled in the cap holder. Further, the air jet has been so precisely designed and fabricated that smaller particles due to impaction stick to the inner walls of glass micro fibre filter. This is operated with 6VAH cap lamp battery of miners and mineral explorers. The instrument, which can be in continuous use, is working on the gravimetric measurement principle. It has been successfully tried in paper, cement and thermal power plants to measure concentration of lungs dust load to minimize occupational health hazards in open cast and under ground mines. A biological study with PM10 exposure in adverse respiratory and cardio vascular effects has also been made in Chandigarh. This study has been found to directly supplement our observations.

Under our community health studies programme, in association with Post Graduate Institute of Medical Research Centre, Chandigarh, a case study has also been conducted by taking measurements at Mandi Gobindgarh and Morinda towns of Punjab State (Fig.3). Mandi Gobindgarh and Morinda are famous for rolling mill industry and drawing steel rods and plates of various thickness and width. Due to continuous use of coal and oil as fuel in furnaces, there is too much dust and gaseous pollution. Mainly, the rising dust in

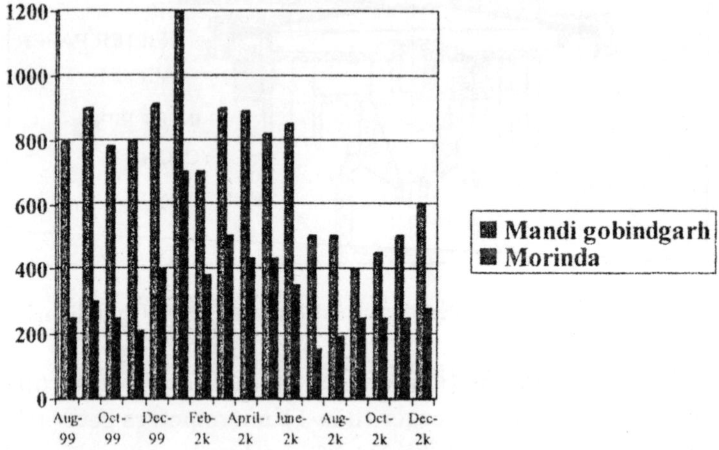

Fig. 3 : Monthly average of Air Pollutants in Rest House Road (Morinda) (μg/m^{-3})

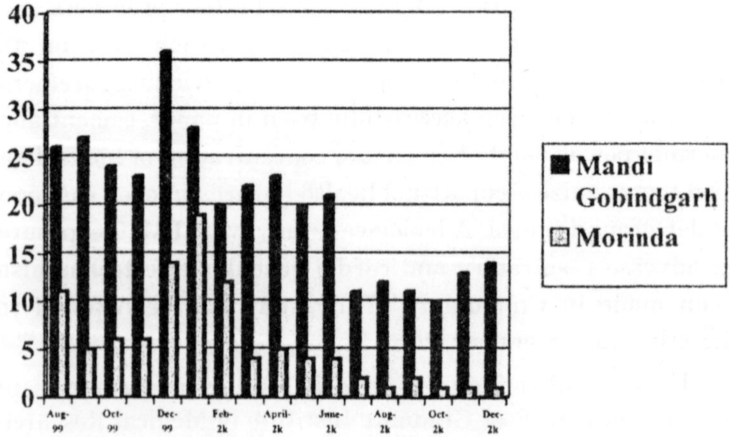

Fig. 4: Monthly Variation of NOx in Mandi Gobindgarh and Morinda (μg/m^{-3})

the atmosphere causes severe lung problems and chronic pharyngitis diseases, which shorten the life span of most of the workers. They often reveal hoofing cough, asthma and pneumoconiosis. Further, this disease gets aggravated while inhaling and exhaling the polluted air. A few cases of tuberculosis have also been reported at Mandi Gobindgarh in particular. Due to gaseous pollution like NOx and SOx, workers often complain of chronic respiratory diseases of vibrational cough, cold and throat pain. (Fig. 4).

Table 1 : Sex and age group-wise distribution of subjects in the two towns of Punjab

Age Grup	Mandi Gobindgarh				Morinda			
	Guru Ki Nagri		Prem Nagar		Rest House Road		Purana Bazar	
	Male	Female	Male	Female	Male	Female	Male	Female
20-29	50	50	50	50	50	50	50	50
30-39	50	50	50	50	50	50	50	50
40-49	50	50	50	50	50	50	50	50
50-69	50	46	50	42	50	50	50	42
70 +	16	15	22	13	20	14	17	13
Total	216	211	222	205	220	214	217	205

Table 2 : Monthly average of Air Pollutants in Guru Ki Nagri (Mandi Gobindgarh)

	Guru ki Nagri (Mandi Gobindgarh)				
Months	**Total SPM ($\mu g/m^3$)**	**NO_x**	**So_x**	**O_3***	**CO***
August, 1999	791.104	26.39	28.27	—	—
September, 1999	886.33	27.03	31.05	—	—
October, 1999	765.96	23.98	24.97	—	—
November, 1999	813.84	21.76	25.88	—	—
December, 1999	969.15	36.1	40.87	0.093	—
January, 2000	1191.72	28.68	25.59	0.22	—

Contd.

February, 2000	775.25	20.35	18.6	0.48	—
March, 2000	884.8	23.42	25.39	0.38	—
April, 2000	933.55	24.15	22.75	0.36	—
May, 2000	915.3	20.88	19.62	0.206	—
June, 2000	917.2	23.74	23.86	0.334	—
July, 2000	501.6	11.79	11.56	0.209	505.5

* Measurement of O_3 and CO were made in November, 1999 and July 2000, respectively

Table 3: Monthly average of Air Pollutants in Rest House Road (Morinda)

Rest House Road (Morinda)					
Months	**Total SPM ($Hg\ mm^{-1}$)**	**NOx**	**SOx**	**Oa***	**CO***
August, 1999	261.78	11.8	12.5	—	—
September, 1999	303.3	5.1	5.4	—	—
October, 1999	259.45	7.45	6.25	—	—
November, 1999	227.86	7.95	13.8	—	—
December, 1999	408.43	13.82	12.8	0.055	—
January, 2000	784.64	19.59	18.38	0.178	—
February, 2000	393.25	12.7	11.7	0.37	—
March, 2000	469.67	4.63	5.42	0.162	—
April, 2000	421.45	5.7	4.3	0.08	—
May, 2000	425.167	3.9	5.5	0.327	—
June, 2000	329.53	4.28	5.38	0.05	—
July, 2000	134.99	2.48	2.28	0.74	62.56

* Measurement of O_3 and CO were made in November 1999 and July 2000, respectively

Conclusions

It has seen that respiratory health problems are associated with increase in fine paniculate matter, which needs to be monitored as best as possible. The reliability and versatility of monitoring instruments can be increased using programmable micro controller, compatible with Personal Computer based monitoring system. In place of monitoring the size and mass concentration of dust ranging from 0.3 to 11 micrometer, we should concentrate more on PMi.s and PMio data. The designed system can be easily supplemented with self-diagnostic and self-repairing electronic circuitry. It is most desirable to initiate suitable steps in this direction in the present scenario to obtain reliable data on pollution mapping and its irradiation. Local area network (LAN) based environment monitoring can provide us most befitting input data on biota of the affected region.

Acknowledgements

I am thankful to Dr.R.P.Bajpai, Ex-Director, CSIO, who allowed me to work on this community health studies programme with PGI, Chandigarh. I also thank Dr.Rajesh, Head Community Medicine Group, PGI to induct me in the team to study the effect in the industrial towns of Punjab. I thank all my colleagues in Environmental Monitoring Instruments Division who extended all timely support to complete this societal mission oriented environmental programme.

References:

Angevine, W., Zagar, M. *et al.* (2004) Transport of urban pollution in coastal News England. Bulletin of the American Meteorological Society, 85(8), 1060-1062.

D'Amato, G. (2004) Urban Air Pollution and Allergic Bronchial Asthma. Internista, 12(1):18-22.

Delfino, R.J. , Zeiger, R.S., Seltzer, J.M. *et al.* (1997b) Env. Health Pers., 105: 622-635.

Delfino, R.J., Mulphy-Moulton, A.M., Bumett, R.T., Brook, J.R. and Beacklake, M.R., (1997a). AM J.Respi. Corit. Care. Med., 155:568 - 576.

Dockery, D.W., and Pope, C.A. III (1994) Annual Review Public Health 15: 107- 132.

Drecher, K.L., Jaskot, R.H., Lehmann, J.R.M. *et al.* (1997), J.Toxicol Env. Health, 50:285 - 305.

Hitsfeld, B., Friendrichs, K.H., Ring, J. and Behredt, H. (1997) J.Toxicol, 120: 185 - 195.

Jalaludin, B.B. and Tule, O. (2004) Acute effects of ambient air pollution on respiratory symptoms, Asthma. Environmental Research, 95 (1):32-42.

Peters, A., Goring, A., Wichmann, H.E., and Koenig, W. (1997) Lancet, 349: 1582 - 1587.

Pope, C.A. III, Thun, M.J., Namboon, M.M. *et al.,* (1995) Am J Resp Corn Care Med., 152: 669-674.

Prasad, Basudeo (1993) Measurement of Inhalable Particulates & Its Effect, Report No: CSIO/TR/93/0046:P.23

Romieu, I., Meneses, F., Ruiz, S. et al. (1996) Am J.Respi. Corit. Care. Med., 154:300-307.

Schwartz, J., Dockery, D.W, and Neas, L.M. (1996) J Air Waste Management Assoc. 46; 927- 939.

Tomei, F., Rosati, M.V. *et al.,* (2004) Urban pollution and Nickel Concentration in Serum. International Journal of Environment Health Research, 14(1):65-74.

Vedal, S (1997) The Canadian Council of Ministers of Environment Report. Air Management Association, 47:551 - 581.

CHAPTER 9

GLOBAL ENVIRONMENTAL ISSUES AND MONITORING INSTRUMENTS

Basudeo Prasad and R.P.Bajpai

Environmental Monitoring Instruments Division, CSIO, Chandigarh - 160 030

ABSTRACT

A paper is presented which deals with various environmental factors that causes pollution to air and surrounding environment.leading to various health hazards. Global issues related to air pollution and their impact on land and vegetation are also summarized. Measures to sustain the environment have been suggested.

Key Words : Monitoring instruments, Environment, air pollution, biodiversity.

Introduction

A few known environmental issues have emerged in the global arena due to the potential threat to the human civilization and bio-diversity during last few decades, irrespective of the fact that significant contributions have been made by individual developed countries or group of developing countries in environmental degradation of the unique planet Earth. India has emerged as the fifth polluter country in the global scenario. In such situation, it is the need of day for all countries to sit together and draw out appropriate action plans and suitable techno - economical control strategies, in order to dilute and abate the threats posed by these issues :

Loss of biodiversity

- Global climate changes,
- Protection and promotion of human health,
- Human settlements,
- Sustainable and diversified agricultural & rural development,
- Protection and preservation of forest wealth,
- Desertification,
- Sustainable management of water wealth, and
- Control on energy intensive life style.

The development of low cost high volume monitoring & control instruments is necessary to curb the rising pollution level for the societal mission programme under environmental awareness compaign 2001 - 2002 in which CSIO has played a major role. It is intensive need of the day for the protection, preservation and control of environmental pollution and natural wealth.

CSIO has been organising brain - storming workshops, seminars, trainings on environmental monitoring practices for safety, health & environment. The intensive programmes have been taken up for monitoring air, water, noise, gaseous & stack emission for various industrial belts and case study.

Environmental Monitoring Instruments Division, CSIO has played a major role in controlling of environmental hazards and in restoring non-polluted environmental conditions for human survival and values of life through its R&D and instruments development programmes.

The role of common man for the protection of safe environment and natural aesthetics has been discussed in detail in the paper.

Although, there may be 30 million life forms on earth, yet there is only one species - *Homo sapines*, the man, who can change the environment as per their needs. It is perhaps this ability of the man, which has now posed a real question as how to plan his future survival.

This is because man's action plan, anthropogenic sources have put threats to environment. The two prime factors responsible for these threats are

(*i*) Population explosion, and (*ii*) Energy intensive life style.

India's population has been steadily increasing on an average at an annual rate of 2% since 1950. It was merely 36.1 crores in 1951, which jumped to more than 100 crores in 2001 AD. At present India's population accounts for about 16% of world's population (world population has crossed marks of 650 crores by 2001). India has now become 5th polluter in the world. According to World Watch Institute, Washington, USA, the pollution level of Delhi City is similar to " London Smog" of 1952", which took lives of more than 4000 people. As per the statistical data of institute, the pollution status of Beijing (China) is also on higher side but lesser than India. The acidic clouds after accumulation, are rising over Indian oceans and disbursing over India's wheat growing tract.

Economic Effects of Air pollution

Damage to property due to air pollution is a very important aspect of environmental pollution. It covers a wide range-corrosion of metals soiling and eroding of building surfaces, fading of dyed materials, rubber cracking, destruction of vegetation, effects on animals, interference with production and services, deterioration of works of art.

Global Issues Related to Air pollution

(*i*) Global warming (*ii*) Acid rain (*iii*) Ozone depletion (iv) Depletion of biotic resources (*v*) Effect of meteorological parameters.

Direction and speed of surface winds govern the drift and diffusion of air pollutants discharged near the ground level. Higher the wind speed, more rapidly are the pollutants carried away from the source. Similarly, the direction depends upon the terrain. Hilly areas and valleys which deflect the air flow horizontally, vertically or both. Thus, wind rose plays a vital role in mid hills of North-west regions and Himachal Pradesh in soil erosion spreading the pollutants and desertification.

Under normal condition for every 1000′ increase in altitude, the temperature decreases by 3.3 °F. This vertical temperature gradient is known as " Lapse rate". During temperature inversion, a dense cold stratum of air at ground level gets covered by lighter warm air at higher altitude (in different regions of Himachal Pradesh), thus stopping the vertical air movement, resulting in concentrated pollution beneath the inversion layer. As a result, the atmosphere is stable and very little turbulence of mixing takes place. Under such conditions, pollutants in the air of hilly regions at higher altitude do not disperse. It takes higher sinking time due to ambiguous dynamics of particles.

Adverse effects of Air pollution on Human Health:

1. Eye irritation.
2. Irritation of respiratory tract.
3. Nose and throat irritation.
4. Hydrogen Sulphide, NH3 and mercaptants released from the factories & chemical industries cause odour nuisance even at low concentrations.

5. Particulates, particularly, pollen and congress grass initiate asthmatic attack. Further, chronic pulmonary disease like bronchitis and asthma get aggravated by high concentration of Sulphurdioxide.Nitrogen dioxide, particulate matter and photo-chemical smog.
6. Carbondioxide attacks central Nervous system.
7. HF causes diseases of the bone (Fluorosis patients are found in Meghalay. Shillong in maximum number).
8. Carcinogenic agents cause cancer.
9. Respiratory dust particle (size 0.3 0.3-11 μm - 11 μm enhance respiratory lungs dust load diseases like silicosis, asbestosis, pneumoconiosis. fibrosis and byosinosis.
10. Certain inorganic and organic pollutants metal, non-metals causes lead poisoning loss of memory, failure of central neverous system, fatigue and restlessness, vomiting and loss of appetite, hoofing cough and loss in breathing efficiency.

Energy Intensive Life Style

During the hunter-gather stage of civilization the total energy requirement of a person was 2000-4000 kilo cal/day. This was obtained through the food chain and his own metabolism and muscular energy while doing the work. Consequently, with the discovery of fire, agriculture & industry, per capita energy consumption has gone high particularly for developed countries. In U.S.A. the per capita energy consumption has reached to $25x10^4$ kcal per day. However, it is still low as 10^4k cal/day in India and other developing countries.

Impact on Resources

Ever increasing pressure of population explosion and eagerness to lead western energy intensive life style involving fast urbanisation & industrialisation have not only resulted in over exploitation of agricultural land, degradation and loss of forest cover, desertification, depletion of bio-diversity, accelerated consumption of limited natural resources like water, petro-chemicals, coal and minerals but have consistently deteriorated the quality of all the three spheres of earth i.e. air, water and soil. Estimated land resources in India has been shown in Table 1.

Table 1 : Estimated land resources in India

S.No.	Category	Subject	Area (10 hectares)
1	Lands fit for vegetation	i) Cultivated land ii) Forest land iii) Culturable wastes/fallow pastures groves	142 67 55
		(A) Total area of cultivable land	214
2	Lands considered unfit for vegetation	i) uncultivable waste lands (permanent ice, snow, rock, out crops, deserts, etc.) ii) Urban and other non-agricultural lands (towns, roads, rivers, etc.) iii) Non-recorded areas	20 20 20
		(B) Total area of unculturable land	65
Total land area (A+B) 4% of world land area			**329**

In an estimate given by Ministry of Agriculture, it has been indicated that about 87 mha out of total 142 mha of agriculture land is prone to degradation by severe water and wind erosion of soil. Soil salinity has also been added considerably in the degradation of agricultural land.

Forest Land

The satellite imageries study of National Remote Sensing Agency revealed that forest area in 1972-75 was 55.5 mha, which has reduced to 46.3 mha in 1980-82 indicating an average depletion rate of 1.3 mha per year. As regards to closed forest area like Himachal Pradesh & N-E region of our country it was found to be only 46.4 mha in 1972-75, which further reduced to 36 mha in 1980-82. Thus, as against our national forest policy, 1988, which aims to achieve 33% of the geographical area under forest cover (66% for hilly regions) the closest forest cover during 1980-82 was just 10%. The degraded forest land is approximately 30 mha out of 67 mha. Deforestation causes series of inter-related harmful impacts shown in (Fig.1)

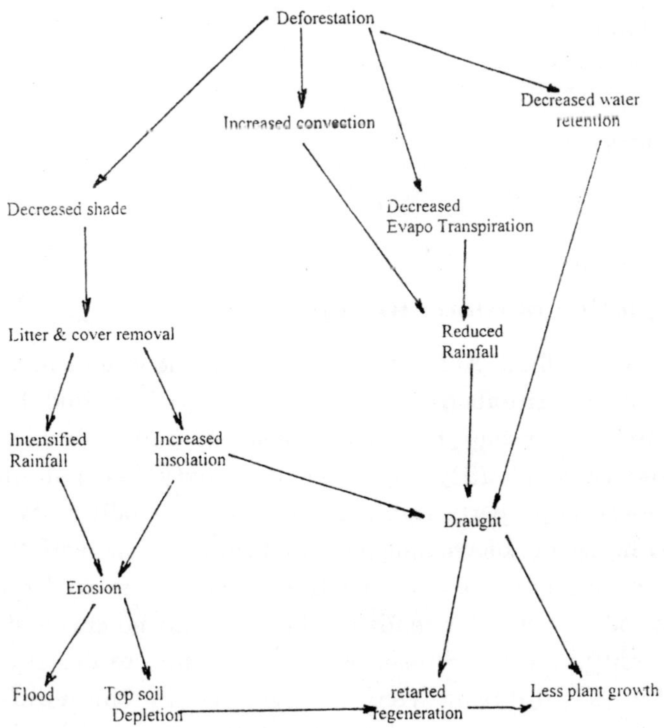

Fig. 1 : Inter-related harmful impacts of deforestation

Table 2 shows environmental benefits derived from a medium size tree of 50 tonnes during 50 years life span apart from its I\timber, fruit & flower value.

Table 2 : Environmental benefits derived from a Medium Size Tree

Env. Benefits	Single tree (Rs. in lacs)	Forest type	
		(Rs/ha in lacs) Tropical	Sub-Tropical
1.Ozone production protein	2.50	22.50	20.50
2.Conservation of animal	0.20	1.18	1.64
3.Control of soil erosion	2.50	22.50	20.50
4.Water cycling & humidity control	3.00	27.00	24.60
5. Shelter for bird. Squirrel & insect	2.50	22.50	20.50
6. Air pollution control	5.00	45.00	41.00
Total	**15.70**	**141.30**	**128.74**

Depletion of Biotic Resources

"Vashudhaib Kutumbkam" has been the sole principle of our life and rituals from ancient times of vedic period. Life & nature of our biosphere have been our immemorable and inseparable identity. We have won sixty five patents & intellectual property rights due to our rich biodiversity. The new horizon of biotechnology linked with our biodiversity is a potential insurance cover for the future human civilization. But today even after realizing the enormous potential of bio-diversity and biotic resources, we continue to destroy the habitats inhibiting rich biodiversity in the name of development and industrialisation. It has been estimated on a global scale that nearly 17 mha of forests (tropical rain forest), which houses about 50 % of total biodiversity are being destroyed every year. (Plants, Indicator of Air Pollution, 2004)

To stream line over all development at global level on sustainable basis and to protect environment from further degradation, a comprehensive global action plan should be drawn for 21st Century. Ministry of Environment & Forest has also identified this vital programme as Agenda - 21. It includes the statement of goals and objectives as well as suitable strategies and action plans for sustainable development :-

- Under protection and promotion of human health, environmental health risks of vulnerable groups (urban poor women and children), control of communicable diseases, nutrition, family planning and child spacing, occupational health, water and sanitation, impact of pesticides must be taken care.
- Under human settlements, food security in urban areas, environmental impact of cities, health problems of poor and housing must be looked into.
- For sustainable agriculture and rural development we must reduce dependency on chemicals. Soil fertility & integrated pest management should be adopted.
- To protect and preserve the biodiversity, a knowledge based indigenous data of important plants, animals and eco system should be created.
- Under sustainable management of water resources programme, we must have energy auditing on water resources and consumption. We should lay emphasis to increase food production from fresh water and oceans. We should revitalise the effluent water

treatment plants of cities for recycling the influent water in the city supply.

To achieve the objectives of Agenda - 21, Central Scientific Instruments Organisation has developed low cost high volume air, water and noise monitoring instruments highly suitable for Indian environment. A few of these are - Personal Dust Monitor, SOz Monitor pH Meter, Soil Salinity Tester & Conductivity Meter, Development of Sulphation Chamber, Portable Stack Opacity Monitor and Automobile Exhaust Monitor for Diesel Vehicles. Apart from environmental pollution monitoring instruments, CSIO has also developed pollution control instruments like Low Voltage Electrostatic Precipitator and lonisor.

Environmental Monitoring Instruments Division, CSIO has core competency in the development of solid - state C - MOS technology and micro - controller based environmental monitoring and control instruments. We have developed following micro - controller based instruments which are PC compatible using serial interface RS - 232C protocol:

(*i*) Micro - Controller based Turbidity Meter,

(*ii*) Micro - Controller based Stack Opacity Monitor, and

(*iii*) Micro - Controller based Automobile Exhaust Monitor.

In addition, we have to our credit the development of many other monitoring and control instruments under National Mission Programme like :

(*i*) Personal Dust Monitor,

(*ii*) Nephelometer,

(*iii*) COH Mass Monitor,

(*iv*) Low - Voltage Electrostatic Precipitator, and

(*v*) Digital Titrimeter,

We have released the knowhow of following four instruments :

- Digital Turbidity Meter,
- Low Voltage Electrostatic Precipitator,
- Continuous Stack Opacity Meter, and
- Personal Dust Monitor and Particle Sampler

(Purchased by Chemical Engg. Deptt., Punjab University)

These instruments are being manufactured in India. Apart from the instruments developmental work, we have also provided technical consultancy services (for air, water and noise monitoring) to various establishments like Punjab State Council for Science and Technology, Pfizer Pvt. Ltd; Chandigarh, Richer Demm. Parwanoo, (HP) & DST, UT Administration, Chandigarh.

Under Human Resource Development programmes, we have substantially contributed by imparting theoretical and practical training to P.G. students of Environmental Engg. and under graduate degree students of Engineering and Technical Institutes. We are competent to conduct training programmes in Environmental Monitoring / control techniques for 3rd world / under developed countries, industries, instrument manufacturers and Entrepreneurs, pollution control boards, NGO's and Environmentalists.

But all round success in the field of environment can be achieved through individuals participation such as :

1. Paryavaran Vahini members and Environmental Society of India should report about violation/environmental degradation and further create awareness for environmental issue
2. One should adopt IMBY (In - my back yard) for waste storage, management & waste recycling instead of NIMBY (not in my back yard).

3. Adopt "Vermiculture" for own flowri - culture. This can be taken up as a community programme.
4. Promote use of organic manure instead of chemical fertilisers and spraying pesticides carelessly.
5. Encourage aforestation. If you cut one plant grow ten in waste land and wetlands.
6. Conservation of waste, petro wood and coal energy should be encouraged.
7. Play your power house and decks on low volume to avoid noise pollution

Conclusions

The technology in this area has undergone considerable change during last one decade. Besides, the national needs have also taken a rapid pace. As such the following R&D futuristic programmes for instruments development is proposed:

1. Automobile Exhaust Gaseous Monitoring Instruments.
2. Piezoelectric crystal based instruments for personal monitoring of air pollutants, H_2S, SO_2, NH_3, HC, CO, SPM, etc.
3. Development of particle analyser, toxic gas analyser and ambient dust analyser for monitoring bio - spheric effect, epidemic and occupational health hazards.
4. Automobiles Exhaust Control Devices.
5. Noise Control Techniques.
6. Satellite based monitoring system, pollutions-mapping using remote sensing techniques (LIDAR systems).

7. Laser and Fiber Optics based environmental monitoring instruments.
8. Acid rain monitors.
9. TOC analyser.
10. Environmental Monitoring mobile van, which can also be used for environmental impact assessment, study & environmental awareness programmes.
11. OZONE Monitor and U-V Radiation meter.

The end results of these programmes are obviously of high societal value. The achievements of the project will lead to a healthy environment and higher quality of life, which a conscious Indian nation now very much expects.

In addition to above, it is proposed to develop on-line BOD monitor for rapid measurement. The present method takes nearly 3 days period. There are technology available now a days with which on line BOD monitoring is possible instantly. Development of rapid water analysis kit and odour sniffer based on conducting polymer are good assets in the environmental monitoring fields in the days to come for socio-techno growth of our nation.

Acknowledgement

We are grateful to Green tech Foundation for allowing to present and publish this paper in Green tech - 2001, International Conference on Environment Management. We also owe special thanks to Shri Mohan Kumar for his kind endeavor and timely support to complete this paper.

References

Cpcb @ alpha. nic. in

Garg, K.K. and Jain, S.C. (1998) Environment Lessons for common Man, pp. 10–15.

Migliareti, G., *et al.* (2004) Urban Air Pollution and Asthma, Pediatric Pulmonology, 38(3):198-203.

Plants, Indicator of Air Pollution (2004) Ozone and Trace elements. Pisa, Itly. Nalic Journal of Environmental Monitoring, 6(7):637-640.

Prasad Basudeo and Garg, Sangeeta (1999–2000) Report on "Environmental Pollution Monitoring", 1999–2000.

Prasad, Basudeo (2000) "Paryavaran Pradushan".1996, pp., 40–48.

Report on Medical Health Status of North - East Region, AIIMS, Delhi, June, 1999.

Sajani S.Z. (2004) Urban air pollution monitoring and correlation properties between fixed site stations. J. Air and Waste Management Association, 54(10): 1236–1241.

CHAPTER 10

WOMEN AS SUSTAINERS OF NATURAL RESOURCES AND ENVIRONMENT

Mahadevi Singh[1], Alka Tomar[2] and K.K.Singh[3]

[1]Sophia Sr. Secondary School, Bikaner - 334001.

[2]Centre for Media Studies, Community Centre, Research House, Saket, New Delhi-110017.

[3]Project Directorate (Research), Agriculture & Soil Survey, Krishi Bhawan, Bikaner (Raj.)-334001.

ABSTRACT

Women are important environmental educators. Young children first learn to see and understand what is happening around them and begin to feel how they are related to it, through contact with their mothers. As they grow older, education at home is fundamentally important in planting ethics and in stimulating change in attitudes. Women can also stimulate changing behavior that would lead to marked savings in food, water and energy consumption. Women's education is therefore, essential for participation in environmental protection and conservation of natural resources.

Key Words : Women, natural resources, environment

Introduction

The preservation of environment through natural and man made resources are important for economic and social development. A balanced and buoyant environment is necessary for continued development efforts. A healthy environment means less pollution, less sickness, less misery, which would result in greater productivity that would lead to development. India from the very beginning have recognized the dependence of survival of all organisms including human beings on the existence of environment. Hippocrates, the Father of Medicine (6th century B.C.) had stressed the influence of environment on health. Buddha taught "the environment changes according to the state of mind. Guru Nanak (1469-1539) also emphasized the relationship of the environment with the life and he said through the harmonious interaction of air, water and earth that the whole universe is being sustained.

Nevertheless, since the mid-1980s, there has been a significant increase in studies and international meetings concerning women and their relationship with such environmental factors as energy, water, population, natural resources and humanization. For the first time, these factors have been linked to their effects on agriculture, child, family and community health and the conservation of natural resources (Gulhati, 1995).

A consensus has emerged on the importance of education and literacy for women as a contribution to the conservation of natural resources and to environmental protection. Women, as the first to suffer from the effects of environmental deterioration and under development, are usually the first to demand changes. Their role in the family and society makes them particularly anxious and concerned about the well-being of planet Earth and of future generations. In this context, women have several roles to play as producers, users, consumers and administrators of water, energy, agricultural products, and housing and natural resources; and as educators of their children, through whom they can transmit knowledge that can encourage rational and farsighted attitudes towards food, water and energy consumption (Singh, 2000).

Environment refers to the sum total of all conditions and influences that affect the living of human beings. A living does not only apply to survival but it also implies to good health, good quality of life, to work and to move about in a healthy environment which consists of both micro as well as macro environment. Further, micro-environment refers to shelter, living space, and the neighbourhood, whereas the macro-environment refers to the surrounding space and cities in the near as well as vicinity of the shelter. All these rapidly growing conditions of stress on environment in rural as well as urban areas threaten the welfare and even survival of human beings. In order to live in a healthier environment, the man-environment relationship needs to be improved in the light of both micro as well as macro-environment (Dhillon and Dhaliwal, 1996).

As a matter of fact, women play a key role in the protection of household environment both in rural and urban sectors. They must lay stress on the household sanitation, viz., having wire mesh door particularly in the kitchens, covered drainage system, proper disposal of water, refuse as well as harmful insect-pests. Proper care and maintenance of household gadgets is equally important to avoid excessive noise which may prove irritating and annoying to family members. They should also make use of good quality of fuel, free of smoke to avoid eye problems as well as gastrointestinal disorders.

Sources of household pollution

The sources of household pollution covers fuel burning, dust through house cleaning, improper disposal of refuse, improper storage of food and water as well as noise from household gadgets TV, radio, foot steps, tap water, etc.

Among the sources of household pollution, the rural housewives gave first rank to fuel burning (3.00) followed by dust through house cleaning, improper disposal of refuse burnt material and inadequate natural light to which they gave second (3.96), third (4.50), fourth (5.94) and fifth rank (6.76), respectively (Table 1).

The urban housewives gave different ranks to the sources of household pollution and ranked first (3.01) to the noise produced from TV/radio/household equipments/tap water/foot steps. They gave second, third and fourth ranks to improper disposal of refuse (3.64), dust through house cleaning (3.73) and poor ventilation (4.13), respectively (Cheema, 1990).

The rural housewives referred fuel burning as the most important source of pollution for the reason that they usually made use of firewood twigs of arhar (*Cajanus cajan*) and paddy (*Oryza sativa* L.) straw, etc. for cooking purpose which produce excessive smoke resulting into ill health of the homemakers and other family members. Similarly, dust through house cleaning also causes ill health (Dhillon *et al*., 1990a, Dhillon *et al*., 1990b)

Table 1 : Mean ranks of sources of household pollution in rural and urban area

Source	Rural	Urban
Fuel burning	3.00	-
Dust through house-cleaning	3.96	3.73
Improper disposal of refuse	4.50	3.64
Ash/burnt material	5.94	-
Inadequate natural light	6.76	5.25
Poor ventilation	6.97	4.13
Lack of artificial illumination	7.16	7.73

Contd.

Improper storage of food and water	7.25	6.76
Insect-pests	7.81	4.34
Contaminated food items	8.30	7.12
Noise from TV/radio/household equipment/foot steps/tap waters	8.61	3.01

Source : Cheema, 1990

The urban housewives gave first rank to noise from TV/radio/household equipments/tap water/foot steps, etc. as they are very much in tune for switching the communication devices at very high volume which causes nuisance to the family members as well as the neighbours. Likewise, urban respondents also gave importance to the dust through house-cleaning ash/burnt material since the spreading of dust and foul smell from burnt material adds to the deterioration of health of the family members (Dhillon *et al.*, 1990a, Dhilllon *et al.*, 1990b).

Sources of neighbouring environmental pollution

Neighbouring environmental pollution included street sweepings, farm yard manure, noise from hankers/railway line/main roads/loudspeakers/traffic and community washing at the water bodies (Table 2).

Table 2 : Mean ranks of sources of neighbouring environmental pollution in rural and urban areas

Rural		Urban	
Source of pollution	**Rank**	**Source of pollution**	**Rank**
Street sweepings	2.76	Stagnant water	2.26
Farm yard manure	2.94	Street sweepings	2.53
Foul smell of human wastes	3.41	Faulty sewage system	2.96
Burning of paddy straw	3.84	Traffic noise	3.58

Contd.

Faulty waste/disposal system	5.68	Noise from hawkers/railway line/ loudspeakers/building construction	4.64
Noise from hawkers/ railway line/main roads/ loudspeakers	6.29	Vehicular exhaust	5.63
Spraying of insecticides on fruits and vegetables	6.97	Industrial smoke	5.85
Application of chemical fertilizers in the fields	7.72		
Community washing at the water bodies (well, streams, canals)	7.50		

Source : Cheema, 1990

The first and foremost factor responsible for pollution of neighbouring environment in rural area was street sweeping (2.76). The next highest importance was attached to farm yard manure (2.94), foul smell of human wastes and burning of paddy straw which earned third and fourth ranks (3.41, 3.84) in order of their importance (Table 2). The other sources like faulty waste disposal system, spraying of pesticides on fruits and vegetables, noise from hawkers/railway line/building construction/main roads and application of chemical fertilizers in the field earned 5th, 7th and 8th ranks, respectively. Community washing at water bodies being a source of pollution obtained the lowest rank (Cheema, 1990).

On the other hand, primary factor indicated by majority of the urban housewives was stagnant water around the residential area (2.26), street sweepings and sewerage system, in the form of open gutters/open drains which were of next importance as pollution sources and earned second and third ranks (3.53, 2.96). Traffic noise attained fourth rank (3.58).

The factors namely noise from hawkers/main roads/railway line/building construction vehicular exhaust and industrial smoke were given 5th and 7th ranks, respectively.

It is clear from the above discussion that in rural area the major source polluting the nearby environment was street sweepings, since majority of the people in villages are used to throw the waste materials/kitchen wastes in the streets. The other important problems faced by them were that of the farm yard manure, foul smell of human wastes and faulty waste disposal system. The heaps of farm yard manure were placed on the very outskirt of the village or in front of the houses which were in the vicinity of fields that ultimately lead to breeding of mosquitoes, flies and other insects along with the foul smell of human wastes as the small children had the ill-habits of easing out themselves in the streets, in front of their houses or at the very outskirt of the village, which were not restricted by their parents to stop this practice. The rural housewives also gave relatively more importance to the problem of burning of paddy straw in the fields as it produced excessive smoke which resulted into the deterioration of the environment along with causing health hazards to the human beings such as eye-irritation and gastro-intestinal disorders.

So far as the urban area is concerned, the respondents faced the problem of stagnant water in the streets, street sweepings as well as faulty sewerage system resulting into breeding of mosquitoes and flies along with other insects, ultimately spreading the infectious as well as contagious diseases in the environment. They also reported the problem of traffic noise which occurred from main tracks/railway line/building construction/markets since majority of the households were located either on the main roads or in the market where noise acted as constantly disturbing factor to the urban inhabitants particularly.

Noise Pollution

Noise is considered to be the major source of pollution within the households. The unpleasant or even pleasant noise which is too loud sometimes leads to severe mental disorientation and in particular causes violent behavior. The noise produced in the households from heavy equipments and appliances as well as outside sources like loudspeaker, traffic noise and agriculture machinery prove to be quite irritating and disturbing (Nagi *et al.*, 1933).

Pollution at Home

While maximum emphasis is laid on outdoor pollution, the indoor environmental pollution is scarcely studied. "Health begins at home", is an usual proverb and the women is the worst victim of indoor pollution as she spends more time inside the home. The following are some of the factors that affect the women.

In addition, the women is the most affected victim due to fire accidents, slips and falls, insect bites, etc. Inspite of all these, the women is neither given nor is taking an active role to avoid such type of internal environment.

Biodiversity plays an important role in the preservation of nature. It also acts as bioindicator to determine the health of a particular habitat and its potential to sustain life. In addition, it is also directly responsible for the soil enrichment, water and climate cycle maintenance, humidity, precipitation, recycling and conversion of waste materials into nutrients.

Women play a predominant role in activities related to preservation of natural resources in turn, has a proportionate impact on women. There is strong line of thought that emphasizes women's special ecological consciousness, which makes them better managers of resources. It is rooted in their roles and are stimulated to develop interest and motivation in the domestic sphere of life while performing and pursuing their roles and responsibilities. While performing their role and obligations in the home they have to depend on the surrounding environment from where they live and maintain health. Women play an important role in control of waste which is of paramount importance for proper development, environmental protection and natural resource management. This is a misconception that the environmental pollution is the responsibility of the industries alone and most of the studies were emphasized on this issue i.e. how to control industrial pollution. There is a big hue and cry about the industrial pollution but this affects only a part of the region or surrounding places. Whereas the pollution in the environment due to improper domestic disposal of refuse affects each and every one. Hence, it is important to collect and dispose refuse and its conversion into plant nutrients. Otherwise, the domestic waste particularly the vegetable waste which will become so large that it would start eating up the population in the form of diseases. Once the diseases developed, it may cost 8-10 times more to correct the condition than to correct it in the beginning itself because prevention is much cheaper than treatment both in human and economic term.

The basic needs of the people are purified water, clean air and sanitation around the homes. The things can be maintained by proper disposal of domestic refuse and maintenance of proper cleanliness surrounding the homes. The process starts from homes particularly by women. Women's consciousness of the environment and therefore, their conservative approach is not something inherent arising out of their being women as it is rooted in their roles. Keeping this concept in view and also relatively little work has been done on this issue, where we see lots of domestic garbage every where on the roads, around the homes and these are the main places for mosquito breeding and growth of other pathogenic micro-organisms/bacteria which affects most of the population.

Women and the Environment

Five years ago in Beijing, the 4th World Conference on Women agreed on a wide range of measures to hasten the removal of such obstacles that hinder the full and equal participation of women in all spheres of life, to protect women's rights and to inadequate their concerns into all aspects of sustainable development. This was to be realized through removal of gender inequalities in all areas but particularly in the management of natural resources and in safeguarding the environment (Women's Studies Quarterly, 1996).

Women-2000 is aimed at taking stock of and assessing the implementation of the strategies and commitments of the **Beijing Platform for Action (1995)** and utilize this review for further advancements. In the platform, India accepted the responsibility to integrate gender concerns and perspectives in policies and programmes for sustainable development. However, even before the Beijing Platform, in community forestry in India, efforts have been made at various levels to institutionalize gender issues from the foundation level. Since, custodianship and ownership of forest is still with the state in the form of forest department, the battle is being fought for equal access to decision making bodies, meeting the priorities of women and individual access to usufructs rights (Ho, 1995).

The government's Forest Policy of 1988, essentially mandated a shift from state-controlled forest management to a decentralized and participatory management, termed as Joint Forest Management. The Forest Policy has been criticized on the ground that it take away the fundamental and age-old rights of the people to gather minor forest produce. Thus, wood, shrubs used for cooking and heating, bamboo and palm leaves used for building, wild grass and shrubs as animal fodder are no longer freely available to the tribals. Thus, under the cover of forest conservation, the government seeks to have undue monopoly rights over the ownership and management of forest lands, both reserved and non-reserved, marginalizing people's participation in forest management and share of forest produce.

Women, Environment and Sustainable Rural Development

Food, fuel, fodder and other biomass play a crucial role in meeting daily survival needs in a vast majority of the rural households in the country. Over the years, the biomass resources have been greatly affected by industrialization, urbanization and advancement in economy at large. The marginal cultures like that of tribals and nomads are the first to face the problems arising from the destruction of biomass. But women, not only in these communities but in all communities, face the maximum threat (Swarnkar, 1988).

Collecting fuel is an important daily chore for most of the rural women. Because of the shortage of fire-wood, women are being increasingly forced to traverse longer distance each day in search of fuels. A study carried out in Pura village of Karnataka shows that each firewood gathering household spends an average of 2.5 hours daily and makes as many as 172 trips (each trip is on an average of 8.5 km) to collect mere 1.7 tonnes of firewood in a year.

In several North Indian households, there is greater reliance on cow dung than fire wood for fuel purpose. But, this does not necessarily mean reduction in time spent by women for such activity. A study carried out on the health of pregnant women in two villages of western Uttar Pradesh shows that they spend long hours in animal husbandry, in collecting animal dung and making them into dung cakes for instance, one pregnant woman who spend a 14 hour working day in which three hours goes for animal husbandry works and half an hour on making dung cakes. In addition, in fetching water, two and half hours for cooking purposes and five hours on other household activities including sifting and milling of grains (Braidotti *et al.*, 1994).

Life of women who live and work in the hills and deserts is even more tortuous. For one, agricultural production and these wood like cow dung and crop wastes are also limited. Available information clearly shows that in the hills and deserts women put in large amount of the time just for searching fuel and fodder. Mr. Madhura Swaminathan, in his study of Dwing village in Chamoli district, Uttar Pradesh, point out that one or more members of each household walk five kilometer steep uphill daily and spent six to ten hours on this back-breaking job. The average time spent by each household is 7.1 hours. In 75% of the households, only women have to go out to collect firewood.

Water is another crucial element for human survival and its availability is related to biomass in a country like ours where rainfall period is only for four months in a year. When the biomass in the surrounding environment disappears, water sources like streams and ponds also to disappear soon after the monsoon.

Water arraying is also an extremely strenuous activity undertaken by women and it consumes an enormous amount of their time and energy. Available information indicates that women spend long hours and traverse long distances especially in the hilly terrain, in the arid and semi-arid areas of the country. In the deltaic plain, the time taken may be less than an hour a day. But this varies in villages of Karnataka.

The time taken can be one to 14 hours per household a day, here as in villages of eastern Uttar Pradesh as much as one to 3.9 hours a day on an average.

Effects of Environmental Degradation

Probably, no other group is more affected by environmental destruction than poor village women. Every dawn brings with it a long march in search of fuel, fodder and water. It does not matter if the women is old, young or pregnant : Crucial household needs have to be met day after day. As ecological conditions worsen, the long march becomes ever longer and more tiresome. Caught between poverty and environmental destruction, poor rural women in India could well be reaching the limits of physical endurance.

The specific difficulties that women face - their extra ordinary work burden or lack of access to health care, for instance - do not arise out of ecological deterioration per se. They are pocketed in the sexual division of labour, marked by a double work burden (at home and outside) and by the specific nature of the task they do, and in the unequal distribution of resources like food within the household, which stems from women's inferior status in the household and from a lack of control over cash and productive resources like land. But given this situation, environmental destruction further increases women's already acute problems in a way very different from those of men. It is worth mentioning that they have less access and less control over resources surrounding them. Third world women, whose way of life is intrinsically linked with the environment bear the brunt of the environment's destruction and, for reasons beyond their control, poor women frequently become the agents of their own resource depletion as they struggle to ensure the survival of their families.

Some of the ill effects are highlighted here :

(a) Air pollution

As regards the air pollution, both rural and urban housewives held the view that polluted air causes irritation to the eyes and reduced visibility which further links with headache, nausea and dizziness. Also, the physical ailments such as bronchitis and asthma are caused due to severe air pollution through indirect inhaling of vapours of fertilizers/pesticides/chemicals used in farms and industries (Dhillon *et al.*, 1990).

(b) Water pollution

The rural and urban housewives were very much aware of the use of clean water, free from impurities particularly for cooking food and washing utensils. The housewives from both the areas reported that use of impure water causes sore throat, tonsils, dysentery, cholera, diarrhoea and typhoid (Dhillon *et al.*, 1991a). It was further observed that the rural housewives were found to be quite conscious for the utensils in which they stored water.

(c) Noise pollution

As regards the ill-effects caused by noise pollution, both rural as well as urban housewives felt irritation in the ears from the traffic noise in urban area and the noise of loud-speakers, agricultural machinery, etc. in rural areas. People also experienced headache because of excessive noise. Also, disturbed sleep, reduced working efficiency, rise in blood pressure and restlessness were the outcome of irritable noise (Dhillon *et al.*, 1991).

(d) Food pollution

Stomachache and food poisoning were reported to be the most common symptoms occurring in the rural and urban inhabitants (Dhillon *et al.*, 1991b). In fact, the ill effects of unhygienic food were quite synonymous with the symptoms of water pollution. The inhabitants did suffer from nausea, dysentery, diarrhoea, vomiting and gastric ulcers, etc. by using stale food, improper ways of cooking foods in the open kitchen as well as unhygienic conditions of kitchen without wire mesh door and windows.

Basic Needs in Rural Areas

In rural areas, the depletion of natural resources by environmental degradation has a significant effect on the daily life of a woman and the well-being of her family. As more people are competing for diminishing resources, women find that each day they must walk further from their homes in search of water, fuelwood and other forest products for their basic needs. This extra distance not only adds to their physical burden, but also means that there is less time for looking after the family for the production and preparation of food.

Deforestation and desertification result in a reduction in the variety and amount of biomass material available for fuel, fodder and supplementary foods. Less efficient fuel makes cooking more time consuming and the need to search for fuel sources also leaves less time for other tasks. Consequently, women may be forced to cook less frequently, or change the traditional diet.

Fish supplies are becoming diminished as a result of environmental degradation and large-scale commercial fishing methods. Fishing is generally done by men, but in some areas, it is also an important part of women's work.

Most food is obtained from farms. Women farmers of the third world are responsible for producing food for their families and increasingly they face the problems of degradation and reduced availability of cultivable land. With the greater emphasis on cash crop production, the cultivation of food crops by women is being relegated to poor, marginal land. Women find themselves working harder to produce food from increasingly over worked land and unlike men, modern farming techniques are not used by them. Insufficient access to and control over the vital resource of land is a central theme in understanding the relationship between land degradation and the deeply degraded areas of Northern India. Women's suicide rates are higher than those of men and this is possibly related to be the deterioration of the natural resource base.

In areas of traditional livestock herding, milk production is largely the responsibility of women. Traditional herders are dependent on their animals for meat and milk, but land available for nomadic herding is increasingly lost to settle farmers and other forms of development. Pressure on the land leads to overgrazing and eventually to desertification and the destruction of the rangelands. The search for water and fodder is also becoming more arduous.

For many women, the daily task of obtaining water for the family is their most pressing problem. As water resources dry up, become chocked with silt or contaminated by pollution, the provision of this essential basic resource becomes increasingly difficult. Not only do women have to walk further, and wait longer at the water points, but also the return journey carrying the heavy load, can damage their health. Research has shown that this task can absorb a quarter or more of the daily food intake, so there are nutritional implications, as well as the danger of physical deformation. To save time, nearer, unsuitable water sources are used, such as ponds, where children bathe and clothes are washed, or irrigation ditches polluted by agricultural chemicals.

In India, there was a dramatic increase in irrigated sugarcane cultivation in the early 1980s. As more water was consumed by this cash crop, women in nearby villages found their water supply diminishing. A newly dug well used to get dried up in a year. Eventually, water for the villages had to be brought from a distance of 15 kilometres.

Children's health is at risk from scarcity of clean drinking water, but adult women are more exposed to hazards of polluted water than men. They are the primary water carriers, they wash clothes and utensils; and when children are sick, women who must nurse them are more likely to succumb to infection than are men. Clearly, poorer households suffer most, as they have less access to clean water sources and are less likely to have help in domestic chores.

Environmental degradation also denies women other basic needs. The reduced number of species means that plants and so on, which provide raw materials for household items, are becoming more difficult to find. The basic construction of the family dwelling is usually men's responsibility, but women, are often involved in the finishing processes and repair work. Plants that provide framework and thatching material become more difficult to find as the processes of deforestation, and desertification take their toll. Scarcity of water is a problem where mud is needed for the walls. In high yielding paddy cultivation, the length of straw is also small which creates problem for thatching and houses.

Women use many natural products in their craftwork. Water is needed to make clay for pottery and for mixing dyes; canes and fibres are needed to make baskets. The loss of medicinal plants is particularly serious, especially in places where other medical care not only increases the demand on women's time as they search for alternatives, but also means spreading money to buy products previously obtained for free, and, too, denying them a source of cash income.

Involvement of women actively in Environmental Decision-making at all levels

The increasing population and the growing demands of modernization as well as economic liberalization have put tremendous pressure on the natural resources especially on the livelihood security of the marginalized groups including women. This has also led to a greater threat of displacement and loss of control over basic resources both land and water by the building of big dams and taking over vast tracts of forest lands for industrial enterprises and development of new export-oriented agricultural industries by private companies on agricultural lands.

Alternate strategies and mechanisms for indigenous women to participate in environmental decision-making, planning and management were devised. This was made possible by accessing information and education in the areas of science and technology and economics in order to develop their skills and opportunities for greater and meaningful participation in the process of conserving and sustaining natural resources. To a large extent the women were empowered as producers and consumers and were able to secure back the land and water resources that had become a long continued struggle for them.

1. Agriculture

Women in India have always part of the work force on agricultural sector, the Eighth Plan (1992-1997) for the first time recognized the need of separate land titles for women and directed state governments to allot 40% of surplus land to women alone, and to allot the rest jointly in the names of both spouses. The newly formulated Ninth Five Year Plan (1997-2002) mentions "there will be a special focus on women in agriculture and its allied sectors as they are in majority (89.5%) and form the major stock of all the agricultural operations". The women-folk of the country will be awaiting for the result of the planning (Singh and Mahlawat, 2002).

The transformation of progressive planning into ground reality needs a very strong movement in terms of awareness of men and women for the rights of women and responsibilities of men, as well as creation of enabling social environment and infrastructure support required for autonomy of women farmers.

2. *Energy*

Another important sector is the energy sector, which has to do much for the betterment of women. The joint study, Parikh, Smith & Laxmi on indoor air pollution shows that women and children below five years are among the most affected due to pollutants released during the burning of bio-fuels in traditional stoves. Several health effects are suspected respiratory infections in children, chronic lung diseases and lung cancer in adults and adverse pregnancy outcomes, e.g. low birth weight and still birth for women exposed during pregnancy while there has been some attempt to reduce such exposures through the introduction of appropriately designed stoves, a better solution, according to the study would be to redesign the petroleum policy so that kerosene is easily available to people at affordable prices. This would not only ease the pressure on forests and other bio-fuel resources but also have a positive effect on the health of women and children. Improved ventilation design and dissemination of truly smoke-less stoves in cost effective manner and increased access to clean fuel have been suggested as the solution (Batliwala, 1983).

The study has given a comparative picture of the programme implementation on improved cook-stove programme (ICP) both in China and India. In both the countries the ICP was initiated in the early 1980s. The Chinese programme covered almost 70% of rural households by 1991 without any direct subsidy by the Government while the Indian programme covered only 15% rural household by 1992; and that too after being highly subsidized by the government.

The reasons of slow progress in case of India are many. It is stated that from the start, there were political and bureaucratic pressures for implementation of the project without taking note of the willingness of people. Local people's requirement, were also not taken into consideration. Lack of monitoring and evaluation in spite of 50% government contribution and in huge flow of money from the center to the state nodal agencies and or down line, and low efficiency and reliability of the stoves are shown to be the main reasons.

3. Women and solid waste management

Another major environmental issue facing the urban community is improper disposal of solid wastes. It is heartening to note that the agencies other than the government are putting great effort to this cause. Exnora International took up solid waste management as the thrust area and developed a methodology for primary collection, resource recovery, recycling and reuse of waste where women played a major role and have been the beneficiaries of activities which have income generating potential too.

One of the modules introduced by Exnora for community based solid waste management is the system of door-to-door waste collection. The local community contributes money to employ a "street beautifier", usually and existing rag-picker. The rag-picker is rehabilitated, given a permanent employment as a street beautifier with a regular income and a tricycle cart to collect waste from each household within the community. The benefit the community derives is that the solid wastes are systematically collected and removed. Though, street beautifiers are usually men, over a period of time it was found that the women in the street beautifier's family resorted to recovery of inorganic material like paper, plastic, metal, glass, etc. from the collected waste and earning money out of sale of the recovered material.

The Narikurava colony (gypsies) in Indira Nagar, Adyar, Chennai is a case in example. About 70 gypsy families in the colony are employed as street beautifiers in various "Civic Exnora Localities". The women of these gypsy families do a fine art of sorting the inorganic waste into different grades of paper, plastic, etc. and selling them to waste recycles. This activity has added more than 50% to the income of these families.

Recently, an appreciation of the work done by this gypsy community, Exnora International constructed a "Community Toilet" for their use with a bio-digester for treating the sewage. The gas from the bio-digester is used for the gypsy women for cooking, the sludge from the bio-digester is composted and sold by the gypsy women for this purpose. Akshaya Colony Civic Exnora is one of the civic exnoras with 100% people's participation. Women involve themselves in segregating organic and inorganic waste and compost the organic waste by aerobic composting.

Waste management has emerged as a primary issue as it imposes an added burden on women's everyday. Homes are the origins for generating solid and liquid waste from kitchen and human excreta. Women can play a vital role in managing the kitchen solid as well as liquid waste. In homes, women are mainly involved in the segregation of waste both biodegradable and non-biodegradable. Moreover, it is the women who is basically involved in the process of reusing and recycling. A lady at home collects all the waste metallic tins/can rather than throwing it. In addition, the disposal of several noxious chemicals such as dioxins and nuclear waste disposal were important issues that seized women's attention. The involvement of women's organizations in these area led women to the forefront to organize and mobilize in the public sphere.

Thus, women play an important role in control of waste which is of permanent importance for proper development, environmental protection and natural resource management. The basic needs of the people are purified water, clean air and sanitation around the homes. The things can be maintained by proper disposal of domestic refuse and maintenance of proper cleanliness surrounding the homes. The process starts from homes particularly by woman. Women's consciousness of the environment and therefore their conservative approach is not something inherent arising out of their being women as it is rooted in their roles.

As a mother she helps the children understand that hygiene and cleanliness lead to prevention of diseases. She makes the children develop the habit of cleanliness and realizes its importance in every day life. She also help them realize that insanitary conditions call for action on the part of those who live in the community. Woman as a mother makes her children aware that qualitative improvement in the environment guarantees a better life.

Women can also play a vital role by :

(*i*) meeting the families in the neighbourhood and to seek their cooperation in removing potential health hazards, (*ii*) by organizing social welfare camps, if possible with the help of some leading personalities of the neighbourhood.

(*iii*) organizing an exhibition to make the proper awareness of the sanitation and health programmes.

4. Mega Dams

Mega dams are the most controversial environmental issue in India. Some 'planned' ecological disasters in the name of technological development have displaced millions of people. The Narmada Valley Development Project is one such environmental disaster. Much before various people's organizations massed into a single organization to give birth to the extraordinary NBA (Narmada Bachao Andolan), there was single women - Medha Patekar, who was deeply concerned about how the displaced villagers should be resettled in an equitable human way. The NBA is a unique example of people's movement for the cause of movement.

Facts and figures show that even though the dam is now where near its eventual, projected height, its impact on the environment and the people living along the river as already severe. Women carrying water pots now walk mile to find a negotiable entry point. In several resettlement sites, people are dumped in rows of corrugated in sheds. Malaria, diarrhoea, sick cattle stranded in slush, when displaced people from two different dam projects have been allotted contiguous land. The economic and social impact is no less than ecological impact. Instead of a forest, from which they gathered everything they need - food, fuel, fodder, rope, gum, tobacco, tooth powder, medicinal herbs, housing material - they earn between ten and twenty rupees a day with which to feed and keep their families. Instead of river, they have a hand pump. People affected are mostly the tribal population who have been cultivating forest land. They do not have legal land titles and hence they are not eligible for compensation. Among, this group women are the worst affected. Rehabilitation of ecological refugees has been one of the prime issues in most large irrigation projects. Hence, the damming of River Narmada has been seriously resisted by women peasants and tribal whose life support systems would be destroyed.

5. Women and Food

Food issues were given priority among the environmental concerns of women in India, since they have been worrying about how to protect their own selves and families from unpolluted foods. Women tend the fields and grow the food that feed their families. Women produce 80% of the food grown in India. They do most of the hard labour in the field together with their other duties.

6. Women and Forest Conservation

As an agricultural country, Indian women have a high degree of participation in developmental and conservational activities. In the case of the Chipko Movement in India (It is the women who started the movement) the treat of deforestation was enough to rally the local women to civil disobedience to protect the ecosystem (Singh and Singh, 2002). The Chipko Movement emerged in the remote Himalayan Hill village in the end of 1972. The Chipko Movement in its evolution of five years declared in 1977 that the main products of the forests are soil, water and oxygen and not the timber as conventionally understood by the foresters. The women of Garhwal created in Chipko slogan;

What do the forest bear?
Soil, water and pure air
Soil, water and pure air
are the basis of life.

7. Women and Water Management

Water is a must for all people to meet the social, economic and cultural needs. No individual or society can survive for long without this vital resource. So, for its efficient and effective utilization, it should be managed properly. Water conservation measures at the individual levels are essential for which women working at the kitchen could have her effective participation and as the problems in water management are on account of deliberate and conscious human behaviour, the women could assist by encouraging the responsible behaviour in the use of water.

Women play a major as well as important role in the water management. Women haul the water and collect the rainfall. Thus, practicing rain water harvesting. She knows very well about various ill effects caused due to water pollution. In almost all the villages, women are playing an effective role in disseminating the useful information about the conservation of water.

In daily life at home, water is used not only for drinking but for many other purposes such as washing clothes and utensils, baths and showers, dish washing and preparation of food, gardening, etc. And it has been noticed that almost all these activities are done by women. A women in the village fetch water for so many hours. She has to work hard to collect water far from her place to meet the daily requirement of water particularly in rural areas. So, she is very much expert in the proper utilization and conservation of water. Also, by effective water management, women could save the water for other environmental uses.

8. Women and Bio-diversity

Bio-diversity play an important role in the preservation of nature. Women play a predominant role in activities related to preservation of natural resources in turn, has a proportionate impact on women.

The women around the world have recognized the need, not only to protect biodiversity but to restore and recreate it. In many societies, women have led the resistance to non-sustainable resource exploitation. Studies shows that many of the voices calling for the protection of biodiversity all over the world are women's voices. Vandana Shiva of India is an internationally renowned experts on the risk of biotechnology and has raised awareness of the potential loss of genetic diversity as a result of the patenting of life forms (Hair, 1992).

In is increasingly recognized that the empowerment of women is an essential component of sustainability. It is less well recognized that women have a special role in relation to the protection of environment. All the issues facing the planet and its creativity are inter connected. Thus, the role and status of women and the environment are inevitably interwined. Women remain the pillars and sustainers of the economic systems of many developing countries. So, there is no way that sustainable development can be achieved without placing them in the main stream of economic planning. Giving a proper priority, women would increase food production (since they are the farmers), safeguard the environment (because they are its main champions) and slow population growth (since improving the welfare of women is the most effective birth control).

In the last it, can be concluded that role of women in protecting the biodiversity provides a bridge between environment and development on the path to sustainability. Also, nothing can be achieved unless women's potential is realized.

9. Women and Socio-Economic System

When women moves forward, the family moves, the village moves, these words of Pandit Jawaharlal Nehru is the central theme in the socio-economic paradigms of the country as it is an accepted fact that only when women are in the mainstream of progress can any economic and social development be meaningful. More than 15 crore of women in the country neither have land nor any asset but still they are nourishing their families. Those families would starve if women stopped toiling. The women in the rural areas of India bear a crushing workload in home and in field but their contribution to rural development is often neglected (Singh, 2000).

10. Women's Involvement in Development Programmes

So far as women's involvement in development programmes are concerned, lack of proper co-ordination between macro-policies and grass-root level realities has resulted in the neglect of age-old institutional structures and this has encouraged people's participation at the grass root level.

Attaining economic growth without exhausting the resources and at the same time fulfilling the basic needs of all people is one of the greatest challenges facing our country. The only way to achieve the balance between development and safe guarding the environment is through environmental education and through women's involvement in the management of natural resources and community properties (Venkateswaran, 1992).

Effective environmental legislation are also required. India, however, has a long history of environmental legislation, starting with the water (Prevention and Control of

Pollution Act, 1986), the Air Act of 1981 which was revised in 1988 and the Environmental Protection Act of 1986. But new legislation need to be introduced. Greater government funding for environmental education, training, encouragement for generation of database and research are some of the initiatives on the part of the government while the NGOs are involved in greater consciousness and awareness programmes on environmental issues. More and more people's participatory movements in ecological activities both in rural and urban areas are also welcome change.

11. Women's Participation in Watershed Development

A participatory programme like watershed development, concerning a sector in which women are major actors, needs to be particularly sensitive to gender disparities. It should address the constraints, which prevent women from participating as equals. Given poor rural women's negligible ownership of private resources, recognizing and strengthening their customary rights to common property resources of which they are major users, needs to be made an explicit objective (Singh and Mahlawat, 2001).

To ensure that women's specific needs and interests receive equal attention in a development initiative, their direct participation in decision making is a prerequisite. However, even direct participation may only enable women to ensure that existing day to day condition is not worsened further. The broader goal of promoting gender equality requires transformative strategies which facilitate long-term changes in gender relations, based on more equal distribution of resources and responsibilities as well as power and authority between men and women (Sharma and Singh, 1993).

Therefore, in watershed management programme participation of women should be ensured right from beginning. Steps should be taken to measure participation through involving women in participatory planning of watershed. Different forms and levels of equality that constitute criteria to assess the level of women's development in a watershed programme are as follows :

Welfare

The level of material welfare of women relative to man, in such matters as food supply, income and medical care is concerned purely with relative level of welfare and is not concerned with whether the women are themselves the active creators or producers of their material needs.

Access

Women's access to the factors of production on an equal basis with means' equal access to land, labour, credit, training, marketing facilities and all publicity available services and benefits on an equal basis with men should be recognized. Here, equality to access is obtained by ensuring the principle of equality of opportunity, which typically entails reform of administrative practice to remove all forms of discrimination against women.

Conscientisation

It involves a belief that the sexual division of labour should be fair and agreeable to both sides and not involve the economic or political domination of one sex by the other. Belief in sexual equality lies at the basis of gender awareness and provided the basis of gender awareness and provides the basis for collective participation in the process of women's development.

Participation

This level of equality is concerned with women's equal participation in decision making process. This means participation in the processes of policy making, planning and administration. It is a particularly important aspect of development project formulation, implementation and evaluation. Equality of participation means involving the women of the community affected by the decision taken and involving them in the same proportion in decision making as their proportion in the community at large.

Control

This level entails not only the participation of women in the decision making process, but women in the decision making through conscientisation and mobilization to achieve equality of control over the factors of production and equality of control over the distribution of benefits. Equality of control means a balance of control between men and women, so that neither side is put into a position of dominance or subordination. Till the early 1970s, Indian development planning continued to be governed by the unchallenging assumption shared widely, that the household is a unit of congruent interest, among whom the benefits of available resources are shared equitably, irrespective of gender. As a consequence, women's needs were presumed to be taken care of by development inputs. The concept of the unitary household and the gender neutrality of development interventions based on it have been increasingly challenged during the last 25 years.

Indicators of Women's Progress

A women's development project may be counted as improving the status of women to the extent that the progress is seen in the following indicators.

Basic needs

Better provision for women of such basic needs as food, water, fuel, housing and health care and proportional distribution of basic needs between men and women.

Consciousness

Awareness amongst women regarding women's needs and women's issues awareness of discrimination against women, ability to analyse issues in terms of women's interest and women's rights.

Needs assessment

Involvement of women in identifying the priority needs of the community and in identifying the special needs of women.

Planning

Involvement of women in project designing, implementation, and evaluation.

Sexual division of labour

Involvement of women in tasks traditionally performed by men, level of involvement of men in tasks traditionally performed by women, number of hours per day worked by the average working woman in comparison to the number worked by the average working man.

Control over the factors of production

Women assess to control over land, credit, distribution of income and accumulation of capital. The order in which these indicators are presented is neither intended to imply an order of priority, nor a sequence of what come first and what should come later. It is merely suggested that a successful programme should include projects which seek to improve women's status across the full range of these indicators. Planning for watershed development programme (WDP) is often shaped by a primary focus on the output of the plan at the expense of the process through which the plan is prepared and designed. A comprehensive and realistic WDP can be prepared depending upon the learning capacity of the agency, how it uses its experience to strengthen institutional capacity and to what extent it shares the knowledge gained with the community. The entire strategy adopted should have following states :

1. Consensus with the community on the values, goals and objectives for watershed interventions.
2. Negotiating agreement on what the community and the PIA have to offer to each other, how the participation strategy should be organized and what will be the role of PIA of community in achieving the jointly planned outcomes.
3. Arriving at a common analysis of the situation so that not just the problems and needs are identified but the reasons are also jointly understood.

12. Women - The Environment Manager

At the end of 20th century, the worst threats faced by the world are : ecological destruction, hunger and poverty of the third world and the danger of war. These have been contributed as on outcome of the prevailing development. But where do the women of the world fit in the process of development that destroys their own environment? Women are half the population of the world. In the given scenarios, they are conscious keepers of the family which in turn encompasses the community society, nation and so on and so forth (Paolisso and Yudelman, 1991).

Women around the world are playing a key role in the protection of environment through their many roles and responsibilities. In fact, they are the best environment manager on this earth. In fact, women should be recognized as environment and development experts. In the rural third world, it is the women who knows and safeguard the genetic resources that scientists are so anxious to catalogue and protect.

The environmental issues in India have been developing and evolving to the extent from the protection and conservation of ecosystem (e.g. bio-diversity national parks, etc.) to problems related to cleaning facilities. The role of women in the environmental protection can be well described under the following headings :

(*i*) The voice raised by the Chipko Movement was the reestablishment of a scientific truth, whose recognition by the society and the state is the need of the hour, especially when we are unable to get rid of the threats from landslides, floods, soil erosion and irregular flow of our rivers.

(*ii*) Studies have shown that tribal women in India know how to use some 300 forest plants as medicines. Also, they know all the plants by name, before they were recognized by the botanists.

(*iii*) In the village of India, they gather the firewood and raise the alarm when the forest dwindles. Traditionally, they aim to conserve the forests, taking branches and deadwood rather cutting down the trees. All over the world women would have been at the forefront of grassroots campaigns to save and plant forests. They knew that the forest provided more than timber; that its dead limbs provided the heat to cook their meals; that the living biomass of the forest provided pure water; that the trees held the soil along the hill sides thus preventing erosion and land slide.

13. Women and Eco-Development

Participation of women in creating healthy milieu and protecting the same is undoubtedly the key to success of the programme "women and eco-development". Therefore, educating women in environment related issues are a shot in the arm for speedy progress and back to roots. Women must be the ambassadresses of environmental issues, for the environment starts from the home.

Women and environment are inseparable. Each women can contribute significantly to protect her environment and it is a bounden duty too. The commons of village especially the women folk have to play a major role in promoting healthy environment. In this line, women should be imparted systematic and scientific training pertaining to day-to-day life situation and issues. However, mere knowledge without practical training pays no dividends and difficult to traverse and transcend the boundaries of commons. Therefore, due importance is given for practical training and for hands on experience to help people believe in what they do and cement the concept (WIN, 1992).

The C.P.R. Environmental Education Centre has been working with women under the programme called Women and Eco-development as a part of the rural eco-development project. The aim and objectives of the programme are :

- To educate the rural women on her environment,
- to help her to identify possible opportunities to enhance their living condition in the context of her environment,
- to help her to acquire some skills to augment her income,

- to help her to take care of her personal and family's health,
- to help her to achieve common community goals through self-help and mobilizing overall participation.

The family is the backbone of any society. In the family, we should not forget the role of woman. A woman is what a family is focused around. She has a lot more responsibility for the way the world is growing than a man does. A culture remains stable if the woman of the society remains stable. Things are preserved, values, emotions and feelings are preserved in the woman first. She has the ability to handle more pain, to absorb more sorrow, a lot more hurt that eventually leads her to greater growth and makes her stronger. She has also the ability to support more, to love more and to strengthen the male and others around her. Hence, it is good for all of us to remember the health of a woman and her role in the family.

Health means not only absence of disease but is a state of well being physically, mentally, socially, environmentally and spiritually. According to WHO Expert Committee on Early Detection of Health Impairment is Occupational exposure to health hazards, "Health .... connotes rather a way of functioning within one's environment (work, recreation, living)". Health develops and is maintained through interaction between the genotype and the total environment.

14. Women, Environment and Sustainable Development

Sustainable development and environment have been the issues and challenges at debate throughout the globe ever since industrialization brought in quick prosperity. In its haste to amass wealth under western influence, the natural environment has been disturbed and the resources have been blindly exploited the result was what we see today environmental deterioration. Deterioration and depletion of resources are due to improper disposal of domestic waste in addition to other factors.

Advocacy and Gender Perspective in Policy and Programmes

In the last five years, two major factors have played an important role in influencing these efforts-building of advocacy on environmental and natural resource management in order to involve women in the process; and policy intervention which has tried to integrate gender concerns and perspectives in policies and programmes for sustainable development.

The first in the 73rd and 74th constitution amendments that have brought in the much needed and long awaited people's participation in planned development programmes. For both rural and urban areas, this is the first experience where issues are being articulated, specially those that have a bearing on the lives of the people. The process has to some extent helped in creating a problem solving platform where the apathy of the people is removed by helping them to overcome the dependency syndrome, by changing their mindset in order to bring back the focus of controlling their own lives (Green, 1994).

There has been a greater effort to evaluate the policies and programmes in terms of environmental impact and women's equal access to and use of natural resources. Adequate research on the hazards to which women are exposed due to environmental degradation of traditional and indigenous resource use and management.

Three decades ago women in the central Himalayas - a region deprived of modern facilities launched a movement for protecting their trees - clinging to the trees, they said **"we will not allow you to cut our trees, let your axes fall on our backs first"**. Trees were their life support and if the process of sacrificing trees for satiating the every growing appetite of forest contractors goes on, the day is not far when all the trees would be gone and this in turn would affect them most adversely. The women created history by initiating the Chipko Movement.

The displacement and loss of land resources has also given a new direction to a view expressed by the women of Andhra Pradesh as one said that women now a days are "increasingly being subjected to violence and so even if not for my sake, having a plot of land in any name is important for the future security of my daughter".

The first and worst victim of deforestation and day to day household work is woman. In Indian traditional society women are the pivot of the family set-up. In hilly regions but in decision-making they play only a secondary role. The scarcity of water, fuel-wood and fodder led the women to raise the question of selling of forest land and demanded their rights.

In the patriarchal policy making institutions, the need to consult women is not even felt. Thus, the participation of women in decision making and solving their problems related to their sustainability became more aggressive. Local wisdom and knowledge can not be bypassed nor discarded for conserving and protecting the environment.

Although, the idea of people's participation in the management of land, water and forests is very old, yet, it is the need of the hour that women are given appropriate opportunities and enough room to bring their strength against various exploiters. In the tribal Santhal area of South Bihar, women are filing cases in the direct courts to secure property rights, the women of Vishakhapatnam district in Andhra Pradesh have organized themselves to reclaim the lands that had been alienated over the past several years and are currently in the possession of the non-tribal people. Quietly but steadily, women have demanded their share in the land and other assets and are aware of their rights. But the crisis of survival has also made them more aware of the economics of the survival options (Agarwal, 1997).

Their sisters in other parts of the country have not been very successful. Despite the Supreme Court's order to remove polluting industries out of the urban city limits, the industrialists have not done so. Those who have taken out their units have inflicted harsh economic pressure and unemployment for women who were employed in their industries. Thus, the policies and initiatives have not been complementary to each other. The struggle, therefore has been a continuous process of bargaining and negotiations in order to retain and sustain themselves.

This issue clearly underlines the women's recognition of the precarious nature of intra household resource sharing in general and of productive resources in particular. In most parts of India, women constitute a disproportionate share of the chronically poor population. According to the Census (1991) figures, approx. 85% of women workers and 75% of men are dependent on agriculture and allied occupations for their livelihood for which they are directly impacted by the usage and management of natural resources.

Trends show that in rural areas non-farm employment and earning opportunities seem to be more focused on men than on women, implying that a large portion of the women continue to be dependent on natural resources while man seek employment in new sectors especially industry and services. Moreover, a large number of rural households are now de-facto female headed (about 25%) whether due to widowhood, desertion or male migration especially in the hilly and backward areas, the dependency and the management of resources is of primary concern for women. Land being the primary source for the majority of people, water management also plays an integral part in this, because even those who had land could not cultivate their land as there was no water, a vital resource constraint in crop production.

Women's involvement changes the texture of the process of development by bringing out the needs of all groups in the community. But several groups of women have also articulated that innovativeness, based on traditional wisdom and knowledge, faces extreme resistance from the state mainly because traditional practices are considered to be qualitatively inferior and the control over resources and major decision making processes lie in the needs of communities. Also, the people's agenda does not match with that of the government which is promoting the values of the resources as commodities.

In these five years, it is also felt that livelihood priorities such as drinking water, food, fuel, fodder, health services, etc. can be managed on a sustainable basis if their overall management is decentralized. Towards the end, NGO's, citizens, the media and government should join together to create an awareness of environment issues, disseminate information to the general public and play a constructive role.

Innovation in Approach and Implementation

Smokeless Chulha

It is a common practice among villages to use firewood for cooking. But they are unaware of the aftermath consequences and damage caused by indoor air pollution. This conventional and traditional practice is hard to change by. It calls for attitudinal change and alternate solution.

Most rural Indian homes use traditional chulhas, which are fuel-inefficient. One of the prime objectives of the installation of the improved smokeless chulha is fuelwood conservation, reduction of health hazards, particularly among women and other benefits like ecological improvement. Employment generation is also a part of this activity.

CPREEC installs smokeless chulhas in the village schools, which is cost effective and easy to handle. The idea behind this operation is that as to enable the villagers to see the difference of the environment by themselves and also the women can replicate the same for the domestic purpose.

Vermi-composting

Extensive bombardment of ad forced the farmers to use chemical fertilizers and pesticides. This make belief concept in the pretext of more yields, had adverse impact on land, water and health. The continuous practice of using fertilizers, which are not indigenous and natural causing unprecedented catastrophe for the agricultural community and for the nation. Therefore, it is imperative to address this issue in its own gamut and unfold a solution that could multiply the problem.

In this background, we strongly motivated villages to practice vermicomposting technique in micro-level to avoid the adverse impact. In order to initiate the operation we launched the programmc in all our operational areas and ensured people practice what was taught to them. It also ensures effective solid-waste management at domestic level, thereby promoting healthy milieu for healthy living.

Wastewater Recycling Unit

Spillover water stagnating around the source is a common sight in villages where a proper drainage system does not exist at all. Apart from creating an unaesthetic sight, it causes environmental pollution, favours mosquito breeding and also leads to contamination of water at the source.

The wastage of water at hand pumps is estimated at 2 litres per pitcher of 12-15 litres capacity. 80% of this water is procurable with the waste-water recycling unit. The water that comes out from the unit is fairly clear and usable for livestock care, gardening and other operations where a high level of purity is not needed.

Sustainability of Interventions

Herbal Garden

The goal behind setting up of the herbal gardens is to re-popularize those species found sporadically in the wild. This concentrated nursing of herbs will be useful to the entire community as and when any need arises. The workshops ensured exchange of the knowledge on use of the herbal remedies. A training by a qualified Siddha physician on their locally available herbs right from practical identification to preparation of women's beauty and health care needs.

Kitchen Garden

Healthy mind in the healthy body thus goes the adage, it emphasizes the importance of healthy body. In recent times, villagers spend their hard earned money in buying vegetables that has less nutritive value. Though, it was common practice earlier to cultivate vegetables for household needs. Of late the practice petered out. CPREEC earnestly propagated and promoted the value of consuming nutritious food and vegetables for healthy life.

In order to encourage people to practice the above said concept we distribute seeds and saplings to ensure that each house has got a small kitchen garden, which is sufficient for household consumption. Our visit to different operational areas reveals that the response is positive and promising. We are proud to state that our onset of the practice enkindle the interest in the villagers to collect more seeds for the kitchen garden rather than depending on us to supply.

Income Generation

Investing in women is important for poverty reduction. Agriculture or horticulture in India does depend on the vagaries of nature. As the project aims to help the women to harness all the skills within her to win over environmental obstacles, certain skills which are indigenous and can be practiced by her within the limiting factors of availability of resources, etc., and are very crucial for an eco-friendly life. Activities as per the topographical advantages of each group of village, i.e. availability of raw materials like herbs, sticks for baskets, etc., are taught to her.

Health and Nutrition

Improving women's health also improves the health of children and other family members. The women's awareness on health had to have multi-dimensional sphere of her role in the family. She was sensitized to nutrients conservation in the available food rather than seeking nutrients from inaccessible sources. She had to be taught to prevent repetition maladies in children, to prevent setback in build up of health as recouping took away crucial vitality both in mental and physical ability of children. She was taught to strengthen the physical state of her limbs equally by physiculture like yoga. She was taught to take care of the aged to supplement crucial build up as lack of these water soluble vitamins were cause for many ailments among the aged (Gulhati, 1995).

Impact and Spread of Programmes

- From the year 1989, there are about 8000 women from 450 villages of 28 districts of Tamil Nadu,

Andhra Pradesh, Kerala and Karnataka were trained on the various aspects of eco-development like nursery raising also, vermicomposting, setting up of kitchen gardens and herbal gardens, paper bag making, eco-friendly income generation activities.

- There are about 41,000 fruit saplings and some 100 kg of vegetables seeds were distributed to set-up kitchen gardens.
- So far 64 community smokeless chulhas and 180 domestic chulhas are installed in our operational areas.
- In the year 1991-92 EEC has taken up the project of distributing 5000 smokeless chulhas in Chennai and Chengai MGR districts, in conjunction with the Department of Non-Conventional Energy Resource.
- The women groups have collected seeds to set up a seed bank for future propagation.
- Women were trained to setup herbal gardens to repopularise the indigenous medicinal practices using locally available medicinal plants.
- Herbal gardens were setup in 3 villages of Thanjur district of Tamil Nadu.
- In 17 villages of Vellore, Thiruvallur and Thiruvannamalai districts community, vermicomposting pits were setup in order to introduce the usage of natural manure in their kitchen garden and for the effective management of domestic wastes.
- After knowing the ill-effects of non-biodegradable wastes the members of women's groups started collecting the polythene bags from each house to send it to recycling unit. After the installation of community smokeless chulhas at the village schools the women from several villages expressed their desire to put up individual chulhas.
- Women of 4 villages of Kancheepuram district were

given training in domestic smokeless chulha making to develop their skill to build their own chulhas.

- Every individual home were provided with domestic smokeless chulhas in the remote and inaccessible tribal hamlets of Sundapatti and vellerikomval of Nilgiris.
- Women of three villages of Vellore district who were trained in herbal product making (face pack, herbal shika powder, tooth powder, hair oil, etc.). It has become a positive commercial venture, where the women has started manufacturing and retailing through selected outlets.
- Bio-fencing at wasteland development site, Trichy.
- Check dam construction and stone wall fencing at Alagark oil wasteland site, Madurai.

Amelioration of Environmental Pollution

Amelioration refers to the improvements to be made in the household as well as the neighbouring environment. The rural housewives gave their priorities to the use of biogas, LPG, installation of smokeless chulha, use of dried fuel which can help to avoid smoke drudgery and ultimately avoid air pollution. They also expressed that there should be inbuilt kitchens having the provision of exhaust fans and chimneys alongwith water facilities, wire-mesh doors and windows, and use of garbage tins which may help to improve the environment (Dhillon *et al.*, 1990). They further expressed that the use of ventilators in rooms, regular white washing and painting of doors/windows are also the important factors which contribute towards attaining healthier environment. The urban housewives also gave the same priorities except the use of gobar gas for the amelioration of environment.

The equipment and appliances which produce a lot of noise unnecessarily may be due to inefficient machinery because of damaged fan blades, blunt saws and worn bearing, through by a slight change in machinery or getting them repaired in time, the noise level can be decreased to a greater extent. Modern houses, fitted and decorated with wall to wall carpeting, curtains, draperies and indoor plants, etc. not only add beauty to the home environment but also help in attaining cleaner atmosphere in the houses. Besides this, the government should also make prime efforts to involve public in the programmes like Van Mahotsav, World Earth Day and World Environment Day celebrations to encourage women to keep environment free from pollution (Dhillon *et al.*, 1990; Esserman, 1992). The mass media projection needs to be introduced to develop attitudes, skills and abilities to solve day-to-day environmental problems. A law should be introduced not to blow horns unnecessarily especially when passing through the residential areas. Also, the local authorities should curb the use of high time loudspeakers at the religious, cultural and social functions.

Conclusions

Women are generally kept behind the scene because women are entrusted with domestic work like care of children, family health, providing food and other social services. Therefore, a clear-cut demarcation is required for production, reproduction and community works of women. Sometimes, the practical and strategic gender needs are not identified in development programmes.

A projection of the needs of food, fodder and fibre for increasing population by the end of this century reveals a very alarming demand. If targets of food production by 2010 AD are to achieved without sacrificing the precious forest lands and without upsetting ecological balance, adoption of sound landuse planning, as a method of scientific upgradation is must. In order to obtain maximum sustained benefits from technological advancements for optimizing production. It is imperative that the precious natural resources of soil and water should be judiciously used.

The world conservation strategy adopted for India, has one major component in the programme that is on the management of natural resources, the soil and water on watershed basis. It is a holistic approach aimed at optimizing the use of land, water and vegetation in an area so as to provide an answer to alleviate drought, moderate floods, prevent soil erosion, improve water availability and increase fuel, fodder and agricultural production on a sustained basis.

Women irrespective of any area/locality, are aware of the environmental degradation that ultimately affects the development of sound mind and sound body. There is still a great deal for realization which can be achieved through women's participation in the amelioration of environment and environmental education. However, it is going to be a long drawn battle that has to be sustained and won with the help of government, local bodies, voluntary organizations and women's participation at all levels of formulation and implementation of various programmes.

Women's role as preservers of forest wealth can be further accentuated by technological knowledge and nursery maintenance, which can generate additional income. These practices can be integrated in the farming system itself so that it can also meet the household biomass needs, their role in protecting bio-diversity and generic conservation has to be strengthened.

All the sustainable avenues can not be harnessed until policy makers, decision managers and women involve themselves in the decision making process. Technological empowerment must be re-enforced by social empowerment. This calls for gender sensitizing field extension personnel at all levels and equipping them with new technological advances, knowledge of ecologically sound farming practices and management skills. The linkage between rural women and women professionals in agriculture, veterinary science and allied areas can be strengthened through formation of gender sensitive location specific, interdisciplinary approach with compulsory involvement of rural women in planning, technology reassessment and evaluation.

References

Agarwal, Bina (1997) Environmental Action, Gender Equity and Women's Participation. Development and Change, 28 : 1-44.

Altman, Irvin and Arza Churchman (eds.) (1994) *Women and the Environment*, New York, Plenum Press.

Batliwala, S. (1983) Women and Cooking Energy, Economic and Political Weekly, 18(52-53) : 2227-2230.

Braidotti, Rosi *et al.* (1994) *Women, the Environment and Sustainable Development : Towards a Theoretical Synthesis*, London, Atlantic Highlands, N.J.

Cheema, H. (1990) Environmental awareness among rural and urban inhabitants of Ludhiana district, M.Sc. Thesis, PAU, Ludhiana.

Dhillon, M.K. and Dhaliwal, G.S. (1996) Women and Environment, Chapter 11 *In : Agriculture and Environment* (Eds. B.D.Kansal, G.S.Dhaliwal and M.S.Bajwa), National Agricultural Technology Information Centre, 89-1, Sarabha Nagar, P.O. Box Bo. 340, Ludhiana-141001, India, pp. 147-160.

Dhillon, M.K., Cheema, H. and Dhaliwal, G.S. (1990a) Sources of environmental pollution in rural and urban habitats - awareness among housewives. Indian J. Ecol., 17(1) : 13-16.

Dhillon, M.K., Cheema, H. and Dhaliwal, G.S. (1991a) Environmental awareness among rural and urban inhabitants of Ludhiana district, Punjab. Environmental Pollution and Resources of Land and Water, Muzzafarnagar, pp. 343-349.

Dhillon, M.K., Cheema, H. and Miglani, S.S. (1991b) Environmental awareness in Punjab. *In : Environmental Management* (Eds. G.S.Dhaliwal and V.K.Dilanari), PAU, Ludhiana, pp. 49-51.

Dhillon, M.K., Dhaliwal, G.S. and Cheema, H. (1990b) Environmental management in rural and urban habitats : A Case Study of Punjab. Indian J. Ecol., 17(2) : 158-161.

Green (1994) *Women and Planning : Creating Gendered Realities*, London.

Gulhati, R. (1995) Strengthening Voluntary Action in India : Health-Family Planning, the Environment and Women's Development, Konark Publishers, New Delhi.

Hair, Jay D. (1992) "Women's voice must be heard at summit" (United Nations Conference on Environment and Development (The National Wildlife View). International Wildlife, 22(3) : 26.

Nagi, G., Dhillon, M.K. and Dhaliwal, G.S. (1933a) Source of Pollution and its ill effects on rural urban habitants. Indian J. Ecol., 20(1) : 67-73.

Paolisso, M. and Yudelman, Sally W. (1991) Women, Poverty and the Environment in Latin America, Washington, D.C., International Center for Research on Women.

Sharma, A. and Singh, R.V. (1993) People's Participation - A Key Tool for Watershed, J. Indian Resources Society, 13(1&2) : 101-104.

Singh, K.K. and Singh, Mahadevi (2002) Saving forests : A social approach. Science Reporter, 39(7) : 52-55.

Singh, Mahadevi (2000) Role of women in Indian society. Environment & People, 7(1) : 14-20.

Singh, Mahadevi and Mahlawat, Manjeet (2001) Women's Participation in Watershed Development. Environment & People, 8(6) : 13-29.

Singh, Mahadevi and Mahlawat, Manjeet (2002) Role of women in agriculture. Environment & People, 8(8&9) : 26-29.

Swarnkar, G.P. (1988) *Women Participation in Rural Environment*, I edn., Chugh Publications, Allahabad.

Venkateswaran, S. (1992) *Living on the edge : Women, Environment and Development*, New Delhi, Friedrich Ebert Stiftung.

WIN (1992) Engendering the Debate on Environment : Women and Ecologically Sustainable Development (Women and Environment). WIN News, 18(2) : 32.